Death and Love

Death and Love brings together notable psychoanalytic and philosophical theorists to explore the connection between death and love.

The book examines how these phenomena shape human existence and relationships, challenging the conventional dichotomy between life-affirming and death-driven dimensions. The volume features contributions from international scholars who illustrate these ideas through various lenses, including literature, film, and theology. The chapters consider the role of the death drive in shaping social bonds, the transformative power of love beyond individual existence, and the notion that, both philosophically and psychoanalytically, love aligns with the realm of death.

Death and Love will be essential reading for academics and students of philosophy, psychoanalysis, existentialism, theology, and psychology. It will also be of interest to psychoanalysts in practice and in training, and to all readers wishing to explore this thought-provoking topic.

Julie Reshe is a Ukrainian-born philosopher and the author of *Negative Psychoanalysis for the Living Dead: Philosophical Pessimism and the Death Drive* (2023). She teaches at University College Cork and the Global Centre for Advanced Studies, Ireland.

Todd McGowan teaches theory and film at the University of Vermont, USA. He is the author of several previous books and co-host (with Ryan Engley) of the *Why Theory* podcast.

Death and Love

Psychoanalytic and Philosophical Perspectives

Edited by Julie Reshe and Todd McGowan

LONDON AND NEW YORK

Designed cover image: Getty Images | KinoMasterskaya

First published 2025

by Routledge
4 Park Square, Milton Park, Abingdon, Oxon OX14 4RN

and by Routledge
605 Third Avenue, New York, NY 10158

Routledge is an imprint of the Taylor & Francis Group, an informa business

© 2025 selection and editorial matter, Julie Reshe and Todd McGowan; individual chapters, the contributors

The right of Julie Reshe and Todd McGowan to be identified as the authors of the editorial material, and of the authors for their individual chapters, has been asserted in accordance with sections 77 and 78 of the Copyright, Designs and Patents Act 1988.

All rights reserved. No part of this book may be reprinted or reproduced or utilised in any form or by any electronic, mechanical, or other means, now known or hereafter invented, including photocopying and recording, or in any information storage or retrieval system, without permission in writing from the publishers.

Trademark notice: Product or corporate names may be trademarks or registered trademarks, and are used only for identification and explanation without intent to infringe.

British Library Cataloguing-in-Publication Data
A catalogue record for this book is available from the British Library

ISBN: 9781032663449 (hbk)
ISBN: 9781032663425 (pbk)
ISBN: 9781032663487 (ebk)

DOI: 10.4324/9781032663487

Typeset in Times New Roman
by Deanta Global Publishing Services, Chennai, India

In memory of Mari Ruti

Contents

Introduction   x
JULIE RESHE

SECTION I
Lacanian Reflections: Love in Literature, Film, and Media   **1**

1   **Between Nowhere and Goodbye: Love Clichés (and beyond) in Literature and Film**   3
GAUTAM BASU THAKUR

2   **Til Death Do Us Part: Lacking in Love or Loving Lack**   16
STEPHANIE SWALES

3   **(Courtly) Love and Death (Drive)**   29
RUSSELL SBRIGLIA

4   **An Ethics of Shame: Love, Media Pleasures, and Monsters**   38
JENNIFER FRIEDLANDER

SECTION II
Through Death to Love: Psychoanalytic, Philosophical, and Theological Insights   **49**

5   **On the Subject of Love**   51
RICHARD BOOTHBY

6 Love and Death under Erasure: Lessons from the Phoenix
   (and Diotima) 59
   MICHAEL MARDER

7 From Death to Love: The Transformative Event in Paul's
   Christian Discourse 69
   LEON S. BRENNER

8 Embracing Suffering Beyond the Death Drive in
   Catherine of Siena's Writings 80
   MARK GERARD MURPHY

9 Death Driven by Love 93
   PETER PROSEN

SECTION III
Beyond the Finite: Existentialism and Psychoanalysis in Interplay 99

10 Existentialism After Finitude: The Transcendence of the
   Unconscious 101
   TODD MCGOWAN

11 Why Is the Death Drive Not Identical with Being-Toward-
   Death? 109
   SIMONE A. MEDINA POLO

SECTION IV
The Disintegrating Power of Love: Spielrein, Weil, and Kristeva 119

12 Simone Weil on Death: Exploring Intersections with
   Freud and Spielrein's Death Drive 121
   WANYOUNG KIM-MURPHY

13 In Search for Adult Sexual Tenderness in Freud, Kristeva,
   and Bersani 127
   STEPHANIE KOZIEJ

14 The Spielreinian Death Drive and Negative Affect Regulation Processes 137
ARVIN BAINS

15 Spielrein's Negative Psychoanalysis: Mother Death Calling 146
JULIE RESHE

Index   *157*

Introduction

Julie Reshe

I'll share a secret right from the start: I initiated this volume because I wanted to read it myself. The themes of death and love, each profound and captivating in its own right, have always held my fascination. By bringing them together, voilà, I believe I have discovered the recipe for creating the most intriguing book in the world.

Besides its extraordinary themes, this volume is also notable for the contributions of some of the most remarkable scholars who share a passion for intertwining the topics of love and death. Heartbreakingly, our beloved Mari Ruti passed away shortly after submitting her abstract for this collection. This volume is dedicated to her memory. Her abstract is included at the end of this introduction as a testament to her contribution, and her spirit and ideas resonate throughout the entire book. I am grateful to Todd McGowan for his unconditional support of my obsession with this topic and for his guidance in co-editing this volume with me. I appreciate his dedication to this project.

In philosophy, particularly in existentialism, the defining and tragic reality of human existence is death. In psychoanalysis, however, this tragic defining reality is more often captured by concepts that can be encompassed within the category of love – desire, drive, eros, and the other. Philosophy's focus on death tends to lack an interindividual dimension – the dimension of love. The tragedy of death in existentialism lies in its individuality, being always one's own death. Conversely, the scope of psychoanalytic love often lacks the dimension of death. In psychoanalytic theory, love and desire are frequently seen in opposition to death, rather than being defined by it.

This volume bridges the divide by adding the dimension of love to the philosophical concept of death and incorporating the dimension of death into the psychoanalytic concept of love. It is not merely an intriguing theoretical elaboration of the concepts of death and love in psychoanalysis and philosophy. Love and death concern each of us in the most direct and intimate ways – both are at the very foundation of our being. Therefore, the book touches the core of each of us, exploring how love and death are eternally intertwined within our souls.

The first section of this collection, "Lacanian Reflections: Love in Literature, Film, and Media," begins with a chapter titled "Between Nowhere and Goodbye: Love Clichés (and beyond) in Literature and Film" by Gautam Basu Thakur. He brilliantly elaborates on Lacan's maxims about love, starting with the famous "Love is to give what one does not have," and explicates them through critical discussions of O. Henry's short story "The Gift of the Magi" and Clint Eastwood's film *Million Dollar Baby*.

Following this, Stephanie Swales in her chapter "Til Death Do Us Part: Lacking in Love or Loving Lack" explores the death drive as an integral part of the social bond, including the love relation. She beautifully illustrates this through the vicissitudes of the relationship between Connell and Marianne in Sally Rooney's novel *Normal People*.

The next chapter, from Russell Sbriglia, "(Courtly) Love and Death (Drive)," builds on the work of the Ljubljana School and Lacan's theory of the death drive as "immortal life" to the literature of courtly love, wherein love is understood as submission to the ultimate Other. This is vividly illustrated through the genre of courtly love, as exemplified by Chaucer's "A Complaint to His Lady" and Dante's *Vita Nuova*.

Concluding the section, in her chapter "An Ethics of Shame: Love, Media Pleasures, and Monsters," Jennifer Friedlander responds to Claire Dederer's dilemma, formulated as "What Do We Do with the Art of Monstrous Men?" Drawing on developments in Lacan's thinking, Friedlander aptly suggests the liberatory potential of our enjoyment of shame and frames her argument for a form of love in tandem with the death drive.

The second section, "Through Death to Love: Psychoanalytic, Philosophical, and Theological Insights," opens with the chapter "On the Subject of Love" by Richard Boothby, which discusses Lacan's account of love, describing it as a depersonalizing experience. His insightful analysis engages Lacan's distinctive interpretation of the death drive as a force that destabilizes the imaginary contours of the ego. Notably, this discussion also includes Mari Ruti's exploration of love and Alain Badiou's emphasis on love's capacity to transcend the self.

Michael Marder's excellent chapter, "Love and Death under Erasure: Lessons from the Phoenix (and Diotima)," explores how death and love coincide by their placement under erasure in the figure of the phoenix.

Leon S. Brenner's chapter, "From Death to Love: The Transformative Event in Paul's Christian Discourse," meticulously examines the relationship between love and death in the writings of Saint Paul through the lens of Alain Badiou's philosophy and Lacanian psychoanalysis. It reveals how, in Paul's discourse, love as a revolutionary force overcomes the limitations of death and offers a new, universal path to salvation.

In his cutting-edge chapter, "Embracing Suffering Beyond the Death Drive in Catherine of Siena's Writings," Mark Gerard Murphy examines the themes of suffering and the death drive in the writings of Catherine of Siena, a mystical theologian from the 14th century. He explores the direct connection between the death drive and Catherine's spirituality, particularly emphasizing bodily suffering.

Peter Prosen's sad essay, "Death Driven by Love," provocatively challenges the conventional notion – represented in Aristophanes' myths in Plato's *Symposium* and similar cultural fantasies – that love is solely a force of affirmation and should not cause distress. Drawing on the thoughts of Schopenhauer, Nietzsche, and Freud, Prosen argues that the real experience of love involves self-alienation and is indistinguishable from anxiety. Love belongs to a dimension of self-destruction; it is a form of death, where the other becomes one's death drive.

The third section, "Beyond the Finite: Existentialism and Psychoanalysis in Interplay," opens with Todd McGowan's groundbreaking chapter, "Existentialism After Finitude: The Transcendence of the Unconscious." McGowan introduces the concept of psychoanalytic existentialism. For this, he removes the emphasis on finitude from existentialism and introduces the idea of freedom – understood as the infinitude of the subject and its embrace of the unconscious – into the deterministic framework of psychoanalysis.

In her chapter "Why Is the Death Drive Not Identical with Being-Toward-Death?" Simone A. Medina Polo argues that the death drive represents a figure of infinity (drawing from Hegel, Freud, and Lacan), whereas being-toward-death represents a figure of finitude (elaborating on Kant and Heidegger). Nonetheless, the chapter brilliantly positions love as the transfinite link that oscillates between the infinite and the finite.

The fourth section of the volume, "Disintegrating Power of Love: Spielrein, Weil, and Kristeva," begins with Wanyoung Kim-Murphy's chapter titled "Simone Weil on Death: Exploring Intersections with Freud and Spielrein's Death Drive." This chapter eloquently reveals nuanced connections between the psychoanalytic concept of the death drive, viewed as a human inclination toward self-destruction and love, and Simone Weil's concept of self-denial as a strategy for channeling the death instinct towards noble causes. It also timely elaborates on how Weil offers a lens through which to understand contemporary wars.

In her exceptional chapter, "In Search for Adult Sexual Tenderness in Freud, Kristeva, and Bersani," Stephanie Koziej explores how an early Freudian concept of tenderness, which predates the death drive, offers insights into positioning self-destruction at the center of life. The chapter also incorporates Kristeva's and queer theorist Leo Bersani's elaborations on the disintegrating dimension of sexuality to support this assertion.

The third chapter in this section, titled "The Spielreinian Death Drive and the Negative Affect Regulation Processes" by Arvin Bains, rigorously explores Sabina Spielrein's influence on affect regulation. It critically examines her challenges to Freud's theories, emphasizing dynamic intersubjectivity and the role of self-sacrifice in understanding love.

In my concluding chapter, "Spielrein's Negative Psychoanalysis: Mother Death Calling," I discuss my beloved Sabina Spielrein, the pioneering psychoanalyst who first introduced the concept of the death drive into psychoanalysis, thereby undermining Freud's initial psychoanalytic framework of thought. Spielrein offers a perspective that diverges from the traditional Freudian view, portraying the human being as both self-destructive and self-sacrificing, driven not by self-centeredness but by love.

Dignum Memoria: Mari Ruti's Abstract
The Death-Repeating Ethos of Creativity

In conventional terms, creativity – in this essay understood to entail not merely intellectual or artistic endeavors but also a Nietzschean poetics of becoming – tends to be regarded as a life-affirming dimension of the human condition. However, Ruti argues that it is better theorized as a death-repeating endeavor: it is only insofar as the subject fails to reach a state of ontological completion and coherence that it retains the capacity, let alone the passion, for sublimatory activities. Were Eros ever to fully triumph over the death-driven aspects of psychic life, the subject would lose its inclination toward the continual reinvention of the conditions of its existence. It would likewise lose its desire to affiliate with others. Ruti consequently proposes that a psychoanalytic conception of creativity as a facet of the (self-)destructive aspects of the repetition compulsion confirms that sublimation is more accurately thought of as a function of negativity than of life-affirming flourishing. Or, perhaps more precisely, the human subject can only – always partially and fleetingly – flourish to the extent that it is able to approach life from the perspective of death.

Mari Ruti was Distinguished Professor of Critical Theory and of Gender and Sexuality Studies at the University of Toronto. She authored over a dozen books, including *A World of Fragile Things: Psychoanalysis and the Art of Living* (2009); *The Summons of Love* (2011); *The Singularity of Being: Lacan and the Immortal Within* (2012); *The Call of Character: Living a Life Worth Living* (2013); *Between Levinas and Lacan: Self, Other, Ethics* (2015); *Penis Envy and Other Bad Feelings: The Emotional Costs of Everyday Life* (2018); *Distillations: Theory, Ethics, Affect* (2018); and *The Creative Self: Against Neoliberal Self-Optimization*, with Gail Newman (forthcoming).

SECTION I

Lacanian Reflections: Love in Literature, Film, and Media

Chapter 1

Between Nowhere and Goodbye

Love Clichés (and beyond) in Literature and Film

Gautam Basu Thakur

Introduction: Lacan on Love

Lacan's commentaries on love are scattered throughout his seminars – from Seminar I to Seminar VIII to Seminar XX and beyond. Often these are no different from Lacan's (general) style of "off-the-cuff comments, looping references to earlier weeks' discussions, bad puns, […] oblique references to literary or theologico-philosophical texts" to aphorisms (Burnham 2021, p. 77).

Notwithstanding the challenge, therefore, of distilling some concrete or concise Lacanian insights on love, I want to begin this essay by, first, focusing on Lacan's Seminar VIII: Transference, and, then, attempt to illustrate a few of his puzzling aphorisms. I want to begin with Seminar VIII because transference is a form of love addressed by the analysand to the analyst in the clinic.

Or, as Bruce Fink (2016) puts it, transference is "love transferred onto the physician from some other real or idealized figure in a patient's life" (p. 2):

> [A]nalysis automatically places the analysand in the position of the beloved. The analysand […] demands to be found lovable, and […] analysts take the analysand as someone who is important and listen to him in a way that no one has ever listened to him before. (p. 46)

For the analysand, the analyst thus becomes the loved one: someone they believe has the answers to all their queries, who will effectively address their gaps in knowledge and memory, and successfully cure them of their "unnatural" thoughts, feelings, and symptoms.

> [By] asking the right questions, we [analysts] highlight the lack in the analysand, who then comes to believe that we [analysts] must have the answers since we have asked the questions [or that] we have the answers and are simply holding out on him. [As such] not finding the answers in himself, he projects them onto us, and comes to love us as possessors of knowledge. (p. 47)

It is important however for the analyst to refuse the analysand's love. That is, to be not reduced to a love object for healing the analysand's lack. Instead, the analyst's task is to push the analysand towards doing the "difficult work of analysis" by himself (p. 47). As Fink clarifies, the analyst must "cut" the mutual reciprocity that commonly underwrites the lover-beloved relationship – "the analyst knows how to love/ask questions, but he does not crave love in return [...] the analysand [...] expect[ing] to be loved by the analyst [...] complains bitterly when he or she feels inadequately attended by the analyst" (pp. 50–51). The analysand's self-love is displaced or transferred love addressed to the analyst acting as (an) initial hurdle in the clinic.

Without entering further into transference, I want to underline here what will be important for my discussion in this essay, namely, the imaginary/assumed reciprocity structuring love relations – the lover thinks the beloved has something that completes him/her and that he/she has to offer to the beloved what the latter might be lacking. Far from being fulfilling and a positive experience, love is a testament to human stupidity. As Lacan reminds us in Seminar XX (1998a), in his first seminar – *Freud's Papers on Technique* – he spoke about "nothing less than love" (p. 11) but within moments of making this observation, he adds: "in that first seminar I spoke of stupidity" (p. 12). I discuss these points below in detail through my readings of O. Henry's short story "The Gift of the Magi" (1905) and Clint Eastwood's film *Million Dollar Baby* (2004). But before that let me turn to a few Lacanian aphorisms about love, which too will aid my analyses of the texts mentioned above.

Lacan's Aphorisms

Lacan's aphorisms about love both intrigue and baffle readers. These include:

1. "Love is to give what one does not have" (2014, p. 108; 2015, p. 34);
2. "Love [is] a reality that manifests and reveals itself in the real" (2015, p. 52);

and,

3. "I love you, but, because inexplicably I love in you something more than you [hence] I mutilate you" (1998, p. 268).

Lacan is not the only "Western" thinker to ponder the meaning of love, but what do these pithy observations mean? As I see it, his thinking being integrally tied to the science and the praxis of psychoanalysis at once echoes and diverges from existing Western thinking about love. This double valence makes his comments difficult to understand. I want to approach therefore the question of how Lacan defines love through another, slightly longer comment from Seminar VIII (2015):

> The hand that extends toward the fruit, rose, or the log that suddenly bursts into flames – its gesture of reaching, drawing close, or stirring up is closely related

to the ripening of the fruit, the beauty of the flower, and the blazing of the log. If, in the movement of reaching, drawing or stirring, the hand goes far enough toward the object that another hand comes out of the fruit, flower, or log and extends toward your hand – and at that moment your hand freezes in the closed plenitude of the fruit, in the open plenitude of the flower, or in the explosion of a log which bursts into flames – then what is produced is love [but] we must not stop there. We must say that what we are looking at here is love [where] you become […] he who desires. (p. 52)

Lacan calls this a "myth" because it is a condensed version of his ideas about love. Hewitson (2016) rightly notes that in "this story is condensed all the things that interested Lacan about love. The themes we can pull from it fuelled [sic] his commentary on the subject over fifty years of his work" (n.p.). For example, if we take this flower or fruit as the proverbial "fruit of knowledge," and/or, just simply, a desired object, such as the strawberries which a young patient of Freud's could not digest leading her to crave strawberries in her dreams, what does reaching out to and immediately being repulsed by this object mean? What does it mean to freeze in the plenitude of the fruit/flower, to be greeted back by another hand emerging out of the love object? Therefore, following Hewitson but not necessarily repeating his explication of this passage, I too will offer a few brief glosses to present my understanding of "love" in Lacan's thinking. And thereafter further clarify some or all of these through my discussions of O. Henry's story and Eastwood's film.

1. **Desire and love.**
   What I desire (unconscious knowledge) and what/whom I love is different. This is because love has a direct object of satisfaction, but desire always deflects this satisfaction by finding some hindrance to satisfaction. However, as Miller puts it (1992), there exists a conjunction between love and desire insofar as the "ulterior object of love is a displacement from the fundamental object," i.e., the love object also never satisfies (p. 19).
2. **What we expect in the beloved, or love, is not desirable but, rather, traumatic.**
   The love object or the beloved is a fantastic object, i.e., they possess an indeterminable Thing that the lover assumes can suture his ontological lack – complete him/her – when in reality love is the acknowledgement and assertion of the lover's lack with the love object or beloved existing only as that which returns to the lover the uncomfortable fact of its lacking existence.
3. **"Love [is] the real" (Lacan 2015, p. 52).**
   Love haunts, love bites, love is a bed of thorns…or, so claim our popular musicians. Love, indeed, as I show below, is a haunting. If we reach out to the other, then what emerges from that space is the mythical severed hand popular across Hollywood horror films. Not a reciprocation we imagined, but a gesture of true love whereby the real or reality of love comes to the fore. That part of the other/beloved which I did not anticipate in the other, but loved something

else in the other, yet at this crucial moment what I encounter is the other's most radical alterity which haunts me.

4. **Narcissism vs. a fundamental asymmetry.**
   Love is always self-love. Different from primary narcissism as Freud defines it, i.e., the animal instinct guiding even humans to self-care/protection, love is secondary narcissism or how we want to appear in the eyes of others. But what separates human-animals from the rest of the world is that we can render in language some terms of our alienation from the world surrounding us. This is because we speak. Therefore, insofar as love can be only conveyed via speech vs propagation of the species, by speaking about why we love another person we inevitably express a demand for being loved back for something we uniquely possess and which the other wants. As such, we enter a deadlock between offering what we do not have and asking in return what the beloved does not possess either.

5. **Love and anxiety.**
   Love protects us against getting close to our desire, which is not for satisfaction but for remaining in dissatisfaction. Like anxiety which cautions us against the constriction of the space between desire and the object we enjoy (*de jouir*), love is the mediating force keeping us alive as subjects of desire or as subjects who are forever unsatisfied.

With these brief glosses in mind, let us now turn to the two "love stories."

A Tale of Two Loves: Love I – The Foolish Couple

O. Henry's "The Gift of the Magi" (1905) is a short story read with delight around the world, and as I read it, the story is an instantiation of what Bruce Fink dubs *symbolic love*. It is a story about conjugal love triangulated by third factors, namely, Jim's heirloom pocket watch and Della's long thick hair. More precisely, the couple's love relationship is mediated by what Della thinks Jim lacks – a chain for his watch – and what Jim thinks Della lacks – a comb for her flowing tresses. These were the couple's treasures, objects of pride and self-worth, even when their daily lives were immersed in severe economic hardships.

Yet, both Della and Jim plan to save money (which does not work out given their penury) to buy Christmas gifts for each other. The gifts they choose – Jim an expensive comb for Della's hair and Della an expensive chain for Jim's watch – imaginably come at costs that neither can afford. But they each persevere: Jim sells off his heirloom watch to buy the expensive comb for Della, and Della cuts and sells off her hair to buy a chain for Jim's watch.

Jim and Della's love relationship is mediated through these objects. They see themselves as kings and queens because of their respective possessions. Yet Della feels that Jim is incomplete without a chain for his watch and that he longs for it. Similarly, Jim perceives Della as incomplete and longing for the combs. They locate in each other a lack that must be filled – a gap that constitutes the other as desiring resulting in the other suffering silently from a lack of satisfaction. Therefore, it is to fulfil the other's lack that they decide to sacrifice their unique possessions – Jim his watch for Della's combs, and Della her hair for buying a platinum fob chain for Jim's watch. This sacrifice – each giving up their prized possessions to fill the other's lack – is their expression of love: they love the other by giving up a part of their self.

Jim and Della's love is *structural*. It begins in the imaginary (what each imagines the other's ideal-self to be), is mediated by the symbolic lack each perceives in the other, and, results in each sacrificing their unique possessions to heal/satisfy the other's lack/desire. What each view as the other's unique possession (*agalma*) is also viewed as the cause of the other's desire, the object cause of the lack and dissatisfaction in the other (Figure 1.1).

Properly speaking, in each of their perspectives the other is not an individual but the objects they possess: For Jim, Della=her hair; and, for Della, Jim=his heirloom watch. This is why Fink (2016) insists that "we view our partners in love as a collection of objects […] rather than as subjects" (p. 191). And insofar as "our own satisfaction is incomplete without the other's satisfaction," we sacrifice, become "altruistic and all-giving" – "our own satisfaction being immediately connected with giving satisfaction to our partner" (pp. 191–192).

Unfortunately, given there's no reciprocity between how Jim and Della love or view each other, their expressions of love or what they offer each other are at cross-purposes.[1] Herein lies one possible explanation of Lacan's maxim: "Love is to give what one does not have" (Sem. X: 108 [translation revised]). Indeed, to this can be added by way of our reading of O. Henry's story, *love is to give what one does not have, to someone who does not want it* (Lacan 1964–1965. Cited in Vighi 2017, p. 67). For Jim sells his family heirloom to give Della the comb but Della no longer needs a comb because she has sold off her hair to buy Jim's fob

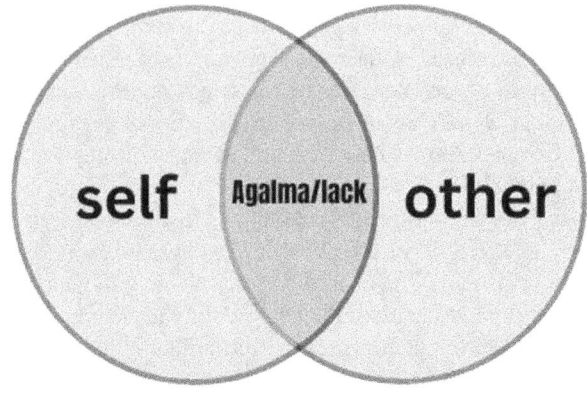

Figure 1.1

chain. And the fob chain she buys for Jim is no longer needed by Jim who has sold his watch.

At this point, I want to jump to that moment at the conclusion of the story when both protagonists are face to face without their personal treasures because they have both sacrificed these in order to fulfil what they conceptualized as the other's lack. This is a moment of truth when the real bursts onto the scene – the reality of love and communication in conjugal relationships as fundamentally structured by an impasse: the impossibility of knowing the other's desire and responding to it. Love "occurs at the point where signification fails," that is, it "manifests [...] outside what can be articulated" (Zeiher & McGowan 2017, p. xi). It is the impediment experienced in loving and/or being loved – the impossibility of being "one" with the other or creating a harmonious One-ness with the other – which, paradoxically, is the signature of love.

This moment of truth is so unbearable and overwhelming that it needs to be veiled, hidden from plain sight so that the dialectic of desire and love can continue. So that humans are not faced with their own abjection as fragmented subjects or alive only because they are forever suspended in chasing impossible or unsatisfactory desires. O. Henry therefore overwrites the real with the fiction of God as the big Other. It is only under the shadow of this mythical big Other and the grand narrative of morals and (self-)sacrifice created around the big Other that O. Henry can give meaning to the foolishness of Jim and Della. He marks his story as "the uneventful chronicle of two foolish children in a flat who most unwisely sacrificed for each other the greatest treasures of their house," only to add:

> But in a last word to the wise of these days let it be said that of all who give gifts these two were the wisest. Of all who give and receive gifts, such as they are wisest. Everywhere they are wisest. They are the magi.

A Tale of Two Loves: Love II – *Mo Cuishle*

Clint Eastwood's 2004 film *Million Dollar Baby* depicts love as a demand addressed to the other but this demand/love is refused by the other who prefers to rather show the loving subject the connection between her demand/love=lack and her desire. The other, boxing coach Frankie Dunn (Eastwood), refuses Margaret "Maggie" Fitzgerald's (Hilary Swank) demand that he trains her to become a professional woman boxer and world champion.[2]

What unfolds in the first half of the movie appears similar to Fink's description of the analysand–analyst relationship in the clinic: the analysand expresses love for the analyst who must refuse this love, and therefore rejecting the analysand's attempt to discover the lack in or desire of the analyst and thus helping the analysand to comprehend her own lack qua desire. However, unlike in the clinic, while Dunn's initial rejection of Maggie's love/demand, often couched in offensive statements like "I don't train girls" or "Girlie, tough ain't good enough," or women's boxing is the "latest freak show," seems unconditional, we soon discover his reasons (though he possible does not know): he does not want Maggie to get hurt because he feels Katy (his estranged daughter) has been hurt by him. That's why, even after he agrees to train Maggie, he keeps reminding her about the most important rule in boxing: "keep your left up [and] protect yourself at all times."

And as the film progresses, beginning with the scene where Dunn finally agrees to accept Maggie as his trainee, he keeps demanding her complete compliance:

> If I take you on, you don't say anything. You don't question me. You don't ask "why" [...] and I am going to try to forget the fact you're a girl. [...] And don't come crying to me, if you get hurt [...] I am going to teach you how to fight. Then we'll get you a manager and I am off down the road. [...] that's the only way we're doing it. I teach you all you need to know, and then you go off and make a million dollars. I don't care. You get your teeth knocked out; I don't care. I don't want to hear about it either way [...] it's the only way I'll do it.

If we closely examine Dunn's words, we see that it's not a simple demand for complete obedience. Rather because he starts with "If I take you on ...," he both accepts Maggie and makes it contingent on her accepting him as who he is. Also, folded into his misogynistic comments is an expression of his own lack – he worries about Maggie getting hurt. In fact, he does not want to hear about it. And though it can be said that Dunn's comment about finding another manager is connected to his former student Willie leaving him before a million-dollar title fight, it can also be understood as Dunn not wanting to see Maggie get hurt in the ring.

Only at the end of the film, when Maggie is dying, does Dunn finally reciprocate her demand/love thus admitting his own lack: specifically, his failure to care for his daughter, and as such submitting to Maggie's demand/love that he pulls the plug of her ventilator support. I will return to this later but before moving ahead let me add a sidenote here: namely, the entire film is a narrative scripted in the form of a letter by Dunn's gym assistant and a former boxer, Eddie "Scrap-Iron" Dupris (Morgan Freeman). Dupris's voice-over guides audiences throughout the film connecting absent storylines and moving the narrative forward; but in reality, it is Dupris reading his letter addressed to Dunn's daughter where he tells Katy about Dunn and Maggie's (love) story. But we only learn about this at the end of the film.

Dunn's direct expression of love for Maggie occurs when Maggie goes to England to fight a younger, experienced, and better boxer. Before the fight, Dunn gifts Maggie a green robe with the words "Mo Cuishle" embroidered in yellow silk. When Maggie asks what it means, Dunn deflects by saying he doesn't know, "It's something in Gaelic." Maggie asks again after she wins the bout and earns the nick name "Mo Cuishle" from the fans: "I can ask someone" she says to which Dunn replies with a dry smile "You find out, you let me know." Does Dunn really not know or is he holding back? If it is in Gaelic, then we have seen him throughout the film learning Gaelic from a book. Could it be that he knows but does not want Maggie to know? At least not at that moment.

The literal translation of "Mo Cuishle" (the correct spelling is *Mo Chuishle*) is "pulse" or "vein." But it is also used as a term of endearment in the way Dunn and the fans use it. It is only at the conclusion of the film that Dunn tells Maggie the meaning of the phrase – "my darling, and my blood." Irrespective of how Dunn uses the phrase – "pulse," vein," "my darling, and my blood," it is clear that through these two words he is connecting Maggie to Katy. Like Katy who is his blood, Maggie too is his blood and beloved. Maggie takes the position of the estranged daughter; she fills the lack in Dunn.

Unlike Jim or Della, Dunn does not address his love to the other. Rather, his love is addressed to his own lack. At the same time, by not disclosing the meaning of the phrase to Maggie, Dunn continues to frustrate her wish to know what Dunn wants. Dunn wants Maggie to fill his lack and restrict Maggie from knowing that she fills his lack at the same time. This aligns with Dunn's general interactions with Maggie. Though he demands her absolute submission in training, during matches, especially at the bout in England, when Maggie was finding it difficult to keep up with the younger experienced opponent, Dunn instead of telling her what to do says: "She's a better fighter than you are [...] she's younger, she's stronger and she's more experienced. Now, what are you going to do about it?" Dunn wants Maggie to find her own unique singularity of being in her lack. If her love is boxing, because boxing can only satisfy her demand to be loved as anything other than "white trash," then Maggie must first embrace her lack for constituting who she can become. This argument finds clear purchase in what happens immediately after – after returning to the US, Maggie visits her family, buys them a new home, but they refuse the new home stating they would prefer cash and that everyone in their trailer park community laughs at Maggie for being a boxer. Dunn wishes Maggie to love herself because of who she is – a boxing champion – and thus suture her lack with self-love. He does not want anyone else healing Maggie's lack with love from the outside just as he does not disclose his affection towards her, that is, does not tell Maggie how she fills his lack as a surrogate daughter – his *mo cuishle*, or, his blood and darling. Loving one's self (narcissism) is the most defining characteristic of love.

As Lacan teaches us, love is always addressed to the self – love is narcissistic (See, 1998a, session 11/1/73; 1967–1968, session 10/1/68). Or, one loves "with his lack" (2014, session 16/1/62). Love is lack positivized; or, it comes from lack (somewhere/symbolic castration) but occupies the place of nothing (or, nowhere). In this sense, love is the objective correlative of our fractured ontology. Even when a subject gains a sense of wholesome self via loving the other, love actually situates the subject in a state of unknowing: does the other love me back? Will the other reciprocate my love or reject it? Can we be united in our mutual love? (We all know how that goes.)

Love is a demand addressed to the other for loving back (Lacan, 2006, p. 853). Desire however is not contingent on reciprocation – "one's desire does not necessarily wither or disappear if one does not feel desired in return" (Fink 2016, p. 36). Insofar as love is a demand for proof of love, something tangible, it is different from desire which is "neither the appetite for satisfaction nor the demand for love, but the difference that results from the subtraction of the first from the second, the very phenomenon of their splitting *(Spaltung)*" (Lacan, 2006, p. 691). Because only speaking beings can love or demand, something is always lost in the words articulating demand (Lacan 2015, p. 356). This residue is desire – impossible to render in speech and always outside of ourselves ("desire is the desire of the Other"). This is why Lacan (1991) says love is on the side of Being (p. 276) – it keeps the subject alive with a sense of purpose and a goal (to be achieved) while distancing the impossibility of satisfying desire, paradoxically, for the subject to unconsciously enjoy (*jouissance*) its un-/non-being.[3]

Dunn tells Maggie the meaning of "mo cuishle" at the end of the film, when Maggie is in the hospital, on respiratory support, her career finished from the spinal cord injury she sustains at the title match against Bellie "the Blue Bear." Unwilling to live out the rest of her life in bed, Maggie asks Dunn to put her out of her misery. Maggie expresses her love to Dunn yet again but this time demanding that he listens to her once. Dunn initially refuses but after Maggie tries to commit suicide by biting off her tongue, he relents.[4] And as he injects a dose of Adrenalin, he tells her the meaning of "mo cuishle" – "my darling, my blood." By telling her what she means to him, Dunn does not offer his love to Maggie as someone who fills his lack. Rather, he opens up to Maggie his own lack, therefore his inability to suture her lack or respond to her demand for being loved, thus effectively giving her nothing and aiding her to a state of nothing (death). But Dunn does not "survive" this encounter either. As Scrap's voice-over tells us:

> [As he] walked out [,] I don't think he had anything left. [...] Frankie never came back at all. Frankie didn't leave a note, and nobody knew where he went. [...] he didn't have anything left in his heart. I just hope he found someplace where he could find a little peace [:] Somewhere between nowhere and goodbye.

The moment when two lacking subjects finally encounter true love, each giving to the other their respective lacks, it results in death: Maggie dies, physically returning to a state of inertia, while Frankie dies symbolically realizing the inadequacy of the symbolic order to find him a meaningful life. Love is mediated by the fantasy of the other as the possessor of the "Thing" (Ruti 2011, ch. 7), which the other can offer to the beloved for suturing the latter's lack; or, find the lovers peace, meaning, and a place to belong. But when the love encounter involves two lacking/loving subjects offering nothing to each other except their own lacks (as the other's lack), then we witness love in the real (Lacan 2015) – to love is to die…for the nation, for the family, for a cause, for the other. Herein lies the symbolic revolutionary potential of love qua the imaginary of the loved object interwoven with love's real adhesion with death. To love is to die with or without knowing.

Conclusion: The Poets Did It!

Literary representations of love regularly underscore the relationship between love and lack – the absence or loss of the loved object. For example, in "Seven Days Have Passed and I Have Not Seen My Lady Love," a love poem from Ancient Egypt (circa 1539–1075 BC), the poet writes,

> Seven days have passed, and I've not seen my lady love; a sickness has shot through me.
> I have become sluggish,
> I have forgotten my own body.

Not too differently, Mira Bai from medieval South Asia (circa 16th century), sings in "Darling Come Visit Me":

> Darling, come visit me,
> give me a vision of yourself – I can't live without you.
> A lotus without water, a night without the moon.
> That's what you look like without your beloved – me.

Or, Emily Bronte writes in *Wuthering Heights*,

> May you not rest as long as I am living; you said I killed you – haunt me then! ... Be with me always – take any form – drive me mad! Only do not leave me in this abyss where I cannot find you! I cannot live without my life! I cannot live without my soul!

All of these excerpts illustrate love as (1) an individual experience that is always unique yet when written or spoken as inevitably displaced, never adequate, and therefore needing metaphors and symbols to convey the real feeling; (2) consequently, literary expressions of love are always cliched, repetitive, and monotonous; and, (3) these expressions commonly depict love taking shape against a sense of a subject's lacking wholesome being ("I am incomplete without my beloved") and/or the subject's feeling of having lost the beloved (heartbreak or death of the beloved), as the reason for making him or her feel incomplete.

I am not suggesting that loss, (failed) recovery or imperfect suturing of experiences of lost love are the only features of love expressed in cultural texts across human history. However, it is indeed possible to make that argument based on the consistency with which these themes as well as the impossibility of writing about love as a profoundly inimitable singular experience appear across texts from around the world. Yet, in any case, what remains often amiss in literary representations is the relationship between love and death and love and enjoyment (of death). But it is the poets who first saw this through and this is attested by Pablo Neruda's poem "Love" where he writes:

> Because of you, in gardens of blossoming flowers I ache from the perfumes of spring.
> I have forgotten your face, I no longer remember your hands; how did your lips feel on mine?
> Because of you, I love the white statues drowsing in the parks, the white statues that have neither voice nor sight.
> I have forgotten your voice, your happy voice; I have forgotten your eyes.
> Like a flower to its perfume, I am bound to my vague memory of you. I live with pain that is like a wound; if you touch me, you will do me irreparable harm.
> Your caresses enfold me, like climbing vines on melancholy walls. I have forgotten your love, yet I seem to glimpse you in every window.
> Because of you, the heady perfumes of summer pain me; because of you, I again seek out the signs that precipitate desires: shooting stars, falling objects.[5]

Neruda guides us toward something often overlooked and/or foreclosed in commonplace ideations of love. In his poem, there is not simply a sense of loss or being incomplete due to the beloved's absence but also a curious facet about the lover-poet's grief over a lost love being entangled with an enjoyment of pain bound to the impossibility of recovering the lost love object.

Developing out of cliched expressions of loss, grief, and haunting are tendrils of an experience of painful enjoyment of separation which risks dissolution only if the loss is recovered; or, the lover suddenly finds satisfaction in the return of the (lost) beloved:

> I live with pain
> That is like a wound; [but] if you touch me, you will
> Make to me an irreparable harm.

It seems the poet wishes to live with the pain of his loss and if that loss is to disappear so will his life and his poem. It is impossible to overlook Neruda's insistence in this poem to refuse wholesome subjectivity by suturing the gap between the lover and the (lost) beloved. The poem's final stanza repeats his enjoyment of this painful experience because the loss/lack galvanizes his desire:

> Because of you, the heady perfumes of
> Summer pain me; because of you, I again
> Seek out the signs that precipitate desires:
> Shooting stars, falling objects.

The loss suffered creates a negative space that makes the lover both suffer and want to love again.

Effectively, within 20 lines Neruda captures a deeply enigmatic character of love – its relationship to loss, pain, enjoyment, and resultant galvanization of new desires for, paradoxically, again, transient or temporal love objects. Love thus seems possible only in its absence, always when the loved object is lost or at a distance, i.e., irrecoverable. The proximity of the loved object, when it comes close to becoming a reality for the subject seeking wholesome existence through reunion with a lost beloved, actually seems threatening; most possibly because such a bridging between the lover and the love object would evaporate the primary condition of love, i.e., the loss or absence of the beloved/loved object. The poet does not want to lose his love, therefore he cannot lose his lack – or, as Miller (2013) puts it, "To love is to admit your lack" (p. 1). To love is to embrace death.

Notes

1 See, Miller's (2013) comments on reciprocal love.
2 But the film also depicts another side to this relationship: Dunn eventually starts addressing Maggie with his demand/love, but she keeps defying him at every opportunity, even if she does not outright reject it. In effect, there is a subterranean tension in their relationship though, given their relationship as trainer (Master/Boss) and trainee (student/fighter), Dunn is determinately in the position of the other to whom Maggie addresses her love/demand. I address this later in the paper.
3 Aristotle (1999) makes the argument in *Nicomachean Ethics* that "entelechy" or fully actualizing all potential is what makes us human. See, Book I, Sec. 1. Freud's and Lacan's departure from this totalizing tendency of European philosophy mark the Copernican Revolution of psychoanalysis as theory and praxis. It is for this reason one has to agree with Badiou's identification of Lacan as an antiphilosopher.
4 The trope of committing suicide by biting off one's tongue is common in literature. It represents a subject, otherwise interred against his will, to regain control over the body and reclaim individual agency. But the act can be also interpreted as a refusal to speak, to withdraw from the symbolic order. I do not have space to discuss this here but for a discussion of the trope in literature, see Skuse (2021) and Flaherty (2014). For a brief history of the tongue, see Crowcroft (2022).
5 "Amor." First published in the magazine *Claridad*, n° 83, 23 de diciembre de 1922, © Pablo Neruda 1922, and Fundación Pablo Neruda.

References

Aristotle (1999). *Nicomachean Ethics*. Tr. W. D. Ross. Batoche Books: Kitchener. https://socialsciences.mcmaster.ca/econ/ugcm/3ll3/aristotle/Ethics.pdf

Burnham, C. (2021). "Lacan's Trash Talk: Three Objects for the Internet." In Burnham, C. & Kingsbury, P. (Eds.) *Lacan and the Environment* (pp. 75–93). Palgrave Lacan Series.

Crowcroft, K. (2022). "The Oddest of Organs: A Brief History of the Tongue." *LitHub*. https://lithub.com/the-oddest-of-organs-a-brief-history-of-the-tongue/

Eastwood, C., Haggis, P., Ruddy, A. S., Rosenberg, T., Swank, H., Freeman, M., Mackie, A., Baruchel, J., Colter, M., Rijker, L., O'Byrne, B. F., Martindale, M., Lindhome, R., & Peña, M. (2004). *Million Dollar Baby*. Warner Bros. Entertainment.

Fink, B. (2016). *Lacan on Love: An Exploration of Lacan's Seminar VIII, Transference*. Polity.

Flaherty, J. (2014). "Violence of Rhetoric: Silencing the Tongue in Kyd and Shakespeare."*Actes des congrès de la Société française Shakespeare*, 31, 89–101. https://doi.org/10.4000/shakespeare.2822

Hewitson, O. (2016). What does Lacan say about…Love. *Lacanonline.com*. https://www.lacanonline.com/2016/06/what-does-lacan-say-about-love/

Lacan, J. (2006). *Écrits: The First Complete Edition in English* (B. Fink, H. Fink, and R. Grigg, Trans.). W. W. Norton.

Lacan, J. (2014). *Anxiety: The Seminar of Jacques Lacan Book X*. Trans. A. R. Price. Polity.

Lacan, J. (1998a). *On Feminine Sexuality, The Limits of Love and Knowledge, 1972–1973: Encore the Seminar of Jacques Lacan Book XX*. Trans. B. Fink. New York: Norton.

Lacan, J. (1998). *The Four Fundamental Concepts of Psychoanalysis*. Seminar Book XI (1973), trans. A. Sheridan. New York: Routledge.

Lacan, J. (1991). *Freud's Papers on Technique: The Seminar of Jacques Lacan Book I 1953–1954*. Ed. Miller, J-A. Tr. J. Forrester. Routledge.

Lacan, J. (2015). *Transference: The Seminar of Jacques Lacan Book VIII*. Trans. B. Fink. Polity.

Lacan, J. *The Seminar of Jacques Lacan. Book XII: Crucial Problems for Psychoanalysis (1964–1965)*, untranslated.

Lacan, J. *The Seminar of Jacques Lacan. Book XV: The Psychoanalytic Act (1967–1968)*, untranslated.

Miller, J-A. (1992). The Labyrinths of Love. Tr. Marie-Laure Davenport. (Les Labyrinthes de l'amour). *La lettre Mensuelle*, 109, 19–22. https://jcfar.org.uk/wp-content/uploads/2016/03/The-Labyrinths-of-Love-Jacques-Alain-Miller.pdf

Miller, J-A. (2013). "On Love." Interview with Hanna Waar. Tr. Adrian Price. https://artandthoughts.fr/2013/12/03/jacques-alain-miller-on-love/

Neruda, P. (1983). *Passions and Impressions*. Edited by Matilde Neruda & Miguel Otero Silva. Translated by Margaret Sayers Peden. Farrar, Strauss and Giroux.

O. Henry (1905). The Gift of the Magi. http://webhome.auburn.edu/~vestmon/Gift_of_the_Magi.html

Ruti, M. (2011). *The Case for Falling in Love: Why We Can't Master the Madness of Love – and Why That's the Best Part*. Sourcebooks Casablanca.

Skuse, A. (2021). "Biting One's Tongue: Autoglossotomy and agency in *The Spanish Tragedy*." *Renaissance Studies: Journal of the Society of Renaissance Studies*. V. 36, Issue, 2, 278–294. https://onlinelibrary.wiley.com/doi/full/10.1111/rest.12747

Vighi, F. (2017). "L-D-L', or: Lacan's Dialectics of Love (in Loveless Times)." In Zeiher, C., & McGowan, T. (Eds.). (2017). *Can Philosophy Love? Reflections and Encounters* (pp. 67–86). Rowman & Littlefield International.

Zeiher, C., & McGowan, T. (Eds.). (2017). *Can Philosophy Love? Reflections and Encounters*. Rowman & Littlefield International.

Chapter 2

Til Death Do Us Part
Lacking in Love or Loving Lack

Stephanie Swales

No psychoanalysis would be worthy of its name without, at its core, consisting of love stories. From speaking about love between parents and children, siblings, friends, romantic partners, unrequited love, and of course the analysand's transference love, the bonds of love can initially seem relatively devoid of subjective freedom. Analysands repeat instead of remember the traumatic failures of the love relation and wish to be freed of its conflict, hatred, jealousy, and destructiveness. If only, they might say, my partner and I could communicate better, really understand each other, stop fighting, and so on, then I would be happy in my relationship, then I could really live. Via the capitalist discourse, neoliberal ideology promises solutions to these relationship discontents. It does so, for instance, by way of subscribing to a dating app and trading in your current partner for a new, improved one or through the promise of good communication and empathy through the purchase of Gary Chapman's immensely popular book *The Five Love Languages* (1992). It is not for nothing that Chapman's book now includes half a dozen versions tailored to different markets – including "The Five Love Languages for Men," "The Five Love Languages of Children," "The Five Love Languages Military Edition" and even "The Five Languages of Appreciation in the Workplace." Via the five love languages rubric, the attainment of a harmonious, happy relationship is reduced to something marketable and teachable – like learning to speak a foreign language and eventually becoming fluent in it. From a Lacanian perspective, however, we might say that each and every speaking being has their own love language; all communication is miscommunication and it is impossible to ever completely understand our own experience, let alone that of the other. Wishes for perfect communication and the cessation of arguments, jealousy, and so on boil down to two fundamental and related fantasies: first, that there is such a thing as a harmonious sexual relationship – or, in other words, that castration and lack are not irrevocably at the heart of existence; second, that the drives, which Lacan tells us are all death drives, could be tamed and peacefully incorporated into the fictions of the ego.

In contrast, the romantic relationship between Connell and Marianne depicted in Sally Rooney's 2018 novel *Normal People* is demonstrative of the impossibility of a symbiotic union of body and soul while simultaneously featuring the rich, satisfying, and at times exquisitely painful singular coupling of their unconscious

DOI: 10.4324/9781032663487-3

death drives. Just as the process of Lacanian psychoanalysis involves the construction of and eventual traversal of the fundamental fantasy, of someone's essential way of positioning themselves in relation to lack and the Other which is repeated ad infinitum, the eroticized shifting dynamics of social status and power between Marianne and Connell play a role in their progressive construction of a fundamental fantasy that is not shared so much as it is in certain respects complementary. Through symptomatic repetitions rife with the jouissance of rejection and nonbelonging, Marianne and Connell gradually assume responsibility for their desire and attain the subjective freedoms associated with what becomes a sinthomatic coupling – or perhaps a sinthomatic uncoupling. As such, the bonds of their love cannot be considered without death drive.

Normality and Belonging vs. Abnormality and Nonbelonging: Fantasies of Taming the Drives

The opening chapters of *Normal People* are set in rural Carricklea, County Mayo in Ireland where we are introduced to Marianne and Connell, two students in their last few months of secondary school who appear to their peers to have very little in common. The two of them are divided by significant differences in class, social status, and physical attractiveness. In terms of class, Marianne is wealthy and lives in a mansion with her cruel older brother (Alan) and her cold lawyer mother (Denise) who employs Connell's mother (Lorraine) as a housecleaner. Not only does Connell live with his single mother in relative poverty in a council house, but he is considered to come from a trashy family; Connell himself was the result of his mother's teenage pregnancy, and his uncles have gone to prison. On the other hand, Connell is a handsome and popular jock whereas Marianne is a fiercely intelligent, unpopular, excluded loner with crooked teeth and a plain face. The on-again, off-again nature of their romantic relationship notwithstanding, what draws and keeps them together is the death drive. Marianne describes something of this: "She feels pleasurably crushed under the weight of his power over her, the vast ecstatic depth of her will to please him" (Rooney, 2018, p. 241). The self-defeating, pleasure-pain of the death drive irresistibly calls them together at the expense of their own social status and of fulfilling what is expected of them.

With its fantasy of normalcy, Connell's brief relationship with his girlfriend Helen serves as an example of the paler pleasures of the pleasure principle-driven iterations of the social bond. Contrasting with Marianne's plain face and crooked teeth, we are told that Helen is beautiful, and "has a great smile, great teeth" (ibid., p. 160). Helen studies medicine, has a full circle of friends, gets along swimmingly with Lorraine, and invites him to spend a holiday with her family. "To be known as her boyfriend plants him firmly in the social world, establishes him as an acceptable person, someone with a particular status, someone whose conversational silences are thoughtful rather than socially awkward" (ibid., p. 161). With Helen, it's easy, normal, to say "I love you, even though it had never seemed possible before" (ibid., p. 161). However, Connell is not so much in love with Helen as he is infatuated in the imaginary with his fantasy of her and the person he becomes with her. "He finds himself rushing to the end of the conversation [with Helen] so they can hang up, and then he can retrospectively savor how much he likes seeing her, without the moment-to-moment pressure of having to produce the right expressions and say the right things" (ibid., p. 160). With Helen he denies the unconscious truths of his drives and playacts a role in which his speech acts, desires, and way of relating fit perfectly within the social order. Connell does not feel truly seen by Helen, which is to say that he does not expose his nothing, his lack to her, and this hiding has a certain steady pleasure to it. This pleasure principle version of the non-rapport of the sexual relation is not truly love, relatively devoid as it is of giving what one does not have, of desire, or of exposing one's lack.

In contrast to how he feels with Marianne, "[w]ith Helen he doesn't feel shameful things, he doesn't find himself saying weird stuff during sex, he doesn't have that persistent sensation that he belongs nowhere, that he never will belong anywhere" (ibid., p. 175). Marianne and Connell are joined together in their abnormality via the lack in the social order, by the death drive, which incites jouissance rather than pleasure. Unlike Helen, Marianne sees Connell in his extimacy, in his lack, and this is what makes their love so alternately compelling, frightening, embarrassing, and maddening. Out of fear of losing face, Connell takes pains to hide, for instance, his intelligence and his interest in literature from his popular secondary school social group, Marianne sees and appreciates this about him, encouraging him to pursue his desire at university – a desire which he had not realized he even had. Likewise, Connell "always thought [Marianne] was damaged" (ibid., p. 189), but yet even while dating Helen, Connell writes Marianne long emails, rescues her from an abusive relationship, kisses her, and pays rapt attention to her, preferring this partner who is lacking from the point of view of the external Other. To love someone means to love their lack, a lack which extimately corresponds to one's own lack. As Lacan puts it in his eighth seminar, to love is to love the object *a* or *ágalma*, as the cause of our desire one locates in one's partner (2015, p. 143).

Connell and Helen's version of the sexual relationship with its supposedly smooth march towards marriage and family testifies to nothing more than the socially held fantasy of what a "normal" relationship should be. Their relationship is bound to self-destruct – not only because of Connell's increasingly obvious love for Marianne and the jealousy incited in Helen, but also on account of its disavowal of the self-destructiveness at the center of the social world itself. By comparison, Connell's love for Marianne is so strong precisely because it is founded by way of the death drive, of the destructive, "terrible hold he'd had over her, and still had, and could not foresee ever losing" (Rooney, 2018, p. 176). At the start, Connell unconsciously desires to have power over Marianne, to function as a master figure for her and enjoy a relation that revolves around the anal and invocatory drives. This denial is the motor force behind his initially treating her so poorly – without realizing it – by refusing to acknowledge their relationship in public. The more we try to deny our castration the more we are unfree and enslaved by repetition compulsions. Correspondingly, there are substantial differences in romantic partnerships depending upon whether the union is founded primarily on the death drive or on fantasies of the exclusive reign of the pleasure principle as well as the degree to which each partner accepts lack and adopts an ethical position of nonbelonging.

In various ways, Marianne and Connell are interpellated as occupying positions of nonbelonging, or as abnormal by the regime of normality. The pleasure principle erects the fantasmatic screen of normality, and Helen temporarily protected Connell from having "that persistent sensation that he belongs nowhere, that he never will belong anywhere" (ibid., p. 175). The death drive, on the other hand, unites Connell and Marianne through their sharing "the same spiritual injury" such that "neither of them could ever fit into the world" (ibid., p. 242). As such, Connell and Marianne are united via their death drives, finding a kindred spirit in each other by way of their "weird" thoughts and pleasures which subvert their efforts to fit in with the crowd and enjoy a confident, smooth inclusion in the symbolic order. "It's not like this with other people" (ibid., p. 242) and never feeling lonely (ibid., p. 239) when they are together are two statements which demonstrate that they are bonded through the lack at the heart of the death drives (Galioto, 2023). Although both Connell and Marianne long for a feeling of belonging and at various times precariously attain it, they ultimately identify with positions of abnormality and nonbelonging. The impossibility of ever fitting into the world has something to do with (albeit not exclusively, to make a pun) being interpellated by the social order as trash: Connell takes on the position of trash via social class and Marianne embodies trash in her masochistic – although ultimately hysteric – fundamental fantasy.

Occupying the position of nonbelonging necessitates a certain assumption of lack – a lack which might be considered as the refuse or trash of the Other. A full consideration of what it is to take up the position of lack necessitates thinking through lack on the side of the subject – with the subject standing in for a lack in being around which the drives revolve – and lack on the side of the Other – of the Other's castration. On the side of the subject, one model for the subjectification of lack is the psychoanalyst. Lacan in *Television* (1974) speaks to the psychoanalyst's occupation of the position of lack, of playing the role of the object *a*, alternately calling the analyst's position as that of the saint or trashitas. Having subjectified lack, the analyst stands in for the unconscious or trash insofar as it is that which the analysand would prefer to throw away. To act like a saint is to embody a way of being comfortable with lack, with the object *a*, and with the unconscious. On the side of the Other, a subjective position of nonbelonging is what Todd McGowan, for instance in his book *The Racist Fantasy* (2022), emphasizes is ultimately an ethical stance that refuses to participate in the surplus jouissance – racist and otherwise – that comes from taking part in the capitalist discourse's disavowal of the lack in the Other. There is thus a certain subjective freedom for a couple united in nonbelonging.

Whereas some couples are united in belonging to the world, enjoying symbolic success or privilege or the community found in religious congregations or fandom of sports teams, other couples find themselves bonded through their shared status as misfits, racialized others, or some other category of reject of the social order. From this latter category we have the prototypical lovers' proclamation "it's us against the world!" A couple who adopts this rallying cry are not necessarily occupying the ethical position of nonbelonging elaborated upon by McGowan, since the social reject can function as a position within the dominant ideologies of the Other, and as such, couples can bring bad faith to their supposed status as rebels on the fringes of society. More commonly, marginalized individuals are interpellated as not belonging anywhere, and marginalized couples can understandably fantasize that if only they were to find some way to belong in the majority group that their suffering would abate and they would live happy lives. In other words, the subjective freedom associated with an ethical position of nonbelonging hinges upon an acceptance of castration – both one's own and that of the Other.

Although the ways in which Connell and Marianne, respectively, feel interpellated by the social order as trash do correspond to positions of nonbelonging, when the two of them initially avoid facing – much less subjectifying – their own desire, these positions of nonbelonging constitute symptomatically restricted subjective positions. Similarly, as though it were a dirty secret, they tend to hide their relationship from the social world, as if their relationship does not exist unless it is sanctioned by social expectations. In other words, for much of the book, neither does their love unite them in a position of nonbelonging nor does it lead to subjective freedom insofar as they do not have the courage to follow their desire and embrace lack. Correspondingly, in *Normal People* not only is there an evolution of the relationships that Marianne and Connell have to one another but also a transformation of their own relationships to the drive. The backdrop for this evolution is provided by shifting dynamics of power and social status, whereby one or the other of them can be seen in the phallic position as having what it takes to belong. Through the process of subjectifying their desire and embracing lack, Marianne and Connell shift from a love which is symptomatic to their love as sinthomatic.

A Child Is Being Beaten

At the beginning of their relationship, although Connell to a certain extent exposes his own lack to Marianne, sharing thoughts and things about himself (e.g., his enjoyment of learning and literature) which do not fit in with the expected profile of a popular jock, he obsessively doubts his love for her and keeps his relationship with her secret. In this vein, after the first time they have sex, Connell thinks that "he seemed to fit perfectly inside her…But why Marianne?…Some people thought she was the ugliest girl in school. What kind of person would want to do this with her?" (Rooney, 2018, p. 25). Connell continues to attempt to hide his lack from his social group, feeling deeply humiliated by what he extimately locates in Marianne, by that within himself which exceeds and does not belong to the figure of a popular male athlete. "[H]is life would be over" (ibid., p. 28), he thinks, if people found out. The cowardly disavowal involved in such a double-life ultimately leads to an eruption of his unconscious and the self-undermining that is characteristic of the drives; Connell represses his desire for a relationship with Marianne such that it never even occurs to him to ask her to the Debs school dance. Instead, he asks Rachel, the most popular girl in school. Although Marianne had until then played along and pretended that she was no one special, her discovery of Connell's betrayal leads her to the abrupt realization of his mistreatment of her, which she can no longer tolerate. In other words, Connell's denial of his own lack led to the self-destruction of the drives and to the destruction – albeit temporary – of their relationship.

Initially, Marianne plays the role of the anal object, of the trash, and idolizes Connell, whose superior attractiveness, athletic ability, and social status render him in possession of the phallus. As a hysteric, "she felt she would do anything to make him like her" (p. 18). Just prior to their first kiss, Connell says "I think it would be awkward in school if anything happened with us" (ibid., p. 15) and Marianne is the one who suggests that the nature of their relationship could be secret, that "no one would have to know" (ibid., p. 15). Marianne initiates this perverse pact of sorts, allowing herself to be alternately treated as loved and as trash to be thrown away as soon as representatives of the socio-symbolic matrix are present. In turn, Connell takes up the role of uncastrated master figure and incarnates the object of the invocatory drive, of the voice as superego, when after their first kiss he commands her to keep their kiss a secret. Marianne gives herself over to Connell and masochistically enjoys the position of the anal object. The first time they have sex, she is "on her hands and knees" and then says "thanks" afterwards as though Connell had rendered her an undeserved favor (ibid., p. 22).

Marianne's formula for a sexual relationship might be said to closely adhere to the formula for the varieties of fantasy in Freud's "A Child is Being Beaten." Although Marianne's father is dead, her remaining family members either ignore her or demean and abuse her in clear demonstrations of *jealouissance*. Marianne is quite literally beaten as well as relentlessly bullied by her older brother Alan. After receiving top exam results, Alan goes into one of his jealous outbursts, saying, "You're so fucking pathetic" followed by "Do you think you're smarter than me?" (ibid., p. 146). After she laughs involuntarily in response to his saying "You should hear what people in town say about you," Alan wrenches back her arm and spits on her (ibid., p. 147). Marianne's mother Denise clearly favors Alan despite his cruelty towards Marianne and his lack of symbolic success. For instance, Denise gives Marianne Christmas money with no card and in the same envelope she uses to pay Connell's mother (Lorraine). In this not-so-festive ceremony of holiday gift-giving, Denise pounds the table, yelling, "You think you're special, do you?" (ibid., p. 148). To the jealous accusations of both her mother and her brother, Marianne responds in the negative: no, she's nothing, nobody special, trash.

The child who is beaten is paradoxically assured of her place in the other's heart through the passion that inspires the beating. She is special precisely insofar as she, as trash, is paradoxically powerful as an object of disgust that inspires jealous rage, beatings, and the pounding of fists. She is the anal object of fascination who inspires men—her brother, her university boyfriend Jamie, her Swedish lover Lukas—to beat her, tie her up, tell her she is worthless trash. Marianne makes herself into the child who is being beaten and thus loved. That being said, she experiences a great deal of suffering, humiliation, and psychic deadening from this position that she is compelled to repeat, with her only respite coming from hiding herself or being ignored by the gaze of the Other; there is little subjective freedom in her vacillation between these two poles of being the Other's trash. This is not to say, however, that Marianne's path to increased freedom will involve mastering the masochism of her death drives and transforming her fantasy from "a child is being beaten" or "a child is being demeaned" by an Other who gets off on beating her to something like "a child is being praised and prized." The death drives are inherently masochistic and destructive, eliciting jouissance precisely from the impossibilities of attaining the object or being perfectly loved and understood by the Other.

First, Marianne begins by unconsciously wanting to be hurt, to be thought of as nothing, seen as nothing special, to be a dirty secret, trash, an outsider not fit for Connell to acknowledge in public. As such, she orchestrates taking up the passive position of the drive, seeking to make herself the degraded object. Her first movement into a more active subjective stance is initiated when Connell asks Rachel to the Debs instead of Marianne. In this symptomatic act, Connell's death drive sabotages his desire to be with Marianne. This desire quickly becomes retroactively clear to him when he "entered a period of low spirits" (ibid., p. 76). "He had recurring dreams about being with Marianne again" (ibid., p. 77) from which he would "wake up feeling so depressed he couldn't move a single muscle in his body" (ibid., p. 77). Connell's depression is here demonstrative of Lacan's formulation of it in *Television* as a "moral failing" or a "moral weakness, which is, ultimately, located only to thought; that is, in the duty to be Wellspoken, to find one's way in dealing with the unconscious" (1974/1990, p. 22). In other words, Connell's depression indicated his failure to acknowledge, take responsibility for, and act in accordance with his unconscious desire. In turn, Connell's symptomatic act awakens Marianne's desire to be acknowledged as special to Connell and her refusal of a position of pure refuse. Marianne removes herself entirely from Connell's gaze and reach through ceasing to attend school – she studies for exams at home instead – and refusing to take his calls. She even stands up to Alan when he angrily insists that she speak to Connell. (How dare she refuse to do something a male has asked her to do?) In these refusals Marianne actively asserts her desire.

Hiding, Saving Face, and the mi-dire of Speech

When we next find the pair in conversation, they are both students at Trinity College, Dublin where through a reversal of their power dynamic Marianne has become an accepted member of a popular social group, "suddenly has a cool boyfriend and Connell is the lonely, unpopular one" (Rooney, 2018, p. 76). Marianne is now regarded as looking pretty and being worthy of having friends, whereas Connell feels ashamed of his poverty and feels his lack of wealth makes him a social outsider. Even as they resume their sexual relationship one drunken night, both of them continue to suffer from insecurities that lead them to try to hide their lack and their desire for one another. Marianne says she thinks she is unlovable (ibid., p. 104), cries when they watch *The Umbrellas of Cherbourg*, turning "her face away so it looked like she wasn't crying" (ibid., p. 105), and fails to tell Connell about her family's mistreatment and lack of love for her. Over a year later, when she finally discloses the extent of the abuse she suffers from her family, she explains she hid it from him because she was afraid he would think she was damaged (ibid., p. 189). Not only do we learn that Connell always thought she was damaged, but seeing her as damaged, as abnormal, may have been the condition for the possibility of his love for her.

After Connell's work hours are cut he can no longer afford to pay his rent. Connell procrastinates and then tries but fails to ask Marianne if he can move in with her so that he does not have to move back home for the summer. Instead, he tells her only that he cannot afford to pay rent in the summer; this part of the truth was itself challenging to admit because in the face of her riches, he dislikes bringing up his relative poverty (ibid., p. 125). Marianne jumps to the conclusion that Connell means he wants to move back home and does not wish to be with her. In the absence of Marianne's direct declaration of her desire to stay in a relationship with him, Connell defensively brings up what he doesn't want and says, "I guess you'll want to see other people, then, will you?" (ibid., p. 129) to which Marianne responds "sure" "in a voice that struck him as truly cold" (ibid., p. 129). Afterwards, Marianne's interpretation of the event was that Connell had said "he wanted to see other people" (ibid., p. 114) to which she had assented because "she was never really his girlfriend, she's not even his ex-girlfriend. She's nothing" (ibid., p. 114). Each of them, in other words, quickly assumes the position of the nothing, of trash, rather than risking the exposure of their desire for the other.

Although in these bungled communications the reader could blame class differences and a lack of clear communication on their breakup – thinking if only they could have said what they truly wanted then they could have lived happily ever after – the material, class-based conditions of their relationship (Owens, 2022) and this and many other misunderstandings cover over the real of the impossibility of the sexual relation. Speech is always a half saying, a *mi-dire*, says Lacan, and so there is no such thing as a perfect transmission of human experience. Neither can the fantasy depicted in Aristophanes' speech in Plato's *Symposium* contribution be realized – that of two people, two hearts, two souls, harmoniously joining together as a perfect sphere. At the same time, there is something to be said regarding the respective failures of the couple to take up the ethics of *le Bien-dire*, the Wellspoken. With each of them shrinking from avowing their desire and exposing their lack, they retreat from the possibilities of love bonded by the drives and their respective repetition compulsions sever their connection once again.

Within a few weeks of Connell's departure, Marianne embarks upon the first of several relationships with explicit sado-masochistic dynamics occurring in the bedroom. Marianne dates Jamie, a fellow wealthy Trinity College student whom everyone in their shared social circle believes is a good match for her despite the demeaning comments he sends her way. In one scene, after remarking on Jamie's insecurity – he is a transparent braggart and intellectually and otherwise Marianne is superior to him – she goes on to tell Connell that Jamie is a sexual sadist (Rooney, 2018, p. 136). Having become more aware of her drives, after they begin dating Marianne initiates their sado-masochistic sexual relationship, telling Connell later that she "wanted to submit to him" and "[i]t's not that I get off on being degraded as such…I just like to know that I would degrade myself for someone if they wanted me to…And it turns out he likes to beat me up" (ibid., p. 137). Marianne goes on to explain that with Jamie she is "acting a part" but with Connell she "actually had those feelings" and "would have done anything [he] wanted [her] to" (ibid., p. 139). In contrast to her relationship with the insecure Jamie, the interplay of power, desire, and love is more compelling with Connell, who moreover says he would not wish to hit her. Although in a sense through beating and choking her during sex Jamie gives Marianne the masochistic jouissance that she seems to want, they are neither aligned in mutual desire nor by way of the circuit of the drives.

When, at a social gathering after Connell and Marianne each win a prestigious scholarship, Connell witnesses Jamie's mistreatment of her, Connell rescues her, walking her out. As such, although it is not Marianne's desire but that of Connell that leads her to walk away from Jamie, she later breaks things off with Jamie. What is more, later that night Marianne shares for the first time with Connell something of the extent of how poorly she is treated by her family. She admits that her brother recently told her she should kill herself, and that her mother stood by and witnessed this without much protest. In this fashion, Connell and Marianne each make progressive moves toward exposing their lack and the subjectification of their own desire through the assistance of one another. Marianne, for instance, had encouraged Connell back in Carricklea to study literature instead of going to university in Galway like all his friends and becoming a lawyer – a career path which did not interest him. Love here appears variously as wanting the other to pursue their desire and as loving the other's lack.

After Marianne ends things with Jamie, she quickly regains her former position as a social pariah. Marianne goes on an Erasmus year in Sweden where she again finds herself in a painful position of nonbelonging – one which is not simply due to her inability to speak Swedish. During this year, Marianne and Connell continue to speak and write to one another, but they shrink from subjectifying their desire. In this, they are paradoxically united in the jouissance of depression (Connell eventually goes to see a therapist), their lack of subjective agency subjecting them to the ravages of their drives. While in Sweden, Marianne's repetition compulsion escalates in harmfulness when she enters into a relationship with Lukas, a Swedish artist. Their visits with one another consist largely of sadomasochistic sexual relations – or what Lukas calls "the game" – during which she is not allowed to talk or make eye contact. Even after the sex is over he likes to tell her

You're worthless...You're nothing. And she feels like nothing, an absence to be forcibly filled in...She experiences a depression so deep it is tranquilizing, she eats whatever he tells her to eat, she experiences no more ownership over her own body than if it were a piece of litter. (ibid., pp. 196–197)

Marianne feels unreal, not feeling hunger, thirst, or desire except in fleeting moments. She has dropped out of agentic subjectivity and reduced her existence entirely to the operations of the anal and invocatory drives. As the object of litter, of the anal drive, the phallic Other, Lukas, brings the voice and she gets herself superegoically commanded and denigrated. In another sense, Connell derives particular jouissance from the invocatory drive – both as a writer and in the delicious silence he enjoys when he is together with Marianne.

Given Lukas's relative lack of consideration for her personhood and Marianne's exclusion from a community, Marianne seems even more closely aligned via the drives with Lukas than she had been with Jamie. But again her heart isn't in it. It is as if she has succeeded in killing both the Other's desire and her own by so completely transforming herself into the object of the Other's demand. With Lukas, Marianne performs the rote repetitions of the drive and doggedly represses her desire. Notably, Marianne leaves this hollow pretense of a relationship on her own account this time. Interestingly, the catalyst for her standing up for her desire occurs when, in the midst of being tied up, Lukas says "I love you...and I know you love me" (ibid., p. 203). Horrified, Marianne demands to be unbound and commands "Don't ever talk to me like that again" (ibid., p. 204). Marianne wonders, "how could he tie the notion of love to the basest forms of violence?" (ibid., p. 204). Marianne's assertion of her subjectivity is incited by her anger at the reduction of love to the level of demand and the destruction of the drives and herself as a mere object. Whatever is between them is not about desire, about giving what one does not have, and not about revealing one's lack. Although the love relation cannot be considered without the jouissance of the drives, it also cannot be reduced to it.

For Connell's part, during Marianne's Erasmus year in Sweden he focuses his efforts on being normal, on belonging, and therefore dates Helen. Through hiding from his desire in this fashion he lays the groundwork for his depression, the onset of which is tied to learning of the suicide of his friend Rob from secondary school. In a clear identification with Rob, he fantasizes "about lying completely still until he died of hydration" (ibid., p. 210). Rob had been "a very insecure person, obsessed with popularity" (ibid., p. 232). Connell visits a therapist, and reveals that he keeps returning to the thought that not only is Rob gone but he cannot have his old life back (ibid., p. 224) – his life in which he felt he belonged and was normal. Connell, like Rob, has been consumed by the inauthentic search for popularity and belonging with the corresponding attempt to have the phallus in the eyes of the social world. The death drive, however, subverts such attempts at every turn. The crisis of his depression therefore announces itself as a crisis of his singular desire and of how he obsessionally relates to his lack and to the death drive.

We Are Gathered Here Today to Witness the Joining of Two Deaths

Connell's depression lifts when he, as a writer, starts writing again, putting suffering into words. Connell has great trepidation for being exposed as a poor writer, and so it is only after much struggle and the encouragement of a friend (Sadie) that he eventually submits a short story for publication in the college literary magazine. Upon acceptance, albeit under a pseudonym, he allows it to be published. He takes another risk and applies for an MFA program in New York. In all of these decisions he acts upon his own desire, thus exercising the subjective freedom opened up by be willing to expose his own lack.

Four months later, Connell and Marianne are in his room together and after some fumbling assumptions that each of them wants Marianne to leave, they are finally able to voice their love and desire for one another. However, this blissful union comes to an abrupt end only minutes later when Marianne asks Connell to hit her and he refuses to do so. Although he does not wish to hit her, he knows he enjoys and has "cultivated" the "effortless tyranny over someone [Marianne] who seems to other people, so invulnerable" (ibid., p. 255). As such, Connell's jouissance and drives do align with Marianne's. One's relationship to the real of the drives can be more or less conducive to the survival of the love relation, because in order for the love—and the lovers themselves—to live on, the death drive cannot completely take hold of the subject. Connell's refusal sets in motion Marianne's own refusal of the extremes of the death drive.

What is more, Connell's refusal of Marianne's request for him to beat her is itself a response of love or of recognition of Marianne at the level of being. Lacan's formula for love from Seminar XIX is clearly relevant: "*I ask you to refuse me my offering, because this isn't it*" (2018, p. 77, italics in original). At the heart of Marianne's beating fantasy is a man, a powerful master figure who could beat her, but instead holds himself back. Connell reads the desire behind Marianne's demand, and there is a correspondence between her lack and his own.

Being seen at the level of being, or having one's desires and one's drives recognized however, does not feel straightforwardly pleasurable as the exposure of one's lack elicits an intense vulnerability. Feeling horrible shame after Connell's refusal to hit her, Marianne insists on walking home. Marianne is met upon her arrival by Alan, who, in a fit of rage ends up drunkenly giving her what she had asked (Connell) for; after Alan throws a bottle against the wall she flees to her room, holding the door handle and the weight of her body against the door to prevent Alan from entering, but the handle slips from her hand and the door bangs open, hitting her square in the face and breaking her nose. Blood streaming out of her face and nose, Marianne makes an important and unprecedented move away from her repetition compulsion and towards subjective freedom. Marianne calls Connell, minimizing what happened at first, but asking him to drive over and get her. Upon arrival, he quickly discerns the nature of what had happened and they leave together after Connell threatens Alan with his life. In admitting that she wanted Connell's help, that she chose the bonds of love with him over the shackles of destruction and degradation tying her to Alan and her mother, Marianne gives her desire as an agentic subject to Connell and – at least in that moment – leaves behind the realm of belonging as the trash object.

Both Connell and Marianne, in turn, set a limit to the extreme of the masochism of the death drive while at the same time accepting more than ever that they are bound together in love by the drives. Seven months later, they are still together when Connell announces that he has been accepted into the MFA program in New York. Marianne, we are told, is now capable of believing that Connell loves her, that she is worth loving instead of trash. In spite of Connell giving her the power to tell him to stay, Marianne encourages him to go to New York, to pursue his desire at the expense of their togetherness. Love, here, is depicted as giving up one's own enjoyment, and even the potential longevity of the relationship itself, for the sake of encouraging the other to pursue their desire. "What they have now they can never have back again" (ibid., p. 273). Accepting the essential flux of life, of the death of each present moment and each fictional idea of what one has or does not have in a romantic relationship paradoxically allows for a sinthomatic love connection—one which is bound together by a couple's singular, or, to make a bad pun, coup-ular ("*coup*" being French for "cut") acceptance of the lack of enjoyment at the heart of the death drive.

A Lacanian psychoanalytic vision of subjective freedom coincides with the construction of and identification with the sinthome: as a knotting together of imaginary, symbolic, and real, it is one's radically individual solution to living in a social world with the ultimate real of death. To make freedom possible in life as well as in love, the death drive, the motor force of the unassimilable real, must facilitate the destruction of the ego's fictions and something of an undoing of the self as well as of the Other. In this process, one must have a certain kind of openness to the horror of the real. Neither the self nor the Other can be seen as having the potential for completion; there is no Other who can provide meaning to life. Instead, one radically assumes responsibility for our actions and lives through identifying with the sinthome, the irreducible kernel of the real that resists symbolization or understanding. In other words, one identifies with the perpetual failure to achieve any substantive presence, knotting oneself together in a way that is more inclusive of the death drive itself. When a couple unites in this failure, in the lack at the heart of the self and the Other, in the impossibility of the sexual relation, the regimes of belonging and normality are revealed in their unfreedom. In contrast to the bonds of marriage, the bonds of sinthomatic love – which may of course also involve marriage – are not forged in the vow "'til death do us part" but instead in an implicit acknowledgement of being in each moment joined together in death.

Since at the end of analysis the individual's enslavement to covering over lack is disrupted, resulting in a savoir-faire regarding the real, the process of psychoanalysis typically reduces the occupation of the social link in the form of aggression. However, sinthomatic love, bound in desire and with the real of the death drive, can absolutely involve jouissance in hitting, physically restraining, or otherwise demeaning one another – especially in, but also outside of the bedroom. As such, perhaps somewhere there is a real-life version of Marianne and Connell who are, at this very moment, yelling vulgar nothings to one another: "You freak!" "You weirdo!" "You nothing!"

References

Chapman, G. (1992). *The Five Love Languages: The Secret to Love That Lasts*. Chicago, IL: Northfield Publishing.

Lacan, J. (1990). *Television* (D. Hollier, R. Krauss, & A. Michelson). New York: W.W. Norton & Co. Original work published 1974.

Lacan, J. (2015). *Transference. Seminar Book VIII*, trans. B. Fink. Malden, MA: Polity Press. Original work published 1960.

Lacan, J. (2018). *…or Worse. Seminar Book XIX*, trans. A.R. Price. Malden, MA: Polity Press.

Galioto, E. (2023). "Prohibition and Power: *Normal People* as Pandemic Pornography," in *Psychoanalysis and the Small Screen: The Year the Cinemas Closed* (Eds. Owens, C. & Meehan O'Callahan, S.). New York & London: Routledge.

McGowan, T. (2022). *The Racist Fantasy: Unconscious Roots of Hatred*. New York & London: Bloomsbury Publishing.

Owens, C. (2022). "Normal People in Abnormal Times: How a TV Show Rocked the Irish Pandemic Lockdown…and Other Fantasies." *Analytic Agora, 1*, 182–199.

Rooney, S. (2018). *Normal People*. London & New York: Hogarth Press.

Chapter 3

(Courtly) Love and Death (Drive)

Russell Sbriglia

Perhaps no other psychoanalytic concept has been subject to as much misprision as the death drive. Typically understood as a will toward self-destruction (Thanatos) that stands in utter contradistinction to the life drive (Eros), the death drive, as Jacques Lacan clarifies in Seminar XI, *The Four Fundamental Concepts of Psychoanalysis*, is not the opposite of life but, on the contrary, "pure life instinct, that is to say, immortal life, or irrepressible life, . . . indestructible life" (Lacan, 1978, p. 198). As such, the death drive is not so much an agent of death as of undeadness, an ensign not of human finitude and mortality, but of inhuman infinitude and immortality. As Slavoj Žižek puts it, the death drive is the reason why "human life is never 'just life,'" why human beings are "not simply alive" but "possessed by the strange drive to enjoy life in excess, passionately attached to a surplus which sticks out and derails the ordinary run of things" (Žižek, 2006, p. 62). Crucial to stress here is that though this "traumatic imbalance" does indeed swerve the *human being* from its "natural" state, rendering the human condition that of "an animal sick unto death," it would be a mistake to think of the death drive as bringing about the death of that immortal being which psychoanalysis designates as the *subject*, for it is only through the death drive that authentic subjectivity emerges – an unconscious subjectivity embodied by the undead, extimate object of surplus-enjoyment (*jouissance*) that is at one and the same time the "object-cause of desire" and the "object-loss of drive": that object which Lacan dubbed "*objet petit a*" (Žižek, 1989, pp. 181, 4; 2006, p. 62). To thus speak, as many other theoretical schools of thought do, of the "human subject" is for psychoanalysis a misnomer, for the term "subject" designates the emergence of an uncanny, *inhuman* being within the very heart of the human being, a death-driven being that ex-propriates the human being from itself, thereby rendering it forever *dis*oriented, forever nonidentical with itself.[1]

Shocking as it may seem to those not well versed in Lacanian psychoanalysis, the death drive, precisely insofar as it disorients and expropriates the human being, compelling it to act contrary to "its own good," against "its own best interests," is an *ethical* agency. As Joan Copjec reminds us, the very ethics of psychoanalysis rests upon the principle of the death drive in that the freedom of the ethical subject is "the freedom to resist the lure of the pleasure principle" – to "*disregard* all circumstances, causes, conditions, all promises of reward or punishment for its actions" – and "submit oneself to the law of the death drive" (Copjec, 1994, p. 96). The Kantian way of putting this would be to say that the ethical subject's freedom is "non-pathological." This is why, as Žižek likes to stress, "freedom hurts": authentic freedom entails submission to an extimate agency that, though it constitutes the innermost core of one's being, that which is "in one more than oneself," one cannot help but experience as a foreign intruder, something fundamentally alien, *autre*, other.[2] True freedom involves "a painful renunciation [of] our spontaneous tendencies on behalf of [a] duty" that nonetheless appears to us as our highest calling, as an "inner necessity," something we "just cannot not do" (Žižek, 2023, p. 124).[3] Hence Alenka Zupančič's characterization of the ethics of psychoanalysis as an "ethics of the Real," an ethics wherein one (as in the case of Antigone, the main subject of Lacan's seminar dedicated to "the ethics of psychoanalysis," Seminar VII) is confronted with "the unbearable burden of a really free choice," a choice that, like the Real itself, is *impossible* (See Zupančič, 2000; Žižek, 2006, p. 60).

In no case is the impossible, death-driven choice of freedom clearer than that of love. As Mladen Dolar has pointed out, though we tend to think that true love cannot exist without "an autonomy of free choice" with respect to one's love object, that "one cannot speak of love if there is no freedom of choice," a mere cursory glance through "the centuries of effusions about love" will quickly disabuse us of this notion, for such works repeatedly suggest that "love and autonomy of the subject rule each other out" (Dolar, 1996, p. 131). Indeed, as a rule, love in these texts appears in the guise of what Lacan termed a "forced choice" or "*vel* of alienation," a choice, he explains, "whose properties depend on this, that there is, in the joining, one element that, whatever the choice operating may be, has as its consequence a *neither one, nor the other*," this "one element" being the "lethal factor" of death (Lacan, 1978, pp. 211, 213). As in Lacan's iconic example of this *vel*, the mugger's demand of "*Your money or your life!*" – a choice which leaves one no choice at all, for to choose money would be to lose both one's money *and* one's life – the lovers in these texts, as Dolar underscores, are fundamentally alienated from themselves insofar as they are "compelled to choose love and thereby give up the freedom of choice," for to choose freedom of choice, paradoxically, would be to lose both freedom of choice *and* love (Dolar, 1996, p. 131).[4] It would thus appear that if the annals of literary love teach us nothing else, it is that to exercise one's freedom with respect to love cannot but be experienced as its very opposite: submission to the ultimate Other, Fate.

To further illustrate that literary love is typically attended by a *vel* of alienation that in one and the same gesture "presupposes the freedom of an autonomous choice and . . . demands its suppression," Dolar turns to the age-old trope of "love at first sight" (Dolar, 1996, pp. 130–131). As he recounts, plots that deploy this trope typically unfold as follows:

> A young hero quite *by coincidence* and *through no endeavor of his* meets a young girl in some more or less extraordinary circumstances. What happened

unintentionally and by pure chance is in the second stage recognized as the realization of his innermost and immemorial wishes and desires. The contingent miraculously becomes the place of his deepest truth, the sign of fate given by the Other. It is the Other that has chosen, not the young man himself who was powerless. . . . It turns out that the pure chance was actually no chance at all: the intrusion of the unforeseen turned into necessity, the *tyche* turned into the *automaton*. The moment of subjectivation is precisely that moment of suspension of subjectivity to the Other (fate, providence, eternal plan, destiny, or whatever one might call it), manifesting itself as the pure contingency of the Real. Indeed, the strange force of love reputedly rules out any other considerations; it does not permit deliberation, the balance of gains and losses, pondering the advantages of a certain choice – it just demands the unconditional surrender to the Other. (Dolar, 1996, p. 131)

Here we see how the forced choice of love throws the lover headlong into an ethics of the Real. Like the non-pathological ethics of psychoanalysis, which rejects all utilitarian calculations and concerns, the "strange force" of love at first sight, a force that appears to the lover as though it were "the sign of fate given by the Other," brooks no "pondering" or "deliberation," no "balance of gains and losses." On the contrary, as with the Kantian categorical imperative, an empty, purely formal command to do one's duty "for duty's sake" only, love at first sight is utterly non-pathological, "motived not by its determinate object, but by the mere *form* of love," "love for the sake of love itself, not for the sake of what distinguishes the object" (Žižek, 2017, p. 269).[5] What Žižek says of freedom thus equally applies to "pure love," or, as we might otherwise put it, "Real love," love as an incursion of the Real: it *hurts*.

That "Real love" hurts is a point that, so far as literature is concerned, is no more clearly illustrated than by the genre of courtly love. In his famous lesson on courtly love in *The Ethics of Psychoanalysis*, "Courtly Love as Anamorphosis," Lacan stresses that, as a rule, the Lady of courtly love poetry is "never characterized for any of her real, concrete virtues, for her wisdom, her prudence, or even her competence" (Lacan, 1992, p. 150). Indeed, so frequently is she "emptied of all real substance" and "presented with depersonalized characteristics" that, as certain scholars of the genre have remarked, "all the poets seem to be addressing the same person" (Lacan, 1992, p. 149). This is because the courtly Lady is "not our 'fellow-creature,'" but rather a woman who has been anamorphically sublimated to the dignity of that non-pathological object of "absolute, inscrutable Otherness" for which Lacan reserved "the Freudian term *das Ding*, the Thing – the Real that 'always returns to its place,' the hard kernel that resists symbolization" (Žižek, 1994, p. 90).[6] Hence the lethal dimension of the courtly Lady, who can be understood as a precursor to the *femme fatale* of film noir.[7] When the Lady appears, "one's time is up," for love of a courtly Lady is "a love too true to be bearable," a love whose motto is not "till death do us part," but "till death do us unite" (Dolar, 1996, pp. 140–141).

A couple of brief examples from the medieval literature of courtly love will suffice to illustrate this point.[8] Consider, for instance, Chaucer's "A Complaint to His Lady," which begins as follows:

> In the long night, when every creature should naturally take some rest, else his life cannot long hold out, then it falls most into my woeful thoughts how I have dropped so far behind that save death naught can comfort me, so despair I of all happiness. This thought abides with me till morn, and forth from morn till eve. I need borrow no grief, I have both leisure and leave to mourn. There is no wight will take my woe or forbid me to weep enough and wail my fill; the sore spark of pain destroys me.
>
> This love has so placed me that he will never fulfill my desire; for neither pity, mercy nor grace can I find. Yet even for fear of death can I not root out love from my sorrowful heart. The more I love, the more my lady pains me; through which I see, without remedy, that I may nowise escape death. (Chaucer, 1912, pp. 353–354)[9]

If, as the old saying goes, love is like a rose, then Chaucer's love would appear to be all thorns. As with the superego, which only becomes crueler the more one obeys it, the more the speaker loves his Lady the more she "pains" him—a pain which, like superego guilt, we should identify with the *jouissance* generated by the death drive. Indeed, the speaker captures the very logic of the death drive when he explains that though he knows very well that love "will never fulfill [his] desire," he is nonetheless unable to "root out" this love from his "sorrowful heart," "even for fear of death." On the contrary, he finds that it is *he* who is rooted out by love.[10] The choice here is thus not that of love *or* death, for, as the poem continually suggests, to find oneself in love is, perforce, to wish for a speedy death. As the lover puts it elsewhere in the poem, "Within my true, care-worn heart there is so much woe, and eke so little joy, that woe is me that ever I was born" (Chaucer, 1912, p. 354).[11] Rather, the choice is that of love *and* death, or, more precisely, love *and* death *drive*.

This very same coincidence of love and the death drive, this "lovesickness unto death," as we might put it, is even more pronounced in another classic work of medieval courtly love: Dante's *Vita Nuova*, a book that begins with just the sort of scene of love at first sight detailed by Dolar above. As Dante recounts, at the "very moment" he first laid eyes on Beatrice:

> the vital spirit, the one that dwells in the most secret chamber of the heart, began to tremble so violently that even the most minute veins of my body were strangely affected; and trembling, it spoke these words: *Ecce deus fortior me, qui veniens dominabitur michi* ["Here is a god stronger than I who comes to rule over me"]. At that point the animal spirit, the one abiding in the high chamber to which all the senses bring their perceptions, was stricken with amazement and, speaking directly to the spirits of sight, said these words: *Apparuit iam beatitudo*

vestra ["Now your bliss has appeared"]. At that point the natural spirit, the one dwelling in that part where our food is digested, began to weep, and weeping said these words: *Heu miser, quia frequenter impeditus ero deinceps!* ["Oh, wretched me! for I shall be disturbed often from now on!"] Let me say that, from that time on, Love governed my soul, which became immediately devoted to him, and he reigned over me with such assurance and lordship, given him by the power of my imagination, that I could only dedicate myself to fulfilling his every pleasure. (Alighieri, 1973, pp. 3–4)

Here we have an iconic instance of the fatal effect of love at first sight, as Love is personified as a godly force (hence the capital "L") that lords over the lover, who suddenly finds himself occupying the position of a bondsman. As in many other works of courtly love, this likening of the Lady-lover (non)relationship to that of a master and slave recurs throughout the text, as when, for instance, in his first ballad to Beatrice, Dante writes that, "so firmly faithful" has he been to her that not only does "every thought keep him a slave" to her, but, what is more, should she wish to "sentence [him] to death," she would "see a faithful slave's obedience" (Alighieri, 1973, p. 19). Such acquiescence to death at the hands of the Lady calls to mind nothing so much as the "will to *jouissance*" upon which Lacan based his riposte to the famous "gallows apologue" from Kant's *Critique of Practical Reason*, the latter of which unfolds as follows:

Suppose someone asserts of his lustful inclination that, when the desired object and the opportunity are present, it is quite irresistible to him; ask him whether, if a gallows were erected in front of the house where he finds this opportunity and he would be hanged on it immediately after gratifying his lust, he would not then control his inclination. One need not conjecture very long what he would reply. (Kant, 1997, p. 27)

Though Kant confidently presumes that no rational individual would *willingly* give up his life to gratify a mere passion, however strong that passion may be, Lacan rejoins that the literature of courtly love offers ample evidence to the contrary (Lacan, 2006, p. 661). Indeed, Dante's willingness to be put to death with "a faithful slave's obedience" illustrates Lacan's very point that "a partisan of passion, who would be blind enough to combine it with questions of honor, would make trouble for Kant by forcing him to recognize that no occasion precipitates certain people more surely toward their goal than one that involves defiance or even contempt for the gallows" (Lacan, 2006, p. 660). As a courtly lover, Dante is all too willing to sacrifice his "bare," mortal life for the excessive "new life" (*vita nuova*) opened within him by the immortality of the love-and-death drive. This is why he associates love with *jouissance*, something that is simultaneously the source of his greatest happiness ("Now your bliss has appeared!") and his abject wretchedness ("Oh, wretched me! for I shall be disturbed often from now on!"). As Chaucer does in his "Complaint," Dante here stages the coalescence of love and the death drive in the form of a disorienting enjoyment (*jouissance*) that, to put things in the Lacanian language of the matheme, transposes the human being from a simple "S," a "'pathological' subject," a "brute subject of pleasure," to an "$, " a non-pathological, barred subject of a sublime enjoyment located altogether beyond the pleasure principle (Lacan, 2006, p. 654). In this sense, the literature of courtly love stages the very same "critique of pure desire" as psychoanalysis.[12]

To thus return to where we started, it is the same with love as with the death drive: in order to achieve authentic, subjective freedom, to progress from S to $, one must paradoxically renounce one's freedom of choice and accept as one's fate the "alien extimate kernel" at which love aims, for this extimate kernel is "the only precarious and evasive hold for the subject" (Dolar, 1996, pp. 149–150). Indeed, as Dolar stresses, the very lesson of "the courtly love that Lacan often takes up" is that "in order to be a subject" the lover must "pawn" his being and submit to the Lady-Thing (Dolar, 1996, p. 142). What is crucial to emphasize here is that the lover submits to the Lady-Thing not as a means of consummating his relationship with her; on the contrary, as Žižek clarifies, though the lover's "'official' desire" is "to sleep with the lady," in actuality "there is nothing [he] fear[s] more than a Lady who might generously yield to this wish" (Žižek, 1994, p. 96). Rather, the lover submits to the Lady-Thing as a paradoxical means of "*detour*" (Žižek, 1994, p. 96), as a means of keeping the sublime object at a perpetual distance, for to come too close to the sublime object is to risk becoming a "pervert" in the vein of the various torturer-executioners that populate the Sadean oeuvre, an expressly *unethical* subject who "compromises his desire" by becoming an object of pure superego, a mere "instrument" or "organ" of the Other's *jouissance*.[13] This is why "the status of the subject as such is hysterical" (Žižek, 1989, p. 181). Authentic subjectivity is tied to that hysterical question which Lacan identified as the "*Che vuoi?*": What does the Other want? What is it in me that the Other desires? In contrast to the sadist pervert, who knows very well what the Other wants and is thus all too willing to become the (surplus-)object of its sickening enjoyment, the hysterical subject retains its autonomy precisely insofar as the Other's desire remains opaque to it, for it is by way of this very opacity that the subject is "thrown back on [it]self, compelled to assume the risk of freely determining the coordinates of [its] desire" (Žižek, 2003, p. 129). Only by reckoning with this "abyss of freedom" is it possible for one to become an ethical subject, a subject of pure desire.

As the literature of courtly love repeatedly demonstrates, tarrying with this abyssal freedom is a painful, anxiety-ridden experience. And yet, this pain and anxiety, this lovesickness unto death, is the very substance of the subject's freedom. This is why the ethics of love and the ethics of the death drive are ultimately one and the same, why Eros and Thanatos are not opposites but, as Lacan insisted, one and the same "drive." To risk putting this dynamic in the form of a Lacanian maxim, we could say that *love is on the side of the death drive.*

Notes

1 In claiming that subjectivity "disorients" the human being, I am drawing on Alenka Zupančič, who, in distinguishing Lacanian ontology from the object-oriented ontology

of Graham Harman and Levi Bryant, explains that if an ontology can indeed be gleaned from Lacanian psychoanalysis, it can only be an "object-disoriented ontology," "an ontology as 'disoriented' by what [Lacan] calls the object *a*." Such an ontology "pursues not simply being *qua* being, but the crack (the Real, antagonism) that haunts being from within." The agent of this haunting is, of course, the death drive (Zupančič, 2017, p. 24).

2 See, for instance, Slavoj Žižek, *Freedom: A Disease without Cure* (2023, p. 124). Worth stressing here is that the "*a*" in *objet petit a* stands for "*autre*."

3 Hence the "deontological" nature of psychoanalytic ethics, which is inextricably linked to the non-pathology of the death drive.

4 Worth noting here is Dolar's clarification that the *vel* of alienation is not merely a simple "absence of choice." Though "the choice is offered and denied in the same gesture," this "empty gesture" is nonetheless "what counts for subjectivity," what brings about the subject's "subjectivation" (1996, p. 130).

5 As Žižek clarifies, "true," non-pathological love entails not "indifference toward its object" but, more precisely, "indifference toward the properties of the beloved object." The logic of true love is not, "I love you because I find your positive features attractive," but rather, "I find your positive features attractive because I love you and therefore observe you with a loving gaze. Consequently, all the 'fullness' of the positive features which I adore in the beloved are a stand-in for the 'emptiness' which I really love – even if each of them were to be obliterated, I would still love you" (2017, p. 271).

6 Lacan famously defines sublimation as the "rais[ing]" or "elevat[ing]" of an object – especially a "feminine object" – to "the dignity of the Thing" (Lacan, 1986, p. 112).

7 Perhaps the best example of this overlap of the courtly Lady and the *femme fatale* is the character of Madeleine from Hitchcock's *Vertigo*. On this point, see Žižek (2003/2004, pp. 67–82).

8 What follows is an extremely brief engagement with medieval courtly love through a Lacanian lens, one that merely scratches the surface. For more sustained examples of such engagement, see, for instance, Kay (2001), Fradenburg (2002), Labbie (2006), and Rosenfeld (2011).

9 For the sake of readers less familiar with Middle English, I have chosen to quote from Tatlock and MacKay's prosified, modern English rendering of the poem. Chaucer's original reads as follows:

The longe nights, whan every creature
Shulde have hir rest in somwhat as by kynde,
Or elles ne may hir lif nat longe endure,
Hit falleth most into my woful mynde
How I so fer have broght myself behynde
That, sauf the deeth, ther may nothyng me lisse,
So desespaired I am from alle blisse.
This same thoght me lasteth til the morwe
And from the morwe forth til hit be eve;
Ther nedeth me no care for to borwe,
For bothe I have good leyser and good leve;
Ther is no wyght that wol me wo bereve
To wepe ynogh and wailen al my fille;
The sore spark of peyne now doth me spille.
This Love, that hath me set in such a place
That my desir [he] nevere wol fulfille,
For neither pitee, mercy, neither grace
Can I nat fynde, and yit my sorwful herte

> For to be deed I can hit nought arace.
> The more I love, the more she doth me smerte,
> Thorugh which I see without remedye
> That from the deeth I may no wyse asterte. (Chaucer, 1987, p. 642)

10 I would here be remiss if I didn't cite Žižek's gloss of the death drive as a "rooting out" (Žižek, 1989, p. 181).
11 Chaucer's original lines read as follows: "In my trewe [and] careful herte ther is / So moche wo and [eek] so litel blis / That wo is me that ever I was bore" (Chaucer, 1987, p. 642).
12 The phrase "critique of pure desire" is Žižek's (Žižek, 1999, p. 299). Also worth noting here – especially given that one of his primary examples of the genre is Chaucer's "Complaint to His Purse" – is Aaron Schuster's notion of courtly love as a "critique of pure complaint" (Schuster, 2016, pp. 1–25).
13 As Lacan explains, perverse subjectivity is "constituted through alienation at the cost of being nothing but the instrument of [the Other's] jouissance" (Lacan, 2006, p. 654). My claim that perversion is an unethical subjective position insofar as it is a "compromise of desire" is a nod to Lacan's maxim from Seminar VII – a maxim that could stand for the ethics of psychoanalysis as such – that, "from an analytical point of view, the only thing which one can be guilty of is having given ground relative to one's desire" (Lacan, 1992, p. 319).

References

Alighieri, D. (1973). *Dante's Vita Nuova* (M. Musa, Trans.). Indiana University Press.
Chaucer, G. (1912). "A Complaint to His Lady." In J. S. P. Tatlock & P. MacKay (Trans.), *The Complete Poetical Works of Geoffrey Chaucer*. Macmillan.
Chaucer, G. (1987). *The Riverside Chaucer*. Houghton Mifflin.
Copjec, J. (1994). *Read My Desire: Lacan Against the Historicists*. MIT Press.
Dolar, M. (1996). "At First Sight." In S. Žižek & R. Salecl (Eds.), *Gaze and Voice as Love Objects*. Duke University Press.
Fradenburg, L. O. A. (2002). *Sacrifice Your Love: Psychoanalysis, Historicism, Chaucer*. University of Minnesota Press.
Kant, I. (1997). *Critique of Practical Reason* (M. Gregor, Ed. & Trans.). Cambridge University Press.
Kay, S. (2001). *The Emergence of the Literary Object in the Twelfth Century*. Stanford University Press.
Labbie, E. F. (2006). *Lacan's Medievalism*. University of Minnesota Press.
Lacan, J. (1978). *The Seminar of Jacques Lacan, Book XI: The Four Fundamental Concepts of Psychoanalysis* (A. Sheridan, Trans.; J.-A. Miller, Ed.). Norton.
Lacan, J. (1992). *The Seminar of Jacques Lacan, Book VII: The Ethics of Psychoanalysis, 1959–1960* (A. Sheridan, Trans.; J.-A. Miller, Ed.). Norton.
Rosenfeld, J. (2011). *Ethics and Enjoyment in Late Medieval Poetry: Love After Aristotle*. Cambridge University Press.
Schuster, A. (2016). *The Trouble with Pleasure: Deleuze and Psychoanalysis*. MIT Press.
Žižek, S. (1989). *The Sublime Object of Ideology*. Verso.
Žižek, S. (1994). *The Metastases of Enjoyment: Six Essays on Woman and Causality*. Verso.
Žižek, S. (1999). "Kant with (or against) Sade." In E. Wright & E. Wright (Eds.), *The Žižek Reader*. Blackwell.
Žižek, S. (2003). *The Puppet and the Dwarf: The Perverse Core of Christianity*. MIT Press.

Žižek, S. (2003/2004). "*Vertigo*: The Drama of a Deceived Platonist." *Hitchcock Annual*, *12*, 67–82.
Žižek, S. (2006). *The Parallax View*. MIT Press.
Žižek, S. (2017). *Incontinence of the Void: Economico-Philosophical Spandrels*. MIT Press.
Žižek, S. (2023). *Freedom: A Disease Without Cure*. Bloomsbury.
Zupančič, A. (2000). *Ethics of the Real: Kant, Lacan*. Verso.
Zupančič, A. (2017). *What IS Sex?* MIT Press.

Chapter 4

An Ethics of Shame
Love, Media Pleasures, and Monsters

Jennifer Friedlander

The Shame of Loving Monstrous Media

In the wake of the #MeToo movement, media consumers face a dilemma, famously characterized by Claire Dederer as, "What Do We Do with the Art of Monstruous Men?" Popular discourse teaches that continuing to love the work created by unlovable artists is at best impossible or at worst, ill-advised. Either our disgust at the artists' behaviors should destroy our love of his work or, if this love should prove embarrassingly recalcitrant, then we are duty-bound to exercise the moral courage to refrain from engaging with it (James, 2020). In both cases, we are expected to feel "shame" about our attachment to the creations of disgraced artists. But, according to Robert Pfaller, we should not mistake today's pervasive and public proclamations of shame as indications that we currently live in a "shame culture." On the contrary, shame itself has now become "shameless" – "one is proud that one has so much sense of shame" (Pfaller, 2022, p. 10) Slavoj Žižek elaborates that "the all-pervasiveness of shame thus at the same time signals its lack: we are not embarrassed by our shame, we shamelessly enjoy it" (Žižek, 2022).

Our enjoyment of shame manifests in two distinct modes. First, as indicated above, when shame prompts us to sacrifice the pleasure of the object, we are rewarded by the return of pleasure to the ego, via our sense of moral satisfaction. Focusing primarily on public expressions of shame felt on behalf another, Pfaller observes that, contrary to our tendency to see shame as a signal of our perceived "inferiority,…weakness or failure," we should recognize that shame emerges as "an emotion of surplus and excess" (Harari, 2023). Shame, Pfaller continues, has now "become a luxury item…. [P]eople now display their shame with the same self-confidence as they once did an exclusive wristwatch or an expensive handbag" (Pfaller, 2022, p. 10). Mary Beth Willard's "thought test" nicely encapsulates this point in the context of our social media renunciations of the work of disgraced artists: would you still forsake the work of the artist if you couldn't post about it? (Willard, 2021, p. 131). This form of enjoying shame follows the conservative logic of the pleasure of sacrifice. Giving up of the loved object does not precipitate an encounter with lack; such sacrifice, rather, works to conceal lack. The renunciation of an object of pleasure to appease the symbolic mandate helps prop up the

DOI: 10.4324/9781032663487-5

illusion of symbolic and subjective wholeness: sacrifice "conceals the abyss of the Other's desire...the Other's lack.... [It serves as] a guarantee that 'the Other exists'" (Žižek, 2008, p. 64).

In what follows, I formulate what I see as a less recognized and more emancipatory path for how we might enjoy shame. The response to shame that I have in mind rejects super-egoic satisfaction that comes from distancing ourselves from the loved object. Instead, it involves committing to that love as a site for identification with the jouissance of the Other. Specifically, I argue that by precipitating a libidinal engagement with the object's contamination by the disgusting jouissance of its creator, shame can put the subject in confrontation with her own unbearable jouissance. In such instances, shame no longer prompts an exchange of the once-loved object for the moral satisfaction of renouncing it. Rather, we retain the object, but our relationship to it is transformed by shame: a relationship once governed by the logic of pleasure changes into a relationship fueled by the insistence of jouissance. This facilitates the possibility for the subject to inhabit the discovery that her lack is shared with the Other, and thus sets in motion the conditions for the emancipatory potential of what Lacan calls "separation" to occur. It is through this process of separation that the subject comes to recognize that the Other, itself, is lacking, thus enabling her to abandon the fantasy that symbolic wholeness is attainable. This recognition of lack's inevitability then leaves the subject free to pursue her own desire.

In developing this position – that our enjoyment of shame is not limited to conservative super-egoic pleasure, but that it can manifest in a liberatory relationship to lack – I bring together two sites of analysis. The first concerns Jacques Lacan's attempt to bring shame to enjoyment in his famous chide, "look at them enjoying!" directed to student protesters in Vincennes in 1969. As Eric Laurent attests, his remark was delivered with "the avowed intention of 'shaming' them" (Lacan, 2007; Laurent, 2006, p. 230). Jacques-Alain Miller elaborates that Lacan attempted to shame the students in order to (re)activate the efficacy of the master signifier. At first sight, Miller's thesis seems surprising in the light of Lacan's insistence that the "analytic operation" involves precisely the work of "separating the subject from its master signifier" (Miller, 2006, p. 8). But this surprise is alleviated by Lacan's diagnosis that the dominant "social link" of this period is the university/capitalist discourse, in which the efficacy of the master signifier wanes. The subject loses her orientation to a "signifier that matters" (p.18). Miller, thus, qualifies that the analytic aim of stripping the subject of its master signifier applies only to a subject who "knows he has one, and respects it" (p. 21).

Miller's claim still leaves us with the question of whether mobilizing the master signifier functions solely as a necessary preliminary step to diminishing the subject's allegiance to it, or whether shame's activation of the master signifier can, itself, accomplish the work of separation. I argue in favor of the latter position. Shame, brought about by what we love, calls attention to the master signifier as that which *fails* to confirm our place within the Other. I argue that the master signifier summonsed by that shame reveals that, as Rex Butler puts it, "it always falls short, proves disappointing, fails to live up to [its] promise" (Butler, 2005, p. 54). By calling into service the master signifier as a shared point of lack between the subject and the Other, this response to shame provides an opportunity for separation by "reveal[ing]" rather than "cover[ing] over" the overlapping "void" between the subject and the Other (p. 58).

Dederer's unexpected encounter with her own defiant media pleasures provides the second site for thinking the liberatory potential of our enjoyment of shame. Dederer attempts to combat her love of the films by the "monstruous" Roman Polanski by mobilizing shame. Her plan, intently studying the grim details of his rape of a thirteen-year-old girl, backfires fantastically. Not only does this effort fail to prevent her from "consum[ing] his work," but it also has the paradoxical effect of making her increasingly "eager to" do so (Dederer 2017). Rather than transform her love of the object into the ego satisfaction of virtuous sacrifice, her growing shame transforms her pleasure of the object into jouissance. Her enjoyment is evidenced by her compulsion to repeatedly watch his films. As Dederer recounts, "the more I researched Polanski, the more I became drawn to his films, and I watched them again and again.... I wasn't supposed to love this work, or this man" (Dederer 2017). Her shame, induced by learning more about his "awfulness," propelled Dederer to identify more intently with him. As she tells us, "something in…me… chimes to that awfulness, recognizes it in myself, is horrified by that recognition" (Dederer 2017). To borrow from Lacan's description of *das Ding* in *Seminar VII*, Dederer's account exemplifies that "*Fremde*" cannot be isolated in the "outside" but exists as an unrepresentable foreignness at the "heart of the [subject's] libidinal economy" (Lacan, 1992, pp. 52, 111). Dederer's discovery illustrates how shame may reveal the master signifier to be a site of identification with the limits of the symbolic, rather than a vehicle for propping up the illusion of symbolic wholeness.

In what follows, I develop these claims first by arguing briefly in favor of the premise that our current cultural moment of fomenting shame around our media pleasures marks a departure from the long-held designation of our pleasures in "bad objects" as "guilty." I then frame my case for a liberatory path in response to contemporary efforts to induce this shame, by drawing on two interrelated developments in Lacan's thinking from *Seminar VII* to *Seminar XVII*. The first is his shift in focus from the relationship between guilt and desire to the relationship between shame and jouissance. The second concerns his rethinking of jouissance from being outside the symbolic realm to being inextricably linked to the function of the signifier. In short, it is my contention that the mater signifier, mobilized by shame, arrives as a bearer of jouissance.

Guilty Pleasures/Pseudo-Shame

In December of 2013, Jennifer Szalai's *New Yorker* essay, "Against 'Guilty Pleasure'" set off a flurry of opinion pieces responding to her account of "guilty pleasures" today. Szalai argues that the term "guilty pleasure" is both disingenuous and detrimental. Rather than refer to media pleasures that induce a guilty conscience, the idiom functions to maintain insidious cultural distinctions. As Szalai pithily puts it, calling something your guilty pleasure, "signals that you're most comfortable in the élite precincts of high art, but you're not so much of a snob that you can't be at one with the people. So you confess your remorse whenever you deign to watch *Scandal*, implying that the rest of your time is spent reading Proust" (Szalai, 2013).

The term, "guilty pleasure," Szalai goes on to note, became "part of the [US] cultural vocabulary" in the 1990s, "right around the time cultural distinctions were ceasing to matter" (Szalai, 2013). But whereas Szalai reads this as suggesting that "postmodern" blurring of cultural distinctions has made it acceptable to admit our love for "bad" media objects, I propose we make the converse point: that the softening of cultural boundaries makes it more *dangerous* to admit our love of bad objects, so much so, that the introduction of a new boundary-resetting gesture is required.[1] In this sense, our confessions of guilty pleasures function similarly to our announcements of (pseudo)-shameful pleasures (the ones that offer ego pleasure in exchange for giving up the object) discussed above in providing a rhetorical shield from becoming tainted by our pleasures.

But, despite sharing this protective function, today's invocation of shameful pleasures of media objects created by "monstrous" men, differs significantly from the use of "guilty pleasures" in the context discussed above. To be specific, describing your pleasure as "guilty," allows you to continue to enjoy the media object with impunity. By contrast, announcing a "shameful" pleasure (due to the behavior of its creator) prevents you from continuing to enjoy the media object. The possibility of salvaging the pleasure of the object is lost, but with that loss comes both the consolation of avoiding being tainted by association with the bad acts of the creator and, more crucially, the reward of ego pleasure produced by the sacrifice.

Many of Szalai's interlocutors argue that what we label "guilty pleasures" should really be called "shameful pleasures," since they, as Mark Dery argues, arise from our "awareness of society's disapproval or – even worse – snickering contempt at what, in the realm of culture, are often innocent pleasures, victimless crimes" (Dery, 2015). John Semley similarly emphasizes that "real guilty pleasures…make us feel bad not because we think we're debasing ourselves by watching some show we think we're above…they make us feel bad because they challenge these carefully curated ideas of what kinds of things we take pleasure in, what sort of stuff we enjoy. They undermine our ideas of who we are" (Semley, 2013). The latter account of the way our media enjoyment can threaten "our ideas of who we are" brings us closer to the second response to shame that I am championing, which we saw at work in Dederer's unsuccessful attempt to give up the tainted media objects.

Dederer's response to shame falls in line with how I read Lacan's intention. As Eric Laurent specifies, Lacan's attempt to inflict shame is directed only at those "who do not make themselves responsible for their own jouissance" (Laurent, 2006, p. 233). Lacan, thus, does not advocate shame as a call to give up enjoyment, but rather as an appeal to enjoy in our own way and to identify with our modes of enjoying. The work of shame, thus, aims to mobilize a position for the subject which is at odds with the position of a subject who responds to shame by renouncing the object. As we have seen, the subject who sacrifices her obscene object of enjoyment is rewarded with the illusion of subjective wholeness. By contrast, the subject who maintains a relationship with the object must accept "responsibility" for her jouissance and thus undergoes the process of assuming her constitutive lack. As Joan Copjec puts it, "to experience shame is to experience oneself…as a subject…. The pain associated with shame…has to do with the fact that one is not 'integrated' with oneself, one is fundamentally split from oneself…[which is the] very definition of a subject" (Copjec, 2007 p. 63).

Lacan: From Guilt to Shame

The distinction between shame and guilt rests upon a series of contested, and often tenuous, distinctions. For example, Miller asserts that "shame and guilt evoke one another while being distinct" and Laurent sees "shame [as] an eminently psychoanalytic affect that belongs to the same series as guilt" (Miller, 2006, p. 12; Laurent, 2006, 231). For the purposes of this argument, I will focus briefly upon two ways in which they are distinguished by Lacan and his interpreters.

First, shame and guilt are often linked to the ways in which different moments with capitalism require subjects to take a specific relationship to enjoyment.[2] At the time of Lacan's 1959–1960 *Seminar VII* (*The Ethics of Psychoanalysis*) Lacan sees capitalism as operating in a "Puritanical" phase in which enjoyment is prohibited and "repressed" (Miller, 2006, p. 12). Our enjoyment, therefore, takes place under the shadow of the shaming gaze of the Other. By the time Lacan gives his *Seminar XVII* (*The Other Side of Psychoanalysis*), a "new mode" of capitalism is afoot – one marked by "permissiveness," or a "prohibition on prohibition" (p. 19). But rather than simply permit enjoyment, now, the Other commands us to Enjoy! (p. 15). With this injunction comes the "eclipse of the Other's gaze as the bearer of shame" (p. 15). Instead of suffering from shame, we now face guilt through our inevitable failure to comply with the impossible superegoic mandate to Enjoy! This trajectory leads Jaco-Bernard Naude to argue that the reintroduction of shame may, thus, function to "short-circuit" the contemporary capitalist superegoic logic of mandated enjoyment. Such a derailment, he compellingly suggests, may open a path through which the subject may pursue her singular modes of enjoyment which "escape" the capitalist symbolic realm (Naude, 2021, p. 1).

The second distinction between shame and guilt involves the subject's relationship to the Other. In the experience of shame, the subject feels herself being *seen* enjoying, whereas when the subject suffers guilt, she feels herself being *judged* by the Other for her desire. The waning of shame today can perhaps be epitomized, Laurent suggests, by the phenomenon that our viewing of "reality tv" does not bring shame to the participants. For Laurent we are now in an "age of the generalized reality show" where, as Russell Grigg puts it, "the gaze has been deprived of its ability to shame (Laurent, 2006, p. 239; Grigg, 2004, p. 8). Grigg suggests that, even though the gaze of the viewers might not have the power to shame, it is nevertheless "a gaze that enjoys" (pp. 8–9). We will build upon Grigg's observation to help illuminate the contemporary situation in which it is not those participating in the spectacle who are shamed, but rather those who enjoy *watching* the spectacle. Social media, through which we are increasingly defined by and displayed in our role as media consumers, plays no small part in making our gaze the locus of shame: shame now resides on the side of those who see rather than those who are seen.

Jouissance and the Signifier

Although at the time of delivering his 1959–1960 *The Ethics of Psychoanalysis*, Lacan characterized capitalism as regulating subjects' enjoyment through prohibition (and therefore aligned more closely with the master's discourse and the efficacy of shame), he nevertheless prioritizes the concept of guilt over shame. He famously asserts that "from an analytic point of view, the only thing of which one can be guilty is of having given ground relative to one's desire" (Lacan, 1992, p. 319). In making this contention, Lacan distinguishes one's singular desire from the notion of the "good." Particularly, he insists, "doing things in the name of the good," does not protect us from guilt. He thus establishes an ethics grounded in our rejection of the demands of the Other rather than in our adherence to them.

How, then, might we understand Lacan's shift from an ethics of guilt based upon the subject's relationship to her desire to an ethics of shame based upon her relationship to enjoyment/jouissance (as he presents in *Seminar XVII*)? I suggest that we consider this shift in terms of another development in Lacan's thinking. As many commentators have noted, the concept of jouissance undergoes a significant departure in *Seminar XVII* from his earlier formulation. Paul Verhaeghe explains: jouissance, in *Seminar VII*, is formulated as "diametrically opposed to the symbolic," whereas in *Seminar XVII*, Lacan proposes a "primordial relation between jouissance and the signifier" (Verhaeghe, 2006, p. 29). Lacan here emphasizes the interdependence of jouissance and the signifier – namely, the signifier functions as both the cause of and impediment to jouissance.

For Alenka Zupančič, it is in this "discursive dimension of enjoyment" that "the political dimension of psychoanalysis" resides (Zupančič, 2006, p. 55). The signifier, in this formulation, is seen as not only incapable of warding off intrusions of jouissance, but also is recognized as introducing into the subject a libidinal investment of its own. The political implications of this position, to which Zupančič alludes, are two-fold. First, this view of the inextricable link between the signifier and jouissance ensures that the symbolic can never be complete, but rather is always and already beset with loss. This insight enables a politics based upon the acceptance of symbolic incompleteness. Once the subject is released from the fruitless quest to satisfy the enigmatic demand of the Other, she becomes free to pursue a desire of her own. Second, since this (perceived) loss can never be recaptured, the subject's attempts to remedy it result in her repeating the loss. The repetition of failed attempts to recover the illusionary "original" jouissance comes to offer a form of jouissance of its own – "surplus jouissance."

Taken together, these two implications of the inextricability of jouissance and the signifier help us recognize how the subject is able to build a creative relationship to the signifier via the process of repetition. In repeating what falls outside of the realm of the signifier, the subject evokes the foreclosed potential of the symbolic. Here, the logic of (death) drive overwhelms the pleasure principle: whereas the pleasure principle leads us to strive for (impossible) satisfaction, which results in our disappointment and suffering, the death drive propels us to repeat disappointment and suffering, which leads to a surplus pleasure. Thus, in place of the pleasure principle's demand for "impossible fullness," in death drive, "we directly enjoy lack itself" (Žižek, 2007). Via the operation of the death drive, we can, thus, understand Lacan's claim that repetition "demands the new" (Lacan, 1998, p. 61). What is gained via the repetition of loss is not only surplus jouissance, but also a challenge to the illusion of symbolic closure via an encounter with palpable symbolic excess.

We now apply these theoretical insights to a brief discussion of Dederer's account of her attempt to cast aside the work she loves. In particular, I argue that her report indicates that she shifts her engagement with this work from one of pleasure (compatible with the logic of the pleasure of the pleasure principle) to one of enjoyment (regulated by the death drive). Dederer's discussion of her attachment to her disgraced loved object, thus, demonstrates one way in which repetition generates the new via a change in how we relate to the object, rather than through a change in the object itself.

Repetition/Love/Death Drive

Although repetition is inaugurated by a perceived loss that can never be recovered, it nevertheless ends up producing excess (surplus jouissance). By repeating the irremediable loss created by the signifier, repetition brings into existence what is "impossible" to include within the symbolic. Dederer's account exemplifies how, by refusing to allow shame to prompt us to renunciate the loved object, shame may drive us into a repetitive relationship with the loved object. This response to shame, I contend, carries emancipatory potential for the subject. Whereas renunciation of the object works to consolidate established symbolic coordinates by casting out a threat to one's subjective coherence, repetitive engagement with the loved object creates a challenge to both subjective wholeness and symbolic closure. Repetition thus carves out a space of lack shared by both the subject and the symbolic order—a condition which sets the stage for the subject's accession from alienation to separation.

Dederer, as we saw, unexpectedly discovers that her love for Polanski's films persists despite being "awed by his monstrousness," a monstrousness she dramatizes as "monumental, like the Grand Canyon, huge and void-like and slightly incomprehensible" (Dederer, 2023, p. 3). That her vivid depiction of Polanksi's monstrousness itself takes on resonances of the Real seems far from incidental, since his work poses for her a problem analogous to the challenge posed by destabilizing irruptions of the Real. In the same way that the Real persists despite all attempts to domesticate its unwelcome intrusions, Dederer's denouncing Polanski does nothing to prevent his work from "still calling" to her – an "insistent calling," that, she tells us, "disrupted my idea of myself" (p. 42). To accept the call which threatens her subjectivity, rather than deploy all available symbolic resources to tame it, is, for Dederer, a way of honoring love. As she tells us: we owe "at least some small degree of fealty" to what we love (p. 75).

At first sight her commitment to taking responsibility for what we love resonates with Lacan's invocation of an ethics based on refusing to "give…ground relative to [one's] desire" (Lacan, 1992, p. 319). But love differs from desire in a crucial way: whereas desire desires its own propagation, love aims for its own return: as Lacan puts it, "To love is, essentially, to wish to be loved" (Lacan, 1998, p. 253). I argue now that this point deepens our understanding of the roles of both identification and betrayal that Dederer invokes.

In the context of discussing her complicated relationship to Woody Allen because of allegations of his abusive behavior, Dederer reveals the complex structure of identification within the realm of love. She vacillates between both being the loved one and having the loved one, telling us that "I felt like Woody Allen…He was me" and that "I felt he belonged to me" (Dederer, 2023, p. 16). Her pronouncement that "I took the fucking [notably "the" fucking and not "his" fucking—it could be hers too?] of Soon-yi [the adopted daughter of Allen's ex-wife, Mia Farrow] as a terrible betrayal of me personally," reveals a duplicity with psychoanalytic implications (p. 16). In particular, the ambivalence Dederer evinces between being and having, and love and disgust can be illuminated by Lacan's reworking of Freud's discussion of the directive to "love thy neighbor." As Zupančič explains, Lacan's innovation was to highlight the subject's nagging sense that the disgusting kernel that necessarily resides in the neighbor, must also "dwell…within me…[that] it is structurally, necessarily unclear whether this excluded kernel of my being is in fact mine or my neighbor's" (Zupančič, 2019, p. 92). Love, Zupančič emphasizes, disrupts the pleasure principle's ability to defend against this subjective disturbance, and is thus capable of opening the door to jouissance beyond the pleasure principle.

Dederer's account of the overriding pull of disgraced loved objects illuminates the relationship between love and jouissance. She equates the tenacity of her love with the disgusting jouissance of their creators, declaring, "we are left with love… we love whether we want to or not—just as the stain happens, whether we want it to or not" (Dederer, 2023, pp. 241–242). Notably, she recognizes that the call of love is not an easy one to heed. Love, Dederer points out, is "too eas[ily]" forgotten when "running the calculus" regarding our socially expected response to work created by "monsters." Zupančič agrees that this is necessarily so, in that "love [is]… situated beyond a certain limit of the calculus of the good" (Zupančič, 2019, p. 95). Although renouncing the object protects the subject from straying beyond the pleasure principle, Dederer nevertheless encourages us to listen to "love['s]…quiet voice next to the louder call of…public shaming" (Dederer, 2023, p. 75). The "fealty" to love, which she champions, opens the gate to the jouissance of repetition.

Yet, despite this commitment, Dederer attempts to scaffold her compulsive repetition of Polanski's work within the logic of symbolic mastery: it was as if by "watching something compulsively…you could somehow change it or take responsibility for it by keeping your eyes on it…as if Watching Could Do Something" (pp. 15–16). Even though Dederer may well have invoked this justification as a defensive attempt to keep within the boundaries of the pleasure principle, she is correct that watching *does* do something. It substantiates a commitment to the loved object, through which the subject is compelled to take responsibility for her excessive enjoyment. Such an engagement, in turn, works to challenge any sense of subjective and symbolic completeness, and thus opens a liberating path for creating attachments outside of super-egoic mandates. Rather than succumb to the conservative logic of sacrifice, which serves to uphold the demand of the Other, this commitment to "sacrifice…sacrifice," Žižek contends, sets the subject on course for separation (Žižek, 2008, p. 68).[3] The rejection of excess, accomplished through sacrifice, upholds the illusion of symbolic completion, which furthers subjective alienation. The road to separation, by contrast, is lined by identification with the excessive real that evokes the necessary incompleteness of both the subject and the Other.

Identification with the excessive element draws attention to the misunderstanding surrounding the stakes of any response to the question of what we should do with the work of "monstrous men." Our very investment in the question cannot help but reinforce the idea that our media pleasures may secure us a place within the symbolic. But Dederer reinforces a key psychoanalytic point regarding the impossibility of the symbolic to ground subjective identity: "the way you consume art doesn't make you a bad person, or a good one. You'll have to find some other way to accomplish that" (Dederer, 2023, p. 242). In this way we see how shame mobilizes the master signifier as a highly resonant site from which to confer a sense of symbolic belonging. But, although it instantiates a structural position from which we see ourselves from the perspective of the Other, this position is ultimately empty, incapable of delivering the assurance we seek. The ethics of shame, gestured toward here, involves accepting the impossibility of having one's morality ratified. The subject is therefore cast out to seek attachments of her own. The master signifier, mobilized through shame, calls the subject into a relationship with a signifier that matters, but that signifier itself, I have argued, is beset with a jouissance of its own.

Notes

1 Szalai implicitly reinforces this view when she notes with curiosity that the more culturally stratified French society has no such term as "guilty pleasure."
2 Joan Copjec cautions against attempts to use "shame" or "guilt" to "define" cultural moments. She argues that shame and guilt should, rather, be used to refer to "a subject's relationship to her culture" (Copjec 61).
3 But this refusal to follow the social injunction should not be seen as an enjoyment of transgression. Transgression compatibly orbits the pleasure principle and tethers

the subject to existing symbolic coordinates by reinforcing their boundaries. Shame, by contrast, can induce the repetition of the enjoyment of the death drive beyond the pleasure principle, and opens up new creative possibilities for the subject beyond the limits of the symbolic.

References

Butler, R. (2005). *Slavoj Žižek: Live Theory.* Bloomsbury.
Copjec, J. (2007). "The Descent into Shame." *Studio Art Magazine* no. 168.
Dederer, C. (2017). "What Do We Do with the Art of Monstrous Men?" *The Paris Review.*
Dederer, C. (2023). *Monsters: A Fan's Dilemma.* Knopf.
Dery, M. (2015). "Let's Put the Guilt Back into Guilty Pleasures." *Boing Boing.* https://boingboing.net/2015/02/02/lets-put-the-guilt-back-in-g.html
Grigg, R. (2004). "Shame and Guilt." Edições Universitárias Lusófonas.oai:recil.grupoluso fona.pt:10437/40
Harari, N. (2023). "Nigel Biggar's Colonialism: Cancel Culture or Shame Culture?" *SublationMag* https://www.sublationmag.com/post/nigel-biggar-s-colonialism-cancel-culture-or-shame-culture.
James, R. (2022). "Must Be Love on the Brain? Feminist Responses to the 'Can We Separate Artwork from Artist' Question in the Era of #MeToo Popular Feminisms." *Journal of Popular Music Studies*, Volume 32, Number 4, pp. 75–94.
Lacan, J. (1992). *The Ethics of Psychoanalysis* (D. Porter, Trans.). Routledge.
Lacan, J. (1998). *The Four Fundamental Concepts of Psychoanalysis* (J-A. Miller and A. Sheridan, Trans.). W. W. Norton & Company, 1998.
Lacan, J. (2007). *The Other Side of Psychoanalysis* (R. Grigg, Trans.) W. W. Norton & Company.
Laurent, E. (2006). "Symptom and Discourse." *Jacques Lacan and the Other Side of Psychoanalysis; Reflections on Seminar XVII.* (J. Clemens; R. Grigg, Eds). Duke UP.
Miller, J-A. (2006). "On Shame." *Jacques Lacan and the Other Side of Psychoanalysis: Reflections on Seminar XVII.* (J. Clemens; R. Grigg, Eds). Duke UP.
Naude, J-B. (2021). "An Ordeal of the Real: Shame and the Superego." *Acta Academica* 53(1).
Pfaller, R. (2022). *Zwei Enthüllungen über die Scham* [Two Revelations on Shame]. S Fischer.
Semely, J. (2013). "In Praise of Truly Guilty Pleasures" *Esquire.com* https://www.esquire.com/entertainment/movies/a23738/truly-guilty-pleasures/
Szalai, J. (2013). "Against 'Guilty Pleasure.'" *The New Yorker.* December 9.
Verhaeghe, P. (2006). "Enjoyment and Impossibility: Lacan's Revision of the Oedipus Complex." *Jacques Lacan and the Other Side of Psychoanalysis; Reflections on Seminar XVII.* (J. Clemens; R. Grigg, Eds). Duke UP.
Willard, M. B. (2021). *Why It's OK to Enjoy the Work of Immoral Artists.* Routledge.
Žižek, S. (2007). "The Liberal Utopia: Against the Politics of Jouissance." *Lacan dot com.* https://www.lacan.com/zizliberal.htm
Žižek, S. (2008). *Enjoy Your Symptom!* Routledge.
Žižek, S. (2022). Abstract for "Figures of Surplus-Enjoyment." A Master Class with Slavoj Žižek. Birkbeck, University of London. (https://www.bbk.ac.uk/events/remote_event_view?id=34734).

Zupančič, A. (2006). "When Surplus Enjoyment Meets Surplus Value." *Jacques Lacan and the Other Side of Psychoanalysis; Reflections on Seminar XVII.* (J. Clemens; R. Grigg, Eds). Duke UP.

Zupančič, A. (2019). "Love Thy Neighbor as Thyself?!" *PROBLEMI INTERNATIONAL*, vol. 3, no. 3.

SECTION II

Through Death to Love: Psychoanalytic, Philosophical, and Theological Insights

Chapter 5

On the Subject of Love

Richard Boothby

In memory of Mari Ruti (1964–2023) – with love

This essay offers a very brief remark on a very big question. It attempts to contrast two fundamentally different dimensions of love, one focused upon by Sigmund Freud, the other illuminated by Jacques Lacan.

Freud repeatedly frames love as an exercise of narcissism. Falling in love is a matter of unconsciously finding in the beloved a mirror that stabilizes one's own ego. The beloved functions to flatter, enlarge, or even produce the lover's sense of self. However much the passion for one's greatest heart-throb appears to sweep the lover off their feet, the primary value of love for Freud is a matter of grounding self-certainty. The ecstatic swoon functions to reinforce one's own identity.[1]

Even when Freud distinguishes between two elementary forms of love – "narcissistic love," routinely found in women who hunger for the body-based self-confirmation inflated by a man's erotic infatuation, and "anaclitic" or "attachment" love, the strain of love that inclines men toward bonding with the figure of a nurturing care-taker – the underlying aim of love is to buttress one's own stabilization of self (Freud, 1955, pp. 69–102).

The "trophy wife" phenomenon illustrates both forms simultaneously. The stunningly beautiful woman draped on the arm of a powerful man basks in the glow of a narcissistic satisfaction that is fed by her husband's obvious attention. For the husband, his wowing spouse broadcasts to every man in the room an unimpeachable enviability. A side-benefit of the whole arrangement is the way the trophy wife allows the lucky husband to squelch any more primitive temptation to cozy up to a caring and protective mother-figure.

Freud's emphasis on the narcissistic dimension of love is what leads him to pose erotic attachment as "object love." What is at stake is the reassuring couplet of object and ego. It is this bond between ego and object that frames Freud's conception of mourning. Mourning is a matter of detaching the ego from the love-object, of withdrawing the ego's investment in that object. But the labor of mourning is hard work. The aggrieved survivor must progressively sever myriad points of attachment to the beloved. In the worst-case scenario, this labor of divestiture

DOI: 10.4324/9781032663487-7

fails to sufficiently free the grief-stricken ego from its bondage to the lost object. Unable to establish a stable independence, the bereaved lover descends into the excruciating state of melancholia, an ego-paralyzing experience of vacuity, numbness, and despair.

The emphasis Freud places on the narcissistic, ego-driven character of love only becomes more firmly entrenched with his mature theory of the life and death drives. In the wake of *Beyond the Pleasure Principle* in 1920, Freud's thinking is dominated by the stark antagonism between the upsurge of organic integration and the inevitability of primal dissolution. Where Eros functions as the binding power of unity and stability, death-dealing Thanatos unbinds and disintegrates, threatening to plunge every coherence into chaos. In this binary scheme, love and ego are clearly lumped together on the side of Eros.

Precisely to the extent that Freud links the psychical dynamics of love to narcissism, his theory is well equipped to explain a primitive psychological resistance to change. The result, as Freud himself points out, is a theory parallel to that put forward in Plato's *Symposium* in which love inevitably spawns a dream of immortality. By its very nature, love longs for the permanence of marriage. At the same time, the Freudian view tends to fall in line with the wide-spread norm of Western culture that focuses on the opening gambit of falling in love, as if "love" refers above all to that initial swoon of passion. "Love at first sight" is its fondest expression. The longing for an enduring relationship thus readily appears to be nothing but a wish that the first fevered pulse of attraction might go on forever.

How, then, does Lacan's viewpoint on love differ from Freud's?

There are multiple reasons to approach this question tentatively, not least of which is the fact that Lacan nowhere presents a single, tidy account.[2] Nevertheless, the basic drift of his view readily appears to be the near opposite of Freud's appeal to narcissistic reassurance. For Lacan, the experience of love potentially opens a unique horizon of transformation precisely to the extent that the unfolding experience of love challenges and reshapes the ego. Lacan forcefully generalizes this point in one of his earliest *écrits*, the essay on the "Mirror Stage." "Psychoanalysis alone," he claims, "recognizes the knot of imaginary servitude that love must always untie anew or sever" (Lacan, 2006, p. 80).

For Lacan, the real core of the psychoanalytic breakthrough lies precisely in pointing to the problematic dimension of ego identity. Among the offshoots of the analytic tradition that Lacan most soundly rejects is that of so-called "ego psychology," a largely American school devoted to strengthening the ego. Even allowing that sanity depends in part on a stable ego, and even assuming that unconscious mechanisms routinely function to shore up and fortify the ego, for Lacan the crucial dynamic illuminated by psychoanalysis concerns the way in which the unconscious operates mostly *against* the ego. The most general name Lacan gives to the source of such challenges to the ego is "subject." Indeed, the most elemental opposition of Lacan's theoretical innovation is arguably that between *le moi* and *le sujet*, the *ego* and the *subject*. As he puts it in his first seminar: "The ego hasn't a clue about the subject's desires" (Lacan, 1988, p. 167).

Lacan emphasizes the way in which love, very much including the special form of love that arises in the psychoanalytic transference, tends to destabilize the ego. As Lacan suggests: "What is really at issue, at the end of analysis, [is] a twilight, an imaginary decline of the world, and even an experience at the limit of depersonalization" (Lacan, 1988, p. 232). The key point at stake is the role of the ego tends to function as the seat of repression. On this point, Lacan is emphatic: "This ego, whose strength our theorists now define by its capacity to bear frustration, is frustration in its very essence" (Lacan, 2006, p. 208).

A companion part of Lacan's "return to Freud" is a fresh endorsement of Freud's theory of the death drive, yet Lacan crucially alters its meaning to align with his own perspective. For Lacan, the disintegrating power of the death drive is not biological but psychical. The "death" at stake is not the disintegration of the organism but rather a radical transformation of the imaginary ego under the influence of unconscious dynamics.[3] Rejecting Freud's comparison of the death drive to "the Nirvana or annihilation principle," Lacan links the Freudian *Todestrieb* to the unfolding of the subject, a process that operates in response to symbolic influences that tend to undermine the imaginary stability of the ego. The death drive, Lacan insists, "is to be situated in the historical domain; it is articulated at a level that can only be defined as a function of the signifying chain" (Lacan, 1986, p. 211). As he obscurely but suggestively puts the main idea: "The death drive is a creationist sublimation" (Lacan, 1986, p. 213).

What is further at stake in Lacan's reconception is the way he refuses to follow Freud in lumping ego identity and sexuality together on the side of Life-seeking Eros. Where Freud tended to conjoin ego and sex, Lacan insists on a crucial tension between them.[4] We might readily relate the point at stake to the common French metaphor about orgasm as *la petite mort*, the little death. Sex is perennially capable of fundamentally challenging the stability of ego.

Lacan is clear that love is the most powerful means by which the death drive operates to restructure the ego. On the most elemental level, the imaginary schema of bodily unity is violated by the sexual act. But Lacan enlarges and generalizes the point in his concept of "jouissance," his catch-all expression for the inescapable excessiveness of the drives.[5] Lacan clearly considers a measured openness to jouissance to be an essential requirement of emerging subjectivity.

In all these areas, Lacan ties love to an experience of creative destabilization, the result of an essentially excessive power, the sort of wild and disruptive force associated by the ancients with the impish trouble-causers, Eros and Cupid. For Lacan, such disruption is what energizes the true psychological value of sex. As he puts it in the seminar on *Transference*: "When love truly becomes the means by which death is tied to jouissance, man to woman, and being to knowledge, love can no longer be defined as *ratage*." Lacan's somewhat oblique point here, turning on the word "*ratage*," is to invite us to see how, when love engages with the extremity of jouissance, it can no longer be dismissed as "failure, botching something up, a slip-up, screw-up, or making a mess of things."[6] On the contrary, such love-in-extremity contributes something essential to the emerging truth of the subject. In his seminar on *Anxiety*, Lacan makes the point in a terse but suggestive formula: "Only love allows jouissance to condescend to desire" (Lacan, 2014, p. 209).

To get a rough illustration of this Lacanian theme of love and ego-upheaval we could do worse than to revisit Jane Austen's *Pride and Prejudice*. The three Bennet sisters are all obsessed with falling in love, but Austen's primary intention appears to consist in showing us how the deepest experience of love demands some fundamental shift of personal character. For the youngest, the shallow and insipid Lydia, achieving a love relationship (or something that minimally looks like one) is mostly a means of arousing her sisters' envy. Her disastrous relationship with the hapless Wickham, far from triggering some significant internal change, appears to reinforce all of Lydia's worst weaknesses. The otherwise endearing eldest daughter, Jane, likewise appears to undergo very little internal change when her quiet dream of love is finally satisfied by her marriage to the sweet, if somewhat witless Mr. Bingley. Elizabeth, by contrast, initially somewhat wary and skeptical of all suitors, above all the wealthy and insufferably self-absorbed Mr. Darcy, is able to enter the full blossoming of love only by opening herself to a fundamental psychical shift. In fact, both Darcy and Elizabeth find their way to an extremely promising marriage only by virtue of having both undergone dramatic internal changes, genuinely detaching themselves from their own habitual resort to ego-flattering indulgences – those of pride and prejudice.

But the question remains: how are we to make better sense of what exactly is at stake in such transformative love?

One useful resource is provided by Mari Ruti's discussion in *The Case for Falling in Love: Why We Can't Master the Madness of Love – and Why That's the Best Part*. Theoretically speaking, a pivotal moment occurs halfway through the book when Ruti links falling in love with Lacan's theory of *das Ding*, the unknown "Thing" in the other human being (2011). Ruti discusses this concept in the chapter appropriately titled "It's All About the Thing." Lacan borrows the term from a brief section of Freud's unpublished "Project for a Scientific Psychology." Freud there proposes that the infant's apprehension of the mother is fundamentally divided between, on the one hand, a reassuring likeness of its own body with that of the mother (exactly the sort of mirror-reflection Lacan locates at the heart of imaginary identity) and, on the other, a distinct sense of something unknown, "something new and non-comparable."[7] This unrepresentable excess, no doubt initially registered in large part by the mother's vocalizations, announces a hidden, inexplicable dimension of what is otherwise familiar. Freud calls that mysterious dimension *das Ding*, the uncognizable "Thing" in the Other. Lacan generalizes the notion, claiming that "the question of *das Ding* is still attached to whatever is open, lacking, or gaping at the center of our desire" (Lacan, 1986, p. 84).

Ruti's primary point is that it is precisely the echo of this cognitive "black hole" in our originary relation to the Other that leads us to fall in love. We are most deeply seduced precisely by something unknown in the beloved. "The Thing," she says, "is what makes love so uniquely entrancing" (Ruti, 2011, p. 144). Hidden in that cloud of unknowing, Ruti contends, is the stuff that dreams are made of. What gives some particular person the power to bewitch us with desire is their capacity to arouse a vague but convincing sense of a lost object that we never possessed, an infinitely precious thing that we can never fully specify. As Ruti puts it, "the Thing relates to amorphous sentiments of incompleteness, deprivation, helplessness, and inadequacy; it connects us to a loss that we cannot name" (Ruti, 2011, p. 149).

This account of the lover as haunted by something undefinable in the Other once again links the psychoanalytic theory of love with the view put forward in Plato's *Symposium* by the enigmatic priestess, Diotima. Eros connects us to something beyond us, something we do not understand. And it is that connection that most fires the heat of passion. Love is thus energized not by overflowing fullness and light, but rather by lack and darkness. Love loves a mystery. "If there's anything "hard-wired" about people," Ruti concludes, "it's not some biological male/female (hunter/prey) mentality, but rather the astonishing accuracy with which they locate their Thing in another person" (Ruti, 2011, p. 151).

Ruti's emphasis on the unknown contradicts a favorite assumption about love. In the fever of early romance, it's quite typical for lovers to feel bowled over precisely by the feeling of *knowing* one another. Perhaps, they muse, they might even have been lovers in some other time, some other life! But, then again, we might well wonder if love's self-certainties are not a cover, even a kind of defense, against a deeper engagement with something that we don't understand. Doesn't the magic of a new romance arise precisely from the encounter with someone who presents us with an enticing mystery? Lacan and Plato agree on this: the thrill of love is sparked most deeply by what we do not know. And it's not hard to see why. Doesn't linking the passion of love to an encounter with something unknown – something unconscious – furnish the most deeply appropriate theory of love from a psychoanalytic perspective?

Mari Ruti offers a valuable and eloquent reminder that love arises from the encounter with something inexplicable in the Other, an experience that strangely calls up something enigmatic in ourselves. Yet her treatment leaves us wanting to know more about love's transformative power. How exactly is the defensive, self-serving ego challenged, enlarged, and restructured by the experience of love?

A more encompassing perspective is on offer in Alain Badiou's slim volume *In Praise of Love*. Badiou there makes more explicit what remains largely implicit in Lacan. "The final transfiguration of love," Badiou claims, "becomes possible when the Ego plunges through its own transparency to meet the power that has created it" (Badiou & Truong, 2012, p. 14). We surely miss the ultimate aim of love when we demote it to an exchange of adolescent flirtations. We seriously misjudge love's true potential when we think of it as merely mutual gratification, a pleasure-dance of one ego with another. Badiou thus reminds us that "Lacan doesn't say that love is a disguise for sexual relationships; he says that sexual relationships don't exist, that love is what comes in to replace that non-relationship . . . In love the individual goes beyond himself, beyond the narcissistic" (Badiou, 2012, pp. 18–19). Far from being merely hyper-sentimentality or over-heated sexual arousal, love for Badiou is an adventure in the real, a risk-taking exposure to what is truly Other. Love is a soul-challenge that leaves the subject of love fundamentally altered. "Love," Badiou insists, "is an existential project: to construct a world from a decentered point of view other than that of my mere impulse to survive or re-affirm my own identity" (Badiou, 2012, p. 25).

According to Badiou, love longs for permanence, but not merely to secure the love-object for oneself as an enviable possession, nor to preserve a special precinct of private pleasure. On the contrary, the deepest and most valuable form of love requires a willingness to embrace change, particularly the change that is brought about by adjusting oneself to a partner who is in some crucial ways different from oneself. The most authentic and precious form of love is an unfolding life-drama in which both partners participate in a bumpy, even painful and threatening process of personal change and development, a process made possible by the very otherness of the Other. Love's passionate engagement is thus a matter of sticking with that Otherness.

Entrance into the greatest gift of love, Badiou insists, involves a movement from the perspective of the One to that of the Two. "Love isn't simply about two people meeting and their inward-looking relationship," he maintains, "it is a construction, a life that is being made, no longer from the perspective of One but from the perspective of Two" (Badiou, 2012, p. 29). It's hard to overstate the profundity of Badiou's intention on this point. What is at stake, he insists, is ontological. For Badiou, the domain of the One names not only the self-referential ego but the global demand for consistency that underlies the function of ego, the unchanging yardstick that offers a single measure of all things. In submitting ourselves to the Two in Badiou's sense, we relinquish our reliance on any one standard of judgment. We open ourselves to living with and through difference.

There's ample reason to suspect that many marriages, perhaps the vast majority of them, fall short of the transformative Two-ness that Badiou has in mind. In fact, well-worn marriages are not infrequently swallowed by one or another dysfunctional co-dependency, a mutual hardening of egos. But Badiou insists that the essential goals of the ego – consistency, self-possession, predictability – must be given up in favor of investing oneself in the adventuring pact between true lovers. In a genuine love relation – the dynamic bond that Badiou approvingly refers to as "the Couple" – the ego relinquishes its own comfortable certainties, abandoning its dedication to its own sovereign preservation, in favor of a duality that demands on-going negotiation and sacrifice. In love, the demands of responsibility, dedication, respect, and mutuality with the beloved elevate the loving subject above egoistic self-concern. But what is ultimately at stake outstrips merely graduating from self-centeredness. What is called for by the love-bond is being re-opened to the challenge of one's own unconscious impulses, a walk on the wild side of one's own unknown.

In Badiou's conception, love forsakes the One of ego in favor of the Two in which subjectivity is expanded by openness to personal risk. The result is a novel appreciation of what intimacy really is. Far from being a matter of knowing the other so well that one can take the love-bond for granted, genuine couple-love dedicates itself of the margin of difference between one's self and the beloved. Such love opens both partners to a challenging intimacy with the Other that uproots and dislocates key elements of one's own sense of self.

For Badiou, the key point is that love-in-Twoness cannot be summarized, cannot be closed. It calls rather for an openness to what we haven't yet come to know, let alone to master, both in the beloved and in oneself. Real love (which might in a Lacanian register be well called "love in the real") is not to be measured by mere comfort with the beloved, as if mature love were comparable to the welcome softness of old shoes. On the contrary, real love remains a question to itself. Love thus requires an enduring respect for what the ego does not and cannot encompass. When the experience of love connects the subject to the dimension of the Thing, the result is a violent shudder of the subject's being. "In the phenomenon of love," says Lacan, "at every step of the way one encounters the wrenching and discordance associated with it. No one needs, for all that, to dialogue or dialectize about love to be involved in this gap or discord – it suffices to be in the thick of it, to be in love" (Lacan, 2015, p. 40).

Perhaps it was having in mind such transformative launching-beyond-self that led Lacan to compare the ontologically-inflected love between subjects with the love of God. What is at stake is the challenge of love in the face of the unknown Thing, in the Other and in oneself.

> In its root and essence, desire is the Other's desire, and this is strictly speaking the mainspring of the birth of love, if love is what occurs in the object toward which we extend our hand owing to our own desire, and which, when our desire makes it burst into flames, allows a response to appear for a moment: the other hand that reaches toward us as its desire. This desire always manifests itself inasmuch as we do not know. "And Ruth did not know what God wanted from her." But in order not to know what God wanted of her, it must still have been clear that God wanted *something* of her. (Lacan, 2015, p. 179)

Notes

1 I'm not suggesting that Freud's focus on link between love and egoistic narcissism is exclusive of other factors. We could, of course, alternatively trace the motivating energies of erotic passions to the unconscious forces of the id. To cite only the most famous reference, Freud follows one of Plato's metaphors that compares the ego's relation to erotic energy to a rider tenuously seated atop a wild horse.

2 For anyone familiar with Lacan's style, in his famous seminars and perhaps even more so in his *Écrits*, he generally refuses to offer definitive, summary accounts of key topics of his thought, apparently preferring to force his students to construct their own appropriation of his teaching. As he put it in "The Instance of the Letter in the Unconscious," his preference is to "leave the reader no other way out than the way in, which I prefer to be difficult" (Lacan, 2006, p. 138).

Relevant to this whole topic of Lacan's reserve in providing summaries of his views on key topics, I recently made an attempt to clarify one of Lacan's most enduring but apparently unsystematic interests – that of the unconscious significance of the religious

experience. The resulting book – *Embracing the Void: Rethinking the Origin of the Sacred* – was published by Northwestern University Press in 2022.
3 I unfold this argument in detail in *Death and Desire: Psychoanalytic Theory in Lacan's Return to Freud* (Routledge, 1991).
4 Relevant on this point is Lacan's insistence in his mature period that "there is no sexual relation." For this concept, see especially *The Seminar of Jacques Lacan, Book XX: Encore: On Feminine Sexuality, The Limits of Love and Knowledge* (Lacan, 1998).
5 Lacan's term here plays upon a reference to sexual orgasm. "*Jouir*" in French slang means to "come" or "have orgasm."
6 The clarification here is offered by Bruce Fink in his work *Lacan on Love: An Exploration of Lacan's Seminar VIII*, Transference (2016, p. 101).
7 Lacan devotes the first half of his 7th seminar, *The Ethics of Psychoanalysis*, to elaborating his theory of the Thing. See Lacan (1986).

References

Badiou, A., & Truong, N. (2012). *In Praise of Love* (P. Bush, Trans.). New Press.
Boothby, R. (2022). *Embracing the Void: Rethinking the Origin of the Sacred*. Northwestern University Press.
Boothby, R. (1991). *Death and Desire: Psychoanalytic Theory in Lacan's Return to Freud*. Routledge.
Fink, B. (2016). *Lacan on Love: An Exploration of Lacan's Seminar VIII, Transference*. Polity Press.
Freud, S. (1955). "On Narcissism: An Introduction." In J. Strachey (Ed. & Trans.), *The Standard Edition of the Complete Psychological Works of Sigmund Freud* (Vol. 14, pp. 69–102). Hogarth Press and the Institute of Psycho-analysis.
Lacan, J. (1988). *The Seminar of Jacques Lacan, Book I, Freud's Papers on Technique, 1953–54* (J. A. Miller, Ed., & J. Forrester, Trans.). W. W. Norton & Co.
Lacan, J. (1986). *The Seminar of Jacques Lacan, Book VII: The Ethics of Psychoanalysis 1959–60* (J.-A. Miller, Ed., & D. Porter, Trans.). W. W. Norton & Co.
Lacan, J. (1998). *The Seminar of Jacques Lacan, Book XX: Encore: On Feminine Sexuality, The Limits of Love and Knowledge, 1972–73* (J.-A. Miller, Ed., & B. Fink, Trans.). W. W. Norton & Co.
Lacan, J. (2014). *The Seminar of Jacques Lacan, Book X, Anxiety* (J.-A. Miller, Ed., & A. R. Price, Trans.). Polity Press.
Lacan, J. (2015). *The Seminar of Jacques Lacan, Book VIII, Transference* (J.-A. Miller, Ed., & B. Fink, Trans.). Polity Press.
Lacan, J. (2006). *Écrits* (B. Fink, H. Fink, & R. Grigg, Trans.). W. W. Norton & Co.
Ruti, M. (2011). *The Case for Falling in Love: Why We Can't Master the Madness of Love – and Why That's the Best Part*. Sourcebooks Inc.

Chapter 6

Love and Death under Erasure

Lessons from the Phoenix (and Diotima)

Michael Marder

In my recent book, *The Phoenix Complex* (Marder, 2023), I diagnose and describe a deep unconscious structure, on a par with the Oedipus complex, the Electra complex, and Gaston Bachelard's "fire complexes," which across cultures and historical periods prompts human beings to identify the outside world and themselves with phoenixes, ever ready to spring back to life after death. The miraculous rebound of the phoenix, ranging from psychic and physical recuperation and resurrection to environmental recovery, is the hope that refuses to die even in the face of utter devastation and extreme loss. This lethal hope persists in numerous guises, affecting our sense of life, love, and death at the individual, species, interpersonal, and cosmic levels.

Classically, the myth of the phoenix is told in two different versions – the first much better known than the second – and in accounts that draw on elements of both, for instance, in the writings of Lactantius, Epiphanius of Cyprus, and the unknown author of the third-century Christian treatise *Didascalia apostolorum*. According to the hegemonic narrative, the phoenix dies instantaneously in a fiery conflagration and is reborn from the ashes as another perfect specimen, who is one of a kind. In the alternative version of the myth, itself told with dozens of variations, the phoenix dies, decomposes in its nest, and later on gradually metamorphoses into a new phoenix from the corpse of the old (sometimes as a result of spontaneous generation, *generatio aequivoca*). Across all the narratives, however, death does not have the last word; if anything, it is but an interval, a bridgeable gap between lives, rather than a point of no return, an abyss or a black hole reflecting neither any light nor meaning.

Reproducing the hegemonic myth shorn of its recognizable narrative elements, the deep-rooted phoenix complex puts death under erasure, leaving it visible, yet undermining its ultimacy. In psychoanalysis, the relation to death it orchestrates is called *disavowal*, the simultaneous acknowledgement and repudiation of reality. But what about love? Does the phoenix complex support any type of love other than narcissism and its attendant desire to perpetuate one's own being, even beyond the threshold of death? After all, in every rendition of the myth of the phoenix, this miraculous bird is said to be utterly unique, not needing a mate to procreate, since it is reborn from its own mortal remains. The disavowal of death goes

DOI: 10.4324/9781032663487-8

hand in hand with the disavowal of love, converting the phoenix (and the relevant complex) into a test case for the knot, in which these two high points in the drama of the living are tied together.

At the end of his poem *De ave phoenice*, Lactantius intuits not just a close connection but the identity of love and death in the figure of the phoenix. "Female or male she is, which you will – whether neither [*neutrum*] or both [*utrumque*], a happy bird, she regards not any unions of love: to her, death is love [*mors illi venus est*]; and her sole pleasure lies in death [*sola est in morte voluptas*]; to win her birth, it is her appetite first to die" (Lactantius, 160–165).[1]

Death and love are interrelated by their placement under erasure; their identity is achieved thanks to their disavowal, mediated both through the absence of sexual difference and through a special sort of sexual desire (*voluptas*) that finds pleasure in death as a harbinger of a new birth. Switching from the mythic register to that of the phoenix complex, we may speculate that this desire goes well beyond poetic license: it works behind the scenes of romantic love and the fear of death alike. Placement under erasure – the psychic act of disavowal itself – becomes fecund, productive or reproductive, reproducing the complex that borrows its name from the unique bird by means of those who carry it in the depths of their unconscious. In other words, the erasure of love and death is hypostatized and leads a life of its own, steering the movements of psychic life.

Another literary instance of associating the phoenix with Venus, despite the bird's rejection of "any unions of love," derives from an obscure Latin poet Laevius, who, in one of the extant fragments, refers to the following words inscribed on the phoenix's wing: "O Venus, who nourishes love and rouses desire [*amoris altrix, genetrix cupiditatis*], by whose favor a clear day stretches before me, your follower and your maid servant" (Laevius, Frg. 22). The praise of the goddess who nourishes love and generates desire (*genetrix cupiditatis*) is expressed by a creature who knows neither of these feelings, or, at best, finds sexual fulfillment in death, as the promise of rebirth, the "clear day" (*diem serenum*) stretching ahead as a symbol of renewed life after death.[2] Essentially conservative, the phoenix's desire is for a continued existence across the rupturing of time, for the recommencement of (more of) the same after the end, marked by death. But death is not merely an obstacle to be overcome; unexpectedly brimming with positivity, it is the material condition of possibility for rebirth, the incubator of new life where the tomb and the womb merge. Which is why second-century CE Greek poet Dionysius Periegetes, writes that the phoenix "makes itself a pyre for death or a nest for life [*puran tina tēs teleutēs hē kalian suntithēsi tēs zōēs*]" (Dionysius Periegetes, I, 32).

Many centuries later, John Donne in his 1604 poem "The Canonization" links "the phoenix riddle" to the phenomenon of two becoming one in love:

> Call us what you will, we're made such by love;
> Call her one, me another fly,
> We're tapers too, and at our own cost die,
> And we in us find th' eagle and the dove;

> The phoenix riddle hath more wit
> By us: we two, being one, are it. (Donne, 2010, pp. 151–152)

When it comes to the phoenix, however, the two who become one are two iterations of the same being – the freshly emanated phoenix and its predecessor. Classical sources are irremediably ambiguous on the subject of the identity or the difference between the two: Tertullian claims that phoenix is "another, yet the same [*alius idem*]" (Tertullian, XIII, 9), while Lactantius contends that the new bird is "the very one, yet not the one [*et ipsa, nec ipsa est*]" (Lactantius, 170). The erasure of sexual difference and of the difference between life and death borders on the erasure of difference as such, a condition that is not propitious to any love except narcissism.

It turns out that myth is much more lucid than the "rational" treatment of love and death, which, in the figure of the phoenix, appear without the obfuscations imposed by the apparatus of consciousness. Their hypostatized mutual erasure overflows mythical narration and percolates into philosophy, including one of the foremost ancient works on the subject of love, Plato's *Symposium*. Diotima's speech, reported by her lover Socrates, reveals a certain *machina mundi*, the machine or the mechanism (as much as a set of machinations) that makes the world of finite beings go round in keeping with the tenets of the phoenix complex. Before unveiling this machine, Diotima establishes, and Socrates agrees, that "love loves the good to be one's own forever [*erōs tou to agathon autō einai aei*]" (206a).[3] There is, nevertheless, a major obstacle to eternal ownership: to possess its object (which is not quite an object, since the good, *to agathon*, is the fugacious highest *eidos*, in the light of which all other Platonic ideas appear and make sense) forever, the possessor must guarantee eternal self-possession – an utter impossibility, to say the least, in the world of finite beings.[4] Hence, Diotima immediately raises the question of method, of a good way or manner (*tropos*) for the lover to follow in order to make the impossible possible, to put the strivings of love to the right use, to put them to work (*ergon*), to lend them a body in this world (206b), despite the finitude that stares us in the face and that we consistently repress, incapable of enduring this stare for too long. I want to suggest that, rather than the famous "ladder of love," which will be featured later on in her speech, it is the *machina mundi* of the phoenix complex that paves the tortuous road presumably leading out of the aporia of love.

Let us backtrack for a moment. The maximalism of love's activity as Diotima sees it – i.e., of *how* love actually loves – demands that love unfold as if death did not take place, or, at least, as if death did not have the final word, leaving the lover's fundamental self-possession undisturbed. At the same time, in its effectiveness, love substantiates this very *as if*. This is quite obvious. What is, perhaps, less so is that the same maximalism stipulates that everything should happen as if love, too, did not take place, as if the singularity of the beloved did not matter, since, at bottom, each instance of love seeks the good, and, furthermore, desires the eternal possession of this universal object. "Love is always for this [*dē toutou o erōs estin aei*]," stresses Diotima, implying that the eternal and tautological nature of love's "object" equally stamps every striving toward this object. Regardless of what or who it is that is loved whenever love erupts on the scene, the good is the final destination, that toward which the lover travels via the beloved. Under the sign of eternity (indeed, of an eternal having), both death and love are put under erasure, or disavowed, such that their erasure and disavowal dictate the rhythms of the world, of the waves of biological reproduction and the peaks of cultural creation, of self-replacement that maintains the illusion that the basis of self-possession remains unscathed.

Diotima is Socrates' guide (and ours as well) to the intricacies of the phoenix's love without love that puts in a clear focus continuous self-possession across the discrete existence of unique specimens, where each is "another, yet the same," in the words of Tertullian. And she leads us down the predesignated path straight to the phoenix's death without death. Picking up the thread of her argument, note that, for Diotima, not only the beloved but also beauty is the means for the accomplishment of the goal of love. "– For you are wrong, Socrates, in supposing that love is of the beautiful. –What then is it? – It is of engendering and begetting upon the beautiful [*tēs gennēseōs kai tou tokon em tō kalō*]" (206e). In the painstaking construction of the machine, which operates with love and death under erasure and which works to keep them under erasure, everything (including the beautiful, *tō kalō*) becomes a means, a mere cog ensuring its smooth functioning.[5] It is for this reason that the ladder of love, extending from one beautiful body to the idea of beauty, leads nowhere – that is to say, nowhere essential as far as love is concerned. The beloved as an instance of the beautiful *and* beauty itself, as that upon which engendering and begetting are put into effect, are secondary vis-à-vis a yearning for immortality.

Inching closer to the unveiling of her vision of *machina mundi*, Diotima concludes that engendering, *gennēseōs*, "is something ever-existent and immortal in our mortal life [*aeigenes esti kai athanaton ōs thnētō hē gennēsis*]. [...] Hence, it necessarily follows that love is of immortality" (206e–207a). Engendering acts by putting the aporetic relation of immortality and mortality to work, it draws an excess, a profit, or an offspring (*tokos*) from this relation, from putting death under erasure. Thanks to engendering (in body and soul, as our text will specify later), death loses its finality; engendering is the practical, psycho-physiological disavowal of mortality right in the midst of mortal existence.

As for love, since it operates by engendering, it gets in touch with the immortal, first, by striving to possess its eternal object – the good – permanently, and, second, by *enacting* immortality through the activity proper to it, the activity said to be "ever-existent and immortal." Yet, the genitive form of love – that of which it invariably is – is not as straightforward as Diotima makes it appear. Although in her speech, love is of the good *and* of immortality, it is doubtful that the former object is actually interchangeable with the latter. While, on the surface of it, love is of immortality because it implies the non-negotiable possibility of possessing the object (namely, the good) forever and this possibility's necessary underside of a permanent *self*-possession, a whole lexicon of revolt against time and death is scrambled here, where differences are more important than ostensible synonyms and homologues.[6] So, the "forever" (*aei*) possession of the good is the same word as in the description of what love is "always" for. The "ever-existent" (*aeigenes*) feature of engendering literally means "always-coming-to-be," read in terms of both the content and the form of this loving activity and undeniably opposed to the eternal nature of ideas, such as beauty or the good, that are neither generated nor undergo any changes nor perish. The "immortal" (*athanaton*) quality added to engendering centers on the negation of death (*thanatos*) in the midst of a state that is admittedly mortal (*thnētō*). Once these distinctions emerge in the semantic and philosophical spotlight, the tangle of love unravels, the "under erasure" of both love and death itself put under erasure.

When the time comes to disclose the contraption for putting death (and love) under erasure, Diotima says:

> In this way everything mortal is preserved, not by remaining entirely the same forever, which is the mark of the divine, but by leaving behind that which is growing old and passing away something other and new after the kind of the [ageing] one [*heteron neon egkataleipein oion auto hēn*]. By this means [*mechanē*], Socrates, what is mortal – the body and everything else – partakes of immortality [*thnēton athanasias metechei*]; but what is immortal does so differently. (208a–b)

The means (*mechanē*), the mechanics and machinations of engendering as self-replacement with another who is ideally the same as the one replaced, bear an uncanny resemblance to the classical myth of the phoenix. Without cancelling death in actuality, self-preservation by letting go of oneself in order to leave behind someone "after the kind of the ageing one" de-activates the main effect of death, which is the irrecoverable disappearance of the deceased. That is: without actually becoming immortal, the engendering being participates (*metechei; methexis*) in immortality, in a similar manner in which the instantiations of a given idea participate in that idea (e.g., a beautiful body in the idea of beauty). And without canceling love in actuality, the mechanics and machinations of self-replacement put it, too, under erasure, seeing that love and the beloved are not ends in themselves; they are the means for begetting, which, in its turn, serves as the means for partaking of immortality.

Diotima realizes that the solution she indicates is imperfect, but it is an imperfection conditioned by the limits of finite beings. In addition to a muddle of terms for eternity, immortality, that which is forever, and an ever-existent tendency, *methexis* is no longer reserved for the interrelation of the universal and the particulars, binding instead opposites that are not even situated on the same ontological plane, namely mortal beings and immortality, rather than mortality and immortality. Through the principle (*logos*) of generation, by means of engendering, Diotima insists, "mortal nature seeks, as best it can, to be immortal [*hē thnētē phusis zētei kata to dunaton aei to einai athanatos*]" (207c–d). Like Diotima's solution, his principle/*logos* is flawed, compared to a homonymous principle operative in the eidetic realm, so much so that Socrates associates her with "our perfect sophists [*hōsper oi teleoi sophistai*]" (208c).⁷

Diotima is not there in person to defend herself from the intellectual stabs and tacit accusations Socrates (or is it Plato peering from behind his back?) levels against her. Her absence speaks volumes, of course, and fatefully marks the unfolding of Western thought since its inception in a series of self-replacements and phoenix-like preservation of thinkers *qua* thinkers: Diotima *dis*places, or predates, the replacement of Socrates by Plato.⁸ Had she been present at the feast of words and physical nourishments where Socrates and his lovers discussed the subject of love, however, she would have perhaps retorted that such sophistry is the sophistry of life itself, inbuilt into the biological and cultural machinery of reproduction. Diotima only unveils the workings of the world machine, which is by no means restricted to human beings alone, without necessarily passing any judgment on it.

The next stage in the unveiling shows how love becomes deadly, how the mutually mediated placement under erasure of love and death imbues them with each other's capacities not as a mere accident but as a matter of absolute necessity. Diotima comprehends love as a sickness and, hence, a harbinger of death: "the desire to beget [*gennan epithumēsē*]" in all animals, "whether going on earth or winging in the air," makes them all sick and prone "to sacrifice their lives, to be racked with starvation themselves if they can but nurture their young" (207a–b).⁹ However fraught the way it is achieved by mortal beings, immortality demands that one give up one's mortal existence in exchange for the promise of eternal life realized. Love and death are two transfer stations in this exchange – the two that, themselves, become one (the same as and other to each other) by analogy with the dynamic *and* static state of affairs they precipitate, as well as with the logic of the phoenix.

The applicability to animals of the apparatus that lends mortal creatures access to immortality leads Diotima toward a curious insight. "As for men," she remarks, "one might suppose they do these things [sacrifice themselves for the young, MM] on the promptings of reason [*ek logismou*], but what is the cause [*aitia*] of this amorous condition in the animals?" (207c). The implication of Diotima's remark is that an overarching cause is behind the doings attributed to human reason and to animal instinct. The cause is a shared desire of all mortals to partake of immortality, which means that, servicing the same universal apparatus, human *logos* is a subspecies in the apparently flawed principle/*logos* of self-preservation through self-replacement with the other who is seen as another version of this self (thus, of the same). The being under erasure of love and death, not least through their *inter*mediation, belongs at the level of this super-*logos* driving the actions of the living.

In the cultural sphere, where the "pregnancy of the body" is supplemented with the "pregnancy of the soul," the sacrificial overtones of a lethal love and an amorous death under erasure grow stronger. For the "love of winning a name" and "fame immortal," "even more than for their children [*hē huper tōn paidōn*], they [men, MM] are ready to run all risks, to expend money, perform any kind of task, and sacrifice their lives" (208c–d). If biological progeny is ranked lower than the perpetuation of one's name by heroic or ingenious deeds, that is because children are the material bridge to immortality, while a great name is an immaterial bridge, made, as it were, of the same stuff as the immortal, wherein mortal beings strive to participate. It is for this reason that Diotima and Socrates (who deems himself, according to *Theaetetus* 149a–150b, "the midwife of ideas") value the pregnancy of the soul over its equivalent in the body. The more intensely death and love are put under erasure in self-replacement by a legendary name or a magnificent work, the greater the readiness to sacrifice one's actual life, to give up finite existence in exchange for an ideal recovery of oneself in posterity.

The comparative thrust of the efficacy, with which death and love are erased in the respective engenderings of the soul and of the body, reaches its apogee when Diotima turns to the works of Homer and Hesiod.[10] The community (*koinōnia*) and friendship (*philia*) of men are said to be stronger when the soul, rather than the body, is the begetter, "since the children of their union are more beautiful and more deathless [*kallionōn kai athanatōterōn*]" (209c). It is questionable whether deathlessness can be a matter of degree, as opposed to an either/or choice: something is either deathless or mortal. Arguably, degrees of deathlessness are conceivable when a fuller or a less full participation (*methexis*) of mortals in immortality is at stake. Diotima's comparison is significant for another reason: it ties together the sublimation of love (a well-established theme in psychoanalysis) and the sublimation of death. The positivity and fecundity of the mutual erasure of death and love in the phoenix complex and its early philosophical reverberations in Plato's dialogue assume the form of sublimation when, overflowing the soul, *erōs* gives rise to great works that translate its impulse into community and friendship. An analogous movement takes place on the side of death: sublimated thanks to the same works, the forgetting, which death connotes, is transformed into memory, or, more precisely, "a glory immortally renewed in the memory [*mnēmēn*] of men" (209d). Even though it may seem that, instead of being sublimated, death and oblivion twist into their opposites (immortality and memory), they lurk beneath the brilliant surface of a glorious name, to the extent that its continued shining depends on the persistent effort of renewal, betraying the ever-present shadow of mortality and forgetting.

To return to the phoenix, whom we have never actually left and who (alas!) has never left us, we can glean from the text of fourth-century Bishop of Verona, Zeno, writing with an unmistakable Platonic flair, that the phoenix reborn is "not a shadow, but truth, not a likeness but the phoenix itself, not the other that, though better, is still the same as the one before it [*non umbra, sed veritas, non imago, sed phoenix, non alia, sed quamvis melior alia, tamen prior ipsa*]" (Zeno of Verona I, 16, 9). Zeno of Verona is anxious to cut through the intolerable indecision, the vacillation of the earlier sources on the subject of sameness or otherness of the phoenix's progeny: for him, the identity of the two birds is a true identity, independent of the technics of copying or reproducing the one as a shadow (*umbra*) or a likeness (*imago*) of the other. According to its hegemonic inner logic, the phoenix *must* appear this way, with the reproductive trail either obfuscated (say, in a bright flash of self-combustion and resurrection) or rendered visible in the form of pure production, that is to say, as self-production. The consolidation of truth (*veritas*) in its absolute veracity (no shadows, no likenesses…) depends on a blatant lie.

Diotima, for her part, lets Socrates in on the dirty secret of bodily and psychic self-replacement. The fault lines of love and death under erasure are slightly more prominent in her depiction of the philosophical phoenix, which requires frantic movement and activity to guarantee that everything stays in its place within the temporal order, irrespective of the passage of time and the passing away of the living. The figure of the phoenix is the incarnation of *stasis* – changelessness and stagnation, *as well as* civil strife (as in Plato's *Republic* 470b: "the name 'stasis' is given to enmity with one's own people [*tou oikeiou echthrai*]"), division against oneself, and willingness to sacrifice one's immediate existence for the sake of perpetuating one's genes or one's name. Resorting to love with the view to solving the problem of oblivion and death accelerates empirical perishing for the sake of posthumous survival, not to mention the disavowal of love itself.

Reproduced for millennia on end, the phoenix complex is still being replayed on a planetary scale, among many others, in the twenty-first century. It imbues the lifeworld and the deathworld (fossils and other dead remains) with *stasis*, as a function of a hypostatized and fecund putting of love and death under erasure. In a sense, then, the contemporary global environmental disaster is one of its most far-reaching repercussions, a non-erasable consequence of putting under erasure the powers of metamorphosis, of becoming-other beyond the rigid confines of *stasis*. That is why sifting through and untying the knots of the phoenix complex formed in myth and philosophy is, far from a quaint archival endeavor, a task oriented to a livable (loveable and finite) future.

Notes

1 Earlier still, first-century CE Roman geographer Pomponius Mela observes that the phoenix is "always unique," *semper unica* (the adjective in the feminine), and that she "is not conceived by copulation nor born through parturition [*non enim coitu concipitur partuve generatur*" (Mela, 1867, III.72).
2 As van den Broek (1972) notes, "Laevius was evidently making a play on the two aspects of Venus – as morning star and goddess of Love" (p. 270).
3 All quotes from Plato's *Symposium* are drawn from the translation by W. R. M. Lamb (Plato, 1925). Occasionally, the English translation is modified to reflect the Greek original more accurately.
4 While it is formally true that Plato does not answer the question "exactly how does one come into possession of goodness?" (Nightingale, 2021, p. 85), self-possession must be guaranteed as a basis of any possession. In fact, as already mentioned, Plato does not answer this question because his other dialogues, including *Republic* and *Philebus* indicate that the possession of the good is impossible *per definitionem*.
5 This applies even to the "highest point" in the ascent on the ladder of beauty and the panoramic vision it opens, although its instrumentality has escaped commentators, even those who are as perceptive as John Sallis: "Therefore, as she [Diotima] now describes it, the ascent would culminate in a beholding of the beautiful itself – that is, in

a vision of the pure, complete beautiful itself, totally absolved from all connection with all that pertains to mortality: a vision of the beautiful that would be set utterly above the realm of human flesh and human mortality"
(Sallis, 2021, p. 57).
6 The reason for this "scrambling is obvious": "Diotima needs a unitary conception of immortality if philosophers, politicians, and biological parents are all to be treated as lovers with a common goal" (Long, 2019, p. 60) and, moreover, if the shared nature of the eidetic realm and of love is to come to light.
7 For more on the ironic nature of praise Socrates heaps on Diotima, refer to Jill Frank's *Poetic Justice: Rereading Plato's Republic* (2018, p. 155).
8 In the context of feminist philosophy, Luce Irigaray has interpreted Diotima's absence in the following way: "She does not take part in these exchanges or in this meal among men. She is not there. She herself does not speak […]. And Diotima is not the only example of a woman whose wisdom, especially about love, is reported in her absence by a man" (Irigaray, 2004, p. 20).
9 Her words resonate with Lysias' take on love, also reported in his absence by Phaedrus in the homonymous dialogue. Refer to Chara Kokkiou, *Eros, Song, and Philosophy in Plato* (2020, p. 31).
10 This would be another bit of hidden irony built into Plato's dialogue. As we know, Plato recommends banning poets from the ideal *politeia*. Poetic "pregnancy of the soul" is evidently, for him, not as valuable as philosophical wisdom (and may be downright dangerous and counterproductive). As Gary Scott and William Welton (2008) put it rather mildly, "There is a kind of wisdom and virtue that poets and craftsmen can beget, and even such wisdom and such virtue have a value. That value remains even if it is the case that when compared to true philosophic wisdom and virtue that of the poets and craftsmen seem to be mere semblances" (p. 128).

References

Dionysius Periegetes. (n.d.). *De aucupio.*
Donne, J. (2010). "The Canonization." In R. Robbins (Ed.), *The Complete Poems of John Donne*. Longman.
Frank, J. (2018). *Poetic Justice: Rereading Plato's Republic*. University of Chicago Press.
Irigaray, L. (2004). *An Ethics of Sexual Difference* (C. Burke & G. Gill, Trans.). Continuum.
Kokkiou, C. (2020). *Eros, Song, and Philosophy in Plato*. Lexington Books.
Lactantius. (n.d.). *De ave phoenice.*
Laevius. (n.d.). *Pterygion phoenicis, Fragment 22.* In Charisius, *Ars grammatica.*
Long, A. (2019). *Death and Immortality in Ancient Philosophy*. Cambridge University Press.
Marder, M. (2023). *The Phoenix Complex: A Philosophy of Nature*. The MIT Press.
Mela, P. (1867). *De chorographia libri tres* (G. Parthey, Trans.).
Nightingale, A. (2021). *Philosophy and Religion in Plato's Dialogues*. Cambridge University Press.
Plato. (1925). *Lysis, Symposium, Gorgias* (W.R.M. Lamb, Trans.). Loeb Classical Library, Vol. 166. Harvard University Press.
Sallis, J. (2021). *On Beauty and Measure: Plato's Symposium and Statesman.* Indiana University Press.

Scott, G., & Welton, W. (2008). *Erotic Wisdom: Philosophy and Intermediacy in Plato's Symposium*. SUNY Press.

Tertullian. (n.d.). *De carnis resurrectione.*

van den Broek, R. (1972). *The Myth of the Phoenix According to Classical and Early Christian Traditions.* Brill.

Zeno of Verona. (n.d.). *Tractatus.*

Chapter 7

From Death to Love

The Transformative Event in Paul's Christian Discourse

Leon S. Brenner

Saint Paul, one of the most renowned apostles of Christianity and a contemporary of Jesus, began his life as a Jew, actively participating in the persecution of early Christians. His missionary calling to spread the Christianity of Jesus emerged at the age of 30, following a divine revelation experienced as a mysterious inner voice on his way to Damascus. Paul's thinking is encapsulated in the innovative Christian discourse he developed amidst the diverse currents emerging within Christianity at the time including the apostle John and the apostle Paul. Appointed as the messenger to both Jews and non-Jews (Gentiles), Paul formulated a Christian discourse marked by a universality that surpasses the confines of any law and transcends any differences that could serve as grounds for exclusion from salvation.

Alain Badiou, in his examination of Paul's writings, explicitly separates Paul's discourse from traditional religious interpretations, viewing him instead as a "poet-thinker of the event" and a "militant figure." Badiou focuses on the human interplay of concepts such as "rupture," "overturning," "thought-practice," and "subjective materiality" (Badiou, 2003, p. 2). Badiou explores how Paul's texts scrutinize the relationship between the position of death and path of love (Latin: *agapë*), facilitating the understanding of the subject's fidelity to the "event," where the only proof, paradoxically, lies in its subjective proclamation and affirmation. According to Badiou, this relationship forms the foundation for exploring universality within a historical context and is pivotal in Paul's development of the novel discourse he advocates (Badiou, 2003, p. 5). Paul's concept of love, therefore, is deeply intertwined with Badiou's philosophy of transformation. It enables Badiou's designation of love in opposition to death as the active force that universalizes and sustains the truth of faith, making it a living reality for all.

This chapter explores the intricate relationship between love and death in Paul's writings, as interpreted by Alain Badiou. By examining Paul's discourse within the context of Badiou's philosophy and Lacanian psychoanalysis, it aims to uncover how Paul's revolutionary concept of love offers a universal path to salvation. The analysis will explore the contrasting discourses of the Father and the Son, illustrating how Paul's emphasis on love overcomes the limitations imposed by the law and paves the way for a new subjective position. Through a discourse analysis, this chapter will highlight the transformative power of the event and its implications

DOI: 10.4324/9781032663487-9

for understanding subjectivity, desire, and fidelity. Ultimately, this study seeks to demonstrate the enduring relevance of Paul's discourse in contemporary philosophical thought and its potential for fostering a more inclusive and universal understanding of love.

Discourse Analysis

Badiou considers Paul's Gospel as a discourse and, therefore, employs discourse analysis to highlight its singularity. Discourse analysis is a research method utilized in various fields such as linguistics, sociology, anthropology, and philosophy to study written or spoken language in relation to its social context. By examining the structure, patterns, and functions of discourse, researchers can uncover underlying assumptions, ideologies, and social relations embedded in the text.

In *Seminar XVII*, titled *The Other Side of Psychoanalysis*, Jacques Lacan implements discourse analysis to explore the structures and functions of various forms of social and psychoanalytic discourse. Lacan introduces the concept of the four discourses: the Master's discourse, the University discourse, the Hysteric's discourse, and the Analyst's discourse. Each discourse represents a different mode of social interaction and a distinct way in which power, knowledge, desire, and subjectivity are organized and communicated. Lacan's discourse analysis reveals how these discourses function to sustain or challenge existing social hierarchies and how they influence the psychoanalytic process.

Badiou follows Lacan's framework to analyze Paul's innovative discourse by comparing it to existing discourses of Paul's era (Badiou, 2003, p. 41). He identifies three main discourses in contrast to Paul's: the Jewish, Greek, and mystical discourses.

The Jewish discourse is characterized by the subjective figure of the prophet. The prophet operates within the realm of signs, testifying to transcendence by revealing and deciphering the obscure. Therefore, the Jewish discourse focuses on exceptional elements such as prophetic signs, miracles, and election that point towards transcendence beyond the natural order (Badiou, 2003, p. 41). These emphasize the exceptional nature of the Jewish nation itself, with each member considered an elect entity.

In contrast, the Greek discourse is characterized by the subjective figure of the wise man. Wisdom (*sophia*) in the Greek context involves understanding and appropriating the fixed order of the world, aligning logos (reason) with being. Greek discourse is described as cosmic, situating the subject within the rationality of a natural totality. It is fundamentally concerned with upholding wisdom as a state of knowledge that harmonizes with the natural order of the cosmos (Badiou, 2003, p. 41). Unlike the Jewish discourse, which focuses on exceptional elements and signs pointing to transcendence, the Greek discourse bases itself on the totality of the cosmic order to adjust and align with it.

The mystical discourse represents a fourth possible discourse alongside the Greek, Jewish, and Paul's own Christian discourse. This mystical discourse is characterized by being subjective, ineffable, and intimate, involving experiences that are unutterable and only known to the individual who has encountered a miracle. It is described as the discourse of glorification, where the subject dwells in silent and mystical intimacy (Badiou, 2003, p. 51).

Paul emphasizes the importance of not allowing the Christian declaration to be justified through this mystical discourse of glorification. He advocates for a discourse without proof, miracles, or convincing signs, focusing on the power of conviction that shatters traditional reasoning (Badiou, 2003, pp. 52–53).

According to Badiou, the mystical discourse, while present – particularly within Christian theology – is marginal. His interest lies in the dialectical relationship he identifies between the Jewish and Greek discourses: two distinct but interdependent discourses, each relying on the other for a complete understanding of reality. In this relationship the Jewish discourse relies on the logic of the exceptional sign, which is only valid within the framework of the Greek cosmic totality, while, correspondingly, the wisdom of the cosmos can only be explored based on its anomalies.

Badiou is a thinker that aims to go beyond Hegelian dialectics. Therefore, he argues that the dialectical relationship between the Jewish and Greek discourses limits their effectiveness.

First, they are limited in their ability to achieve universality independently. Both discourses rely on specific frameworks and modes of understanding that are rooted in their respective traditions and worldviews. The Jewish discourse emphasizes the exceptional nature of signs and prophetic revelations, while the Greek discourse focuses on wisdom and the rational ordering of the cosmos. These distinct approaches, while valuable within their own contexts, do not offer a singular universal message, preventing a truly universal understanding of truth and salvation.

Another limitation arises from the division of humanity into separate categories based on adherence to either the Jewish or Greek discourse. Badiou critiques this division, as it creates a binary distinction between Jew and Greek, reinforcing the idea of exclusivity. By categorizing individuals according to their affiliation with a particular discourse, the potential for the realization of a universal message that transcends cultural, religious, or philosophical differences is compromised. This split contributes to a fragmented view of humanity, where individuals are defined by their adherence to specific traditions rather than their shared humanity.

Discourse of the Father

Badiou continues to explore the structure of the discourses in Paul's time. He argues that, while humanity is split into Jew and Greek, both discourses provide a homologous path towards subjectivation that is inherently exclusive; that is, dependent on the exclusion of some-One from its scope. In the Jewish discourse, a member of the Jewish nation can become a subject by excluding themselves from the Gentile group. In the Greek discourse, a subject gains its relation to wisdom by excluding the irrationality of the Barbarian from the group. Accordingly, Badiou argues that both discourses provide a path towards subjectivation through the relationship between a totality and its exception.

The subject constituted on the basis of a relationship between totality and exception has been extensively elaborated by Jacques Lacan in *Seminars XIV* and *XX*. There, Lacan describes this type of discourse in reference to the paternal function in the Oedipus complex and, particularly, the masculine subject he charts out in his schema of sexuation. Masculine logic is instated through the prohibition of the father, symbolically designating the lack introduced in the libidinal child-mother economy. The paternal function, according to Lacan, instates this prohibition and marks out a place for the metonymic sliding of desire on the chain of signifiers. According to this logic, the dynamic function of lack establishes its relationship with the totality of signifiers in the symbolic order through its exclusion from the chain, thereby establishing signification as an organizing law that governs the subject's relationship with reality.

Lacan bases this theory on Freud's account of the "*Wahrnehmungszeichen...the first registration of the perceptions*" (Freud, 1953–1974, p. 234). According to Freud, in order for memory to be organized into conscious subjective history, an initial registration of perception, that is inaccessible to consciousness, has to take place (Lacan, 1993, p. 181). Addressing this issue in linguistic terms, Lacan analogously claims that for the symbolic order to provide a coherent basis for the inscription of the masculine subject, an initial instatement of a "primitive" form of "signifying material" – inaccessible from the vantage point of the subject's reality – has to be affirmed (Lacan, 1993, p. 156). The basic assumption grounding this framework is that, for a closed semantic network to systematically and coherently convey meaning that is universally attributed to its domain, an element has to be excluded from this network and function as its limit point.

Badiou identifies a similar logic conditioning both the Jewish and Greek discourses. This is why he defines them both as discourses of the Father, referencing Lacan's engagement with the "paternal function" situating the subject in relation to the symbolic law (Lacan, 1993, p. 204).

Within the Jewish discourse, the symbolic law can be understood as adherence to a set of divine commandments, rituals, and traditions that govern the community and establish a sense of order and belonging. The Jewish nation is bound by the Mosaic law, which recognizes the covenant between God and the chosen people. The relationship to the law of the father establishes a sense of continuity, tradition, and covenantal responsibility, defining their subjective position within the framework of divine commandments and cultural practices.

In the Greek discourse, the symbolic law can be interpreted as the alignment with the rational order of the cosmos and adherence to philosophical principles that govern knowledge and understanding. The Greek wise man seeks to embody the principles of rationality, harmony, and cosmic order, reflecting a commitment to the laws of nature and reason. The Greek subject's engagement with the symbolic law establishes a framework for understanding the world, seeking truth, and embodying a state of intellectual and moral virtue.

Path of Death

Badiou's reading of Paul associates the discourses of the Father with a particular type of desire (*epithumia*) that entails a "lethal" function in terms of the subject's agency. Badiou states that "The law is what gives life to desire. But in so doing, it constrains the subject so that he wants to follow only the path of death" (Badiou, 2003, p. 79).

Here, Badiou relies on Lacan's simple formula which states that prohibition is the precursor to desire. According to Lacan, it is not the case that first there is a desire that goes too far and then a law is instated to prohibit it. Instead, for Lacan, the law, in its prohibitive character, molds desire; it creates it. According to this framework, desire is transgressive in its nature, and the law (in its paternal modality) is what defines a limit to be transgressed. Therefore, one desires simply because a limit is imposed on them.

Paul posits that the law introduced in the Jewish and Greek discourses intrinsically incites a desire to deviate from the law. This desire is propped up by the fantasy of deviating from the paternal prohibition (Badiou, 2003, p. 79). He argues that situating the object of desire outside the confines of the law grants desire autonomy beyond the subject's "will," fully subsumed under the law. Thus, under the law, the object of desire is given life instead of the subject, thereby transgressing the subject. In Paul's words: the object of desire is inscribed as "life" and the subject as "death." This trajectory in the aim of the object of desire, which Paul terms the "carnal path of death," embodies this dynamic (Badiou, 2003, p. 79). The subject on the path of death navigates around an object of desire that dictates its direction externally and beyond its control—as a subject stripped of agency. This autonomous vivacity of desire, beyond the subject, is what Paul labels "sin" (Badiou, 2003, p. 79).

Badiou, extending beyond Paul's thesis, notes that the operation characterizing the path of death involves shifting the subject's center of gravity. This shift animates the path of death and extinguishes the subject as an entity capable of will and agency: "The law vivifies death, and the subject as life...falls into the realm of death" (Badiou, 2003, p. 82).

To this, Alenka Zupančič adds that the law of the Father displaces the subject's center of gravity and situates desire on the side of the Other (Zupančič, 1998, p. 286). Zupančič employs the geometric concept of "ex-centering," contrasting it with "concentricity," to elucidate how the subject's desire is positioned outside the domain of the subject. She uses the metaphor of concentric circles, which share a common center, to explain how an "ex-centering" operation disrupts their shared locality, relocating it to a different focal point and resulting in circles that no longer share the same center. This geometric analogy precisely illustrates how the inaccessible surplus or the object-cause of desire is shifted from the subject's position to that of the Other, becoming "ex-centered" (see Fig. 7.1).

In both discourses of the Father the lost object cause of desire *ex-sists* in a concealed, exotic realm beyond the reach of the subject. For the Greek it is "wisdom,"

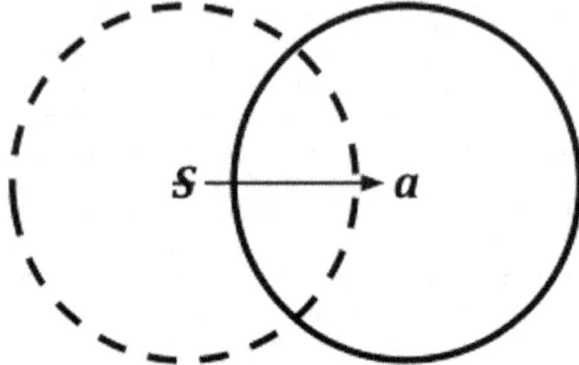

Figure 7.1 The subject's center of gravity is ex-centered, shifted to the position of the object-cause of desire on the side of the Other.

and for the Jews it is "ritualism and prophetism" deciphered in the sign (Badiou, 2003, p. 42). This fantasy, driven by the excluded element, propels the subject's dynamics around the object of desire.

Badiou argues that Paul's examination of the relationship between desire and death in the Father's discourse precisely encapsulates the problematic of unconscious desire as portrayed in psychoanalysis. This is because the autonomy of desire, as ordained by the law, mirrors the autonomy of the death drive (Badiou, 2003, p. 79). Through this correlation Badiou demonstrates the profound connection between psychoanalytic theory of the death drive and Paul's discourse on the path of death and desire.

Badiou posits that within both configurations, the subject is relegated to a dead (frozen) entity resembling the ego, while the being of the subject is situated elsewhere – in the autonomy of desire. He describes a bifurcation that aligns knowledge and will with the Self, and agency and action with the Other. This dichotomy, according to Badiou, epitomizes the subject under the Father's discourse: the disjunction between being and thinking (Badiou, 2003, p. 83). Badiou asserts that this divided subject, torn between a dead Self and autonomous desire, represents a form of powerlessness in thought – a thought estranged from its being.

Discourse of the Son

In contrast to the discourses of the Father, Paul's Christian discourse is described by Badiou as the "discourse of the Son" (Badiou, 2003, p. 42). This designation extends beyond Jesus's identity as the Son of God and refers to the novelty that the Son might introduce into the Father's discourse. Badiou emphasizes that Paul's discourse is primarily characterized as such because it introduces a completely novel structure, one not anchored in the past but oriented towards new possibilities. The incarnation of Jesus as the Son of God signifies a pivotal historical juncture, marking a profound departure from the discourse of the Father and, by extension, from traditional Jewish and Greek discourses. This departure heralds the feasibility of adopting a new subjective position which is epitomized in Paul's concept of love (Badiou, 2003, pp. 43–44).

According to Paul, Christian redemption takes form in a trajectory of subjectivation that is accessible to every human being, without exception. Therefore, Badiou stresses that the gospel, as conveyed in the discourse of the Son, is distinguished by its universal invitation to all of humanity, transcending inherent distinctions such as those between Jewish and Gentile.

Badiou interprets Paul's endeavor as an effort to demonstrate that the logic underpinning Christian redemption does not conform to the dialectic relationship between totality and exception, which is a hallmark of the discourse of the Father. To transcend the logic of exception and its relation to the object of desire and the path of death, the subject must unequivocally traverse the law that initially establishes it (Badiou, 2003, p. 42).

For Badiou, the radical nature of the gospel of the Son's discourse lies in its association with a different type of object (Badiou, 2003, p. 55). It is not concerned with the object of desire but relates to a "pure event" which, according to Paul, alters the relationship between the possible and the impossible in the world (Badiou, 2003, p. 29).

The event that emerges in the historical context for Paul is the "resurrection" of Jesus. For Paul, Jesus is neither a person nor a compendium of knowledge or prophecies that draws us nearer to God. For Paul, "Jesus" signifies a transformative event for humanity, which disrupted the prevailing discourse and heralded the possibility of a new beginning (Badiou, 2003, p. 36).

Badiou contends that the event "Jesus" defies description by philosophical knowledge or prophesy of signs; it is something that can only be affirmed by a subjective declaration of fidelity to its universal call. This fidelity is established through a stark rejection of the law and the endorsement of a discourse that transcends the law. Such an affirmation renders the subject a "son" of that event, and consequently, a "son-subject," dissipating the particularity of the Father's discourse (Badiou, 2003, p. 59). In Badiou's words: "It is the event alone, as illegal contingency, which causes a multiplicity in excess of itself to come forth and thus allows for the possibility of overstepping finitude" (Badiou, 2003, p. 81). This position enables the subject to transcend the finite and step into the realm of the infinite. Badiou describes this as a fidelity that is not supported by knowledge or contingent upon any particular law, but rather an act that necessitates a wager and a perpetual labor in the aim of its materialization.

An "event" for Badiou signifies a disruption in the normal order of things – that is, in the manner in which culture, hegemonic discourse, the law, or what Badiou terms the human "historical situation," establish in the relationship between words and things in the world. The event does not represent an element that "exists" – that is, it cannot be recorded or recounted – in the historical situation as an objective possibility, but belongs to the realm of occurrences that produce a new objective possibility for what, until the event – from the narrow perspective of the law – was considered impossible. Such an occurrence can never be fully registered under the law, making it, according to Badiou, essentially "illegal." Further, it represents a radical break from the law that reconfigures the possible and the impossible, challenging the prevailing order and opening new avenues for thought and action.

Badiou identifies various conditions within the situation that facilitate the possibility of an event. He outlines four such conditions in the human historical situation: politics, art, science, and love. Each condition manifests different expressions of the event in the human context, yet all are characterized by a radical departure from the established order. In the realm of love, the event is manifested initially in an "encounter." What is intriguing in Badiou's analysis of the event that underpins Paul's Christianity is that he categorizes it within the realm of the "encounter." For Paul, it was the encounter with the voice on the way to Damascus, urging him to spread Christianity.

The event initiates a "truth procedure" that is capable of radically altering the entirety of the situation's landscape. The truth procedure is a process of subjectivation that scrutinizes every element in the situation under the hypothesis of the event's encounter and redefines them in relation to it. This transformative process is not merely additive; it does not simply introduce a new element into the mix of existing elements. Instead, it fundamentally alters the structure of possibility itself.

Badiou's philosophy, particularly his conception of the event and the "truth procedure," underscores a radical commitment to the possibility of genuine novelty and transformation in the realm of human experience and knowledge. The event, by manifesting as something that exceeds the anticipatory capacity of the situation's laws, opens a space for a new form of universality – one that is not predicated on exclusion or the hierarchical ordering of elements but on a radical form of inclusion. This vision is inherently egalitarian, as it asserts the potential for universal significance and transformative agency to emerge from conditions of indeterminacy and marginality, challenging the status quo and inviting a reimagining of what constitutes the realm of the possible.

The "Jesus" event is the catalyst that subverts the path of death, enabling a new possibilities for the subject in the Christian trajectory that indicate the potential for victory over death through love (Badiou, 2003, pp. 37, 86). The new possibilities that the event "Jesus" opens up manifests in two distinct paths of subjectivation that Paul delineates as flesh and spirit (see Fig. 7.2). These paths correspond to two different subjective positions, which he labels death and life, respectively. If the law of the Father confines the subject solely to the "path of death," then the event introduces the prospect for the subject to not be wholly subsumed under the law. This means not only embracing "flesh" – tantamount to the "path of death" insofar as it relates to the object of desire – but also having access to the "spirit," which Paul relates to the object of love. The Christian subject is thus a split subject *par excellence*, divided between these two trajectories, and nestled between them lies

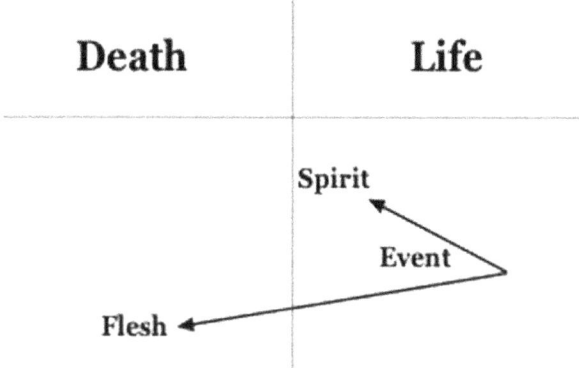

Figure 7.2 The two distinct paths of subjectivation that Paul delineates as flesh and spirit that correspond to two different subjective positions named death and life[1]

the novel, real object: the pure event of the resurrection (Badiou, 2003, p. 75), "a point of the real that puts language into deadlock" (Badiou, 2003, p. 46).

The Principle of Love

Badiou articulates the principle of love, which underlies Paul's discourse, as follows:

> [love's] principle is this: when the subject as thought accords with the grace of the event – this is subjectivation (faith, conviction) – he, who was dead, returns to the place of life. He regains those attributes of power that had fallen onto the side of the law and whose subjective figure was sin. He rediscovers the living unity of thinking and doing. This recovery turns itself into a universal law. Law returns as life's articulation for everyone, path of faith, law beyond law. This is what Paul calls love. (Badiou, 2003, pp. 87–88)

In this pivotal statement, Badiou posits that the involvement with an event catalyzes a subjectivation process, in which the subject's center of gravity is ex-centered for the second time, positioning it anew on the side of life, as a subject split between two incommensurable trajectories – the paths of flesh and spirit, of thought and being. This procedure bestows upon the subject a universal law – the law of the spirit – applicable to each-and-every human being. The material affirmation of the trajectory of life – through the fidelity to the event – as a universal statute for humanity epitomizes what Paul interprets as love (Badiou, 2003, p. 90). Badiou underscores that while the declaration of the event constitutes the subject, without love – the driving force of the enduring affirmation of the event's universal call – such declaration would hold no significance.

For Paul, redemption is not instantaneous and, therefore, the affirmation of the event's universal appeal to all of humanity through love is not a mere moment of dialectical negation. The subject is required to actively engage in "labor" to affirm the event's universal truth within the fabric of reality. This endeavor is identified with the "labor of love," offering another perspective on the meaning of love for Badiou. The labor of love traverses both tradition and logos, thus aiming to redefine humanity as a whole. Accordingly, Badiou accentuates that love constitutes the labor of the militant, manifested in the relentless affirmation of the universal, embracing all diversities – Jew, Greek, man, woman, slave, and citizen alike (Badiou, 2003, p. 90). Love is characterized by this universal appeal that comes to affirm the trans-positional truth of the path of life, and, as Badiou denotes, the real of faith (Badiou, 2003, p. 88). Accordingly, he states that "Love alone embodies the essence of truth, the joy found within truth" (Badiou, 2003, p. 91).

Being infinite and universal, as opposed to the finite and particular law of the Father, the law of the spirit cannot be articulated negatively – such as "thou shalt not murder" – but rather must be posited as an affirmative, singular maxim. This maxim targets not a fantasy derived from the prohibition of the written law (the exclusion) but from an affirmative act which substantiates the spirit's law. Firstly, because it does not incite desire for the object through law's prohibition (Badiou, 2003, p. 89). Secondly, it aims to construct reality positively – as a happening or a procedure that affirms the event's truth. Badiou exemplifies such a law with the maxim "Love your neighbor as yourself," an imperative devoid of prohibition but a pure affirmation demanding faith and relentless endeavor to authenticate it within one's reality. This type of affirmative endeavor aligns with Paul's principle of love.

On a final note, we might add that the labor of love is akin to the "labor" of psychoanalysis, per Lacan, as it focuses on deciphering the signifier's impact on the body – an effect that, while conceptually elusive, is palpably transformative, altering the subject's relationship with reality. This labor is not simple, as it does not culminate in the creation of an understanding. Accordingly, we can characterize the labor of love with the help of Lacan as "not understanding, not a diving at the meaning, but a flying over it as low as possible without the meaning's gumming up this virtue, thus enjoying [*jouir*] the deciphering" (Lacan, 1990, p. 22). This type of enjoyment is not reducible to the construction of meaning. It resides at the paradoxical juncture of the disconnect between the signifier and the letter, masculine and feminine. This dimension elevates love to the status of a universal emblem in its absolute sense – a singular universality as defined by Badiou.

Note

1 This schema corresponds with Lacan's schema of sexuation from *Seminar XX*.

References

Badiou, A. (2003). *Saint Paul: The Foundation of Universalism.* Stanford University Press.

Freud, S. (1953–1974). *The Standard Edition of the Complete Psychological Works of Sigmund Freud* (J. Strachey, Trans., Vol. 1). Hogarth Press.

Lacan, J. (1999). *The Seminar Of Jacques Lacan: Book XX. Encore.* (B. Fink, Trans.; J.-A. Miller, Ed.). W.W. Norton & Company.

Lacan, J. (1993). *The Seminar of Jacques Lacan: Book III. The Psychoses 1955–1956* (R. Grigg, Trans.; J.-A. Miller, Ed.). W. W. Norton & Company.

Lacan, J. (1990). *Television: A Challenge to the Psychoanalytic Establishment* (D. Hollier, R. Krauss, & A. Michelson, Trans.). W. W. Norton & Company.

Lacan, J. (2023). *The Seminar of Jacques Lacan: Book XIX. ...or Worse.* (A. R. Price. Trans.; J.-A. Miller, Ed.). Polity Press.

Zupančič, A. (1998). "The Case of the Perforated Sheet." *Parallax*, 4(2), 286.

Chapter 8

Embracing Suffering Beyond the Death Drive in Catherine of Siena's Writings

Mark Gerard Murphy

Introduction

Catherine of Siena emerged as a central figure in Christian mystical theology during a period marked by the Black Death, political unrest, and a schism within the Church. Her commitment to the Catholic Church and her mystical experiences, including visions and stigmatic phenomena, mark her importance in religious history. Recognised through her canonisation and later designation as a Doctor of the Church, Catherine's influence on Christian thought and mystical theology is important. Sigmund Freud's theory of the death drive delineated in "Beyond the Pleasure Principle" (1920), posits an instinctual pull towards self-destruction and a return to an inorganic state, counterbalancing the life-preserving drives. This concept, although emerging from a psychoanalytic perspective, finds relevance in Catherine's embrace of suffering. Through self-denial, fasting, and the contemplation of hell, she sought closeness to God and spiritual enlightenment, practices that resonate with the death drive's themes of negation and radical negation. As we know, Lacan's thinking evolves from initially focusing on the mirror stage to exploring the relationship between the signifier and the body, particularly how the signifier can lead to the body's mortification. In his later work, Lacan undergoes a conceptual shift, viewing these earlier ideas through the lens of what he terms "the structural clinic." This new perspective reimagines the body's relationship with the signifier in a more life-affirming way, suggesting that structure revitalises rather than suppresses the body (Mäki, 2023). This framework is particularly relevant to understanding Catherine's work, which has been interpreted in ways that either neglect the body or overly simplify it. The later theories of Lacan offer a fresh approach to Catherine's work, moving beyond the binaries of theological liberalism and conservatism to provide a nuanced view of the body and its afflictions.

This chapter thus proposes that Catherine's mystical writings present an opportunity to reflect on the spiritual practice with the psychoanalytic concept of the death drive in relation to the very last Lacan and his concept of the speaking body. The consequent concept of jouissance resonates with a negation of negation that results not in an affirmation of Eros, nor does it reflect an iteration of Thanatos, but

DOI: 10.4324/9781032663487-10

rather shows a conception of enjoyment that goes beyond the binary clinic. The progression of my argument will be as follows. I will:

- Initially, examine the superficial connection between Catherine's spirituality and the death drive;
- Discuss the potential misinterpretations of Catherine's practices as either a negation of the body or a masochistic focus;
- Introduce Lacan's reimagining of the Drive and propose the concept of the toric body as a new framework for understanding bodily engagement in spiritual practice; and
- Conclude with the emergence of a spirituality in Catherine's work that recognises the body as the site of social bonds, challenging contemporary perspectives on spirituality and psychoanalysis.

Background

Catherine of Siena, born into a large family in 1347, dedicated her life to religious devotion and public service from an early age (Vauchez, 2018, p. 25). Rejecting societal norms, she joined the Third Order of Saint Dominic, choosing a life of prayer and penance over marriage or a conventional religious community. Catherine's spiritual practices were intense and deeply personal; she engaged in prolonged fasting and physical mortification, believing these acts brought her closer to Christ (Curtayne, 1980, pp. 1–10). Her mystical experiences began early in life. Catherine reported her first vision of Christ at the age of 6, and these encounters grew in frequency and intensity as she aged. Among the most significant were her mystical marriage to Christ, during which she received a wedding ring visible only to her – which was made of Christ's foreskin – and later, the stigmata, wounds reflecting those of Christ's crucifixion, which, according to her wishes, remained invisible to others (Baldwin, 1987, p. 63). Catherine's spirituality was not solely introspective. It propelled her into active ministry, caring for the sick and poor, and involvement in the politics of her day, advocating for peace and the return of the papacy from Avignon to Rome. Her letters and prayers, collected in various works, including "The Dialogue," reveal a theology grounded in love, humility, and an unyielding devotion to God and the Church (Vauchez, 2018). These practices and experiences define Catherine's life as a mystic and theologian. Her commitment to experiencing God's presence through suffering and service highlights her as a figure who lived her spirituality both in contemplation and in action, embodying an embodied connection to the divine that transcended the ordinary experiences of faith and devotion (Beattie, 2013). However, it can be said that Catherine's embrace of suffering and self-denial directly aligns with Freud's concept of the death drive. Her practices and experiences serve as a vivid illustration of this Drive; it is important to express how it goes beyond the negativity of the Drive toward something more.

Death Drive

Death was central to Freud. Pontalis suggests that Freud's personal and theoretical engagement with the concept of death-work significantly influenced his entire body of work. It challenges the idea that Freud only confronted death at life's end, proposing instead that an insidious presence of death underlies much of his and, by extension, everyone's existence (Pontalis, 1981, pp. 184–193). It places the theme of death on par with sexuality within Freudian psychoanalysis, hypothesising that the prominence of sexuality might have partly served to obscure the more unsettling undercurrents of death (Pontalis, 1981, pp. 184–193). The chapter asserts that understanding Freud's conceptualisation of the death drive is crucial for comprehending the full spectrum of psychoanalytic theory and its implications for clinical practice (Pontalis, 1981, pp. 184–193). Indeed, as we know, Freud introduced the concepts of Eros and Thanatos to describe fundamental forces driving human behaviour. Eros, or the life drive, encompasses instincts for survival, reproduction, and pleasure, including basic needs such as hunger and thirst, and is powered by libido. Initially, Freud posited that these instincts were countered by the ego's forces, but later revised his theory to introduce Thanatos, the death drive, which he believed worked in opposition to Eros (Gourgouris, 2010, p. 35).

In "Beyond the Pleasure Principle" (1920), Freud first articulated the idea of Thanatos, suggesting an inherent human inclination towards self-destruction and aggression (Freud, 2003). This Drive, he proposed, could manifest outwardly as aggression towards others or inwardly as self-harm. Freud's observations of repetitive compulsion in trauma survivors, notably World War I veterans reliving their experiences, led him to theorise an underlying unconscious desire for death tempered by life instincts (Freud, 2003).

Religion, in Freud's perspective, serves as a societal mechanism to channel and mitigate the destructive potentials of the death drive (Grunbaum, 2010, pp. 3–44). Through its doctrines and moral codes, religion seeks to curb the inherently aggressive and self-destructive tendencies of humans, directing these energies into socially acceptable forms and providing a psychological buffer against the bleakness of mortality. Furthermore, religious rituals and beliefs offer a way for individuals to deal with the fear of death and the finality of existence, creating a sense of continuity and meaning that counters the nihilistic pull of the death drive. But there are expressions within Catholic Christian spirituality – especially of the medieval variety – that have a focus on death and suffering (Grunbaum, 2010, pp. 3–44).

Death Drive in the 14th Century?

Tina Beattie explains that in the late Middle Ages, Europe saw the rise of laywomen's movements, with Catherine aligning herself with these groups. Notably, the Beguines were prominent in northern Europe, while in Italy, similar collectives were identified as pinzochere, or penitent women (2013, p. 367). These movements often came under the spiritual care of Dominicans and Franciscans, who provided guidance, confession, and theological instruction to safeguard the women against heresy and ensure the preservation of their virtue. However, this period was marked by intense scrutiny for heretical beliefs, leading to tragic outcomes for some, like Marguerite Porete, who was executed by burning (Beattie, 2013, p. 367).

In the 14th century, the cultural and religious landscape was deeply imbued with the notion that suffering was a conduit to spiritual depth and closeness to the divine. This era, marked by the Black Death, political instability, and ecclesiastical discord, saw individuals like Catherine of Siena, alongside contemporaries such as Julian of Norwich and Bridget of Sweden, engaging in ascetic practices as a means to mirror Christ's suffering and passion. These mystics viewed mortification – through fasting, self-flagellation, and other forms of penance – not merely as acts of devotion but as integral pathways to experiencing God's presence and grace. As Egan states, "in the medieval mind, there was a connection between weakness, self-abnegation and holiness – a connection that originated in Christ's shame and suffering on earth" (1999, p. 3). Their writings and teachings reflect a broader acceptance within the Christian mystical tradition of the time, which held that through the crucible of the suffering body, one could purify the soul, renounce worldly attachments, and achieve a union with God.[1]

Her asceticism, including fasting and physical mortification, aimed to emulate Christ's suffering. She engaged in several extreme acts of mortification such as prolonged fasting, only consuming the Holy Eucharist for sustenance, wearing a hair shirt as a constant source of discomfort and reminder of her devotion, and abstaining from sleep or resting on bare ground to share in Christ's suffering. She also practised self-flagellation, viewing physical pain as a means to purify and discipline the body, aligning her suffering with that of Christ's passion (Curtayne, 1980).

From a Freudian perspective, these acts might be interpreted through the lens of the death drive (Thanatos), which suggests an inherent drive towards masochistic self-destruction and a return to an inorganic state. Catherine's rigorous self-denial and embrace of suffering can be seen as manifestations of this Drive, sublimated into religious devotion. In modern times, ascetic practices are often viewed with scepticism, seen as potentially harmful extremism rather than pathways to spiritual enlightenment. Catherine's intentional embrace of suffering as a form of self-denial for spiritual growth diverges sharply from current health-focused paradigms that typically classify such behaviour as self-destructive. However, understanding Catherine of Siena's extreme mortifications demands more than a naive interpretation. Such a perspective ignores the fact that the 14th century was vastly different from today, characterised by omnipresent death, short and brutal lives, and widespread suffering due to the Black Death and famine. Catherine saw the suffering and limitations experienced by others as her own, using these as opportunities for transformation and connection with others. Taking her actions at face value, as something to be mimicked in a fundamentalist manner today, misses the broader point. It's not about replicating the historical and worldly limitations she faced but understanding how our current world imposes limits on our bodies. It's this structural understanding of the body and its limitations that holds significance.

From the Drive to the Toric Body and Sinthome

Thinking through the place of the Drive and how it relates to the structure of the body as a place of resistance and enjoyment is what led thinkers like Lacan to think about what they call Other Jouissance and later the toric body. This position, I argue, offers a theologically informed psychoanalysis that goes beyond the foreclosure of the horror of the body that we find in liberal spirituality and a conservative masochistic embrace of suffering. And it starts by locating the symptom as that which is integral to the structure of the body.

In the later Lacan, the Drive becomes "the hole in the real that is the sexual relation," which becomes a core component of his theory regarding the structure of the subject. And in Seminar XXIV, he speaks about two conceptions of the body that work with absence. The first is the spherical body, which puts absence outside itself completely, and the second is the toric body, which internalises absence as being integral to the structure of the body (Lacan, 1977).[2] The torus, a surface with a hole through its centre, serves as a metaphor for the structure of the human subject. Lacan uses this geometric shape to illustrate how desire is not a simple linear trajectory but involves a circular motion that returns to its starting point without ever being fully satisfied. This model reflects the endless and self-perpetuating nature of desire, highlighting the impossibility of fully capturing the object of desire. Lacan's torus suggests that the body itself is structured around a central lack or void. This void is symbolic of the fundamental lack in the subject, the *"manque-à-être"* (lack-of-being), which drives the perpetual motion of desire. The body, then, is not a complete, self-contained unit but is defined by its incompleteness, by what it lacks. The toric body sees an absence or a gap at the very heart of itself that cannot be negated. No matter how much one engages in speech, it circulates this primordial void and causes the body to resonate beyond meaning; it is this resonance that becomes Other Jouissance and later Jouissance-one.[3]

This relationship to the body, as we understand it, is fundamentally anchored in the structural misalignment inherent to sexuality due to this hole of the body. There's an absence of any innate harmony or proportion in the body, meaning the interaction with the body always confronts the reality of what it lacks. This highlights that the body's integrity isn't defined by its solidity but rather by its inherent incompleteness, marked by a "toric" or hollowed nature in which the endless positing of demands creates the infinite circulation of desire.

The pursuit to "possess" a body, to forge a viable connection with it, emerges frequently in clinical practice. It is the place of the Sinthome. In Seminar XXIII, Lacan elaborates on the Sinthome (Lacan, 2016). And later in Seminar XXIV, he suggests that it is a way of making a signifier that stabilises the flow around the rim of the torus:

> [the unconscious] only repeats things by going around in circles. In order to say things, reason repeats the symptom. And the fact that today I have to present

myself before you with what is called a physical *Sinthome* does not prevent you from asking quite rightly whether it is not intentional.

And a little earlier,

> The unconscious is an entity that I try to define by the Symbolic, which is only, in short, an extra entity. An entity with which one must know how to deal. Knowing how to deal with it is not the same thing as a knowledge, as the Absolute Knowledge of which I spoke earlier. The unconscious is what precisely makes something change, what reduces what I called the *Sinthome*. (Lacan, 1977, pp. 112; 87)

Unlike symptoms that psychoanalysis traditionally aims to interpret and resolve, the Sinthome does not dissolve under analysis. *Instead, it becomes a "know-how" related to stabilising our identity, an irreducible core that underpins the speaking being's unique psychic structure* (Moncayo, 2019; Thurston, 2022). The Sinthome represents a departure from the goal of symptom resolution, suggesting that living with and managing one's Sinthome is a viable path of existence, even if this – from an outside perspective – looks like it entails some suffering.

Psychoanalytically, Catherine of Siena exemplifies an individual transitioning from the impossibility of a relationship with the Other to engaging in the sole viable relationship: that with her own body and its limitations as the primary condition of relating to the Other. As Terry Eagleton states,

> [such limitation] lays bare the indissoluble core that shows the self up as non-relational. It is one's irreplaceability that is illuminated by one's mortality. In Lacanian idiom, the Real is that starkly irreducible singularity at the core of the human subject, excessive of all cultural features and contingent qualities, which is where we are both most solitary and most universal and of which death is the primary signifier. The only form of relationship that will prove durable is one which can accommodate this radical non-relationality – which is to say that all valid relationships in some sense involve a relation to death, encountering the other at his or her most needy and desolate. (Eagleton, 2018, pp. 99–100)

As is expressed by Lacan, there is no such thing as a relationship, but there is something of the One (Lacan, 1977, p. 119).[4] What One-Jouissance – as development of the Drive – does here is allow a movement away from looking at the extremity of her acts in the imaginary to looking at the structure of acts in relation to the signifier in stabilising the toric body. It is important to note that Catherine's Dominican background significantly influenced her view of the soul's relationship with the body. In her view, the soul essentially shapes the body, suggesting an integration of spiritual and physical aspects of being. The body serves as more than just a container for the soul; it acts in concert with the soul as its integral structure. Catherine states in her Dialogue:

So it is not the body that gives bliss to the soul, but the soul will give bliss to the body because the soul will give of her abundance and will re-clothe herself on the Last Day of Judgment, in the garments of her own flesh, which she had quitted. For, as the soul is made immortal, stayed and established in Me, so the body in that union becomes immortal, and, having lost heaviness, is made fine and light. (2016, p. 49)

She writes of embracing suffering of the body with joy as a means to share in Christ's passion, viewing it not as a punishment but as a privileged path to closeness with God. Egan explains that Barbara Newman, a professor at Northwestern University specialising in English and religion, emphasises the notion that women's bodies were considered more permeable than men's, making them more open to various influences. This "permeability" meant that women were thought to be more easily tempted by the Devil but also more receptive to the Holy Spirit (1999, p. 10).

Consequently, Newman points out, male clerics found it difficult to outright dismiss women's prophetic visions (Egan, 1999, p. 10). She adds that women represented a critical voice from the margins, embodying Christ's judgment on societal power structures (Egan, 1999, p. 10). For Catherine, therefore, the body is always pierced – it is always fragmented; it is never whole: it is toric. As Beattie explains,

> [For] Catherine of Siena [...] "sin is a nothing." For Catherine, those who sin suffer because their desire is compulsively directed towards nothingness [at the centre of ourselves], but God tells Catherine that "from this nothingness of sin, a thorn that pierces the soul, I pluck this rose to provide for their salvation." (Beattie, 2006, p. 250)

As Verhaeghe & Declercq suggest, it is our commitment to speaking from the rim that allows a way of framing the body. This creates a way of relating and "holding suffering" that stops life being completely unliveable (2016). Other jouissance – as lalangue – is thus defined as a way of inventing a body by impacting and holding it with the Sinthome (Porcheret, 2007). And it is this toric speech that is seen as the end goal of analysis for any and all. The end of analysis is feminine (Verhaeghe & Declercq, 2016).

And if there is a body to be invented, then it is a body that will be a speaking body that stands beyond mere affirmation or sheer negation.[5]

The Body That Speaks/Dialogues

In a famous line in her Dialogues, in a vision, Christ says to Catherine, "you are she who is not." Make no mistake, this expression is a way of affirming her feminine body by negation via the Word. And only she who speaks on the side of the not-all can affirm this. There is a negation of her existence as Woman so that she can be revealed as the "feminine not-all." Beattie expresses this beautifully:

God (who is not a forbidding phallus but the crucified body of Christ which opens a fleshy passage between heaven and earth); the subject ("I," Catherine – the words with which she begins many of her letters); the non-subject/not-all ("she who is not," the soul that is lack, emptiness, ecstasy, and longing before God); and the real (the blood and fire of the mystical body of Christ which, like the burning bush of Moses, sets the soul ablaze in a non-consuming fire of rapture). (Beattie, 2013, p. 376)

In this passage, Beattie argues that Catherine positions herself as the subject in her correspondences. She embarks on a personal narrative that begins with her own identity, "I." Contrarily, she introduces the concept of the "non-subject/not-all," referring to herself as "she who is not," to express the soul's state of lack and longing in the presence of the divine. This state encompasses emptiness and fullness, capturing the paradoxical nature of the mystical pursuit where the soul is both absent in its desire for the One and present in its intense yearning. The Real in Catherine's vision is embodied in the mystical body of Christ, marked by blood and fire.

Indeed, we know that Lacan states in Encore that Woman does not exist:

That is what analytic discourse demonstrates in that, to one of these beings qua sexed, to man insofar as he is endowed with the organ said to be phallic – I said, "said to be" – the corporal sex *(sexe corporel)* or sexual organ *(sexe)* of woman – I said, "of woman," whereas in fact *woman* does not exist, woman is *not whole (pas toute)* – woman's sexual organ is of no interest *(ne lui dit rien)* except via the body's jouissance. (Lacan, 1999, p. 7)

This is a way of expressing the loss of the fake body of wholeness: what Lacan calls the "All" or – later – the illusion of the spherical body. Man can only have such a body as a fantasmatic habit he chooses to put on through his relationship to a muse-like figure: Woman. Man gains fake wholeness by relating to his own fantasy he projects onto the body of the sexual other. As such, man only relates to himself and thus exists even less than the Woman who does not. The declaration "you are not" in Catherine's Dialogue negates the fantasmatic status of Woman and introduces a feminine body-all-alone impacted by the Word in the Real. Thus, this toric body, manifesting an existence beyond mortification, openly bears the impossibility of existence between absence and presence. This impossibility is what is known as ab-sense (hors-sense) as expressed in the *Autre Écrit*: ... *ou pire*, specifically in the seminar report of 1971–1972 (Lacan, 2001). And it is this "beyond the binary" that we can call Other Jouissance. The toric feminine structure reveals that we are conscious due to parapraxis, and because of the unconscious (as parapraxis), there is no utopian completeness of being – at least not here on earth! – nor is there a cynical entering the void. The void is impossible in both a negative and a positive sense. Yes, it is the perennial "stone in the road" we perpetually stumble over qua non negativisable jouissance (Miller, 2023, pp. 10–13), but it is also that which is impossible to enter. We can only circle it and create a Sinthome to stabilise the circling. So, it's not about Jungian therapy or morbid existential encounters with absurdity but an oscillation between absence and presence.

Beyond the Binary of Hope and Despair

But what is the point of all this? If we can see both in Catherine's work a place where the body speaks and the later Lacan a movement from the desire to drive to the speaking body that enjoys, then what does a dialogue between the two offer? If we can see in Catherine's mystical theology a place whereby the speaking body comes to the fore, then what new theological insights does this offer?

This is a disruptive speaking-being that operates by being of the world but not in it: an embodiment of jouissance, non-negatable and manifesting as the spiralling of the rim of the hole held by a Sinthome signifying the Lacanian evolution of what was formerly known as the Drive that – as Mäki suggests – takes it beyond negativity and positivity (Mäki, 2023). Yes, the speaking toric body primarily refers to a speaking individual, yet it maintains a continuous connection with the body's expression of its limitations through symptoms: the symptoms speak.[6]

So, it is precisely this body as not-all that speaks that allowed Catherine to speak and disrupt symbolic structures. Metzger explains that Raymond of Capua's – Catherine's spiritual director – "Legenda Maior" details a crucial episode where Christ calls Catherine of Siena to reform the Church. This instruction propels her from a desire for hidden service to a command to preach and spread divine grace and justice publicly (2022). Catherine's acceptance echoes Mary's response to the angel Gabriel, though Catherine herself harbours reservations, emphasising her unworthiness and contrasting her existence as nothingness and folly against God's light and wisdom (Metzger, 2022).

This humble self-assessment is not a philosophical negation of her being but an acknowledgement of her comparative insignificance to God's omnipotence. Catherine's apprehensions about her societal role as a woman and the potential dismissal she might face are addressed directly by Christ. He assures her that divine will transcends gender distinctions, highlighting that her femininity – as opposed to projected Womanhood – rather than a barrier, is precisely why she is chosen for this task. Her mission is to serve as a "medicinal shame" to the prideful and arrogant, leveraging her marginalised status to enact divine wisdom, thus challenging and transforming the Christian community from the margins. Christ's selection of Catherine underscores a deliberate divine strategy to humble the haughty, using the unlikely to lead spiritual renewal (Metzger, 2022). As Terry Eagleton explains, in such a speaking-body, poison and cure are aspects of the same reality (2018, p. 124).

Conclusion

In reflecting on a line from Lacan's *Television*, François Regnault challenges the conventional understanding of sainthood, suggesting that the true role of a saint is not rooted in the practice of charity but rather in embodying a concept Lacan coins as "trashitas." This idea introduces a contradiction against the backdrop of common perceptions, which typically align sainthood with acts of benevolence. According to Regnault, saints actively seek to divest themselves of this association with charity, thereby unburdening themselves from the expectations of benevolence. In this discussion, "trachity," a neologism that fuses the concepts of trash and charity (and echoes the notion of "discharge"), serves as a symbol for this redefined mission of sainthood. Regnault exemplifies this theory through exploring the life of Catherine of Siena. He highlights Catherine's extreme devotion to charitable acts, which led her to the brink of physical exhaustion and sacrifice. This narrative prompts a revaluation of the ultimate significance of such a life, questioning whether these acts of charity encapsulate her entire legacy or final message (2010, p. 1). In challenging Regnault's interpretation, it's important to propose that the extremity of Saint Catherine's charitable acts and sacrifices might align with the Lacanian concept of the Sinthome. This concept, which Lacan introduces as a fourth ring supplementing the Real, the Imaginary, and the Symbolic in his topology of the psyche, signifies a mode of jouissance and formation that is utterly personal and singular to an individual.

In this sinthomatic framework, the spiritual journey involves a pragmatic embrace of the body's limitations, echoing Catherine's lived experience of spirituality through bodily engagement and suffering – not as something to be sought out but something *that is always already prefigured by way of our speaking a structure*. Speaking from the rim acts as a medium through which the body finds its space to exist – an apparatus of jouissance – challenging the need for a spiritually sanitised or "masochistically pierced" theology. Instead, it emphasises recognising our "toric existence" – as a revaluation of the death drive – where being pierced is intrinsic to consciousness and embodiment as such. This perspective connects the inevitability of the symptom (bungles) with the reality of our speaking, embodied existence and how we can recognise others who are also alone with their own symptom. What was once the condition of a drive toward death now becomes the very condition of a toric life. It starts from the "one of the Sinthome" as being that which allows the creation of a social bond (Murphy & Kim, 2023, pp. 99–109).[7]

Today, there is resistance against the tyrannies of prosaic enjoyment and regulations of happiness that contort and control the body. And in many ways, part of our liberation is about freeing ourselves from this injunction toward "wellness," which if followed blindly, leads to more pain (Wright, 2014; Reshe, 2020). Just as today, we see the psychoanalyst who promises a treatment beyond such injunctions with suspicion; we do the same with the suffering saint of the past. Their embrace of the wounded self is just as challenging today as it ever was. Their lived embodied spirituality moves it away from an abstract idealism towards a grounded, lived practice – a know-how – that acknowledges the body as central to our experience of the divine and communal life (Lacan, 1977, p. 28).[8] This interpretation encourages a revaluation of the death drive, positioning our fragmented body as critical element for our engagement with the divine, creating a more integrated understanding of suffering and transformation and its place in the structure of the speaking body that speaks beyond despair, and beyond worldly hope, but certainly not beyond faith, a faith that psychoanalysis operates on also. As Lacan states, "Psychoanalysis, it must be clearly said, turns round in the same circle. It is the modern form of faith" (Lacan, 1977, p. 14).

Notes

1 Within the Christian mystical tradition, suffering and self-denial are central themes viewed as pathways to spiritual enlightenment and closeness to God (Merton, 2013, p. 10). This tradition values ascetic practices, such as fasting, chastity, and voluntary poverty, as means to transcend physical desires. Catherine of Siena's life and teachings are illustrative of this tradition (Vauchez, 2018).
2 In Seminar XXIV Lacan states that "Space seems to be extension when we are dealing with Descartes. But the body founds for us the idea of another kind of space. This torus in question does not immediately seem to be what is called a body, but you are going to see that it is enough to turn it inside out, not in the way that one turns a sphere inside out, because a torus is turned inside out in a quite different way" (p. 6); "The world system up to now has always been spheroidal. Perhaps we might change! The world has always been painted, up to the present, like that, as regards what men have enunciated, has been painted inside a bubble. The living being considers himself as a ball, but with time he all the same realised that he was not a ball, a bubble. Why not recognise that he is organised, I mean what one sees of the living body, that he is organised at what I called the other day a rod [torus]" (p. 15).
3 As Goetzmann et al. explain, this absent centre represents the "navel of the real" and acts as a pivotal connection to reality. It is the evolution of imagery and language within three dimensions: the unrepresented real, the visually imagined, and the symbolically expressed. This unseen real is metaphorically the torus's empty centre. The imaginary aspect emerges from our perception of our bodies, leading into the realm of symbols through language. The torus, then, is not just a physical shape but a symbol of how unrepresented realities and the concept of a "lost" foundational object connect to our psyche. In Freud's view, both the sphere and torus underpin the ego's roots in our bodily existence, with the torus embodying physical openings and interiors that fill and empty, mirroring life's cycles. Its surface, blending external skin with internal membranes, creates a single, continuous form akin to a Möbius strip, merging the internal with the external. This unity of surface, erotically alive through interpersonal connections, forges a bridge from the physical to the psychological, transforming the body's outer layer into a mental construct and integrating the tangible with the psychological, embodying our deepest, often unarticulated, structures (Goetzmann et al., 2023).
4 "This indeed is why women, are more man than men. They are not-all (*pas-toutes*), as I said. These *all* therefore, have no common trait; they have nevertheless this one, this single common trait, the trait that I described as *unary*. They are comforted by the One. *There is something of the One*, I repeated it just now to say that there is something of the One, and nothing else" (Lacan, 1977, p. 119).
5 This Sinthomatic activity can also be seen in her young life. Catherine has divine instruction to form a "mental cell" and perceive her family as the Holy Family was a direct call to find sanctity amidst her daily life. This direction aimed to teach Catherine that connection and living a sanctified life need not be sought in isolation but can be rooted in and through her interactions within her household, even if her family were causing her frustration. By situating them as signifiers in her body, she can create her own singular way live in a social bond. Catherine effectively crafted a personal

Sinthome that allowed her to harmonise her devotion with her worldly duties. This Sinthome, a symbolic and imaginative reconfiguration of her immediate relationships and environment, served as a foundational element in her spiritual and psychic life, enabling her to maintain her connection to God while fully engaging in her familial responsibilities.
6 Beattie further explains that Catherine's era placed the body at the forefront of religious devotion and daily existence. Surrounded by the vivid realities of human life in Siena, she navigated a world filled with desire, suffering, and the stark presence of disease, poverty, and mortality (Beattie, 2013, p. 377). Her work brought her into close contact with those enduring the deepest forms of misery against a backdrop of widespread ecclesiastical misconduct, which she vehemently criticised. Living amid such palpable corporeal challenges, Catherine's experiences and writings reveal a raw, unfiltered engagement with the physical aspects of existence, starkly contrasting with the more sanitised views of the body found in some contemporary theologies (Beattie, 2013, p. 377).
7 Catherine, facing family pressure to marry at 12, briefly conformed to societal beauty standards, only to reject this vanity soon after and yearned to be-all-alone. Despite her family's attempts to disrupt her solitary devotion by burdening her with tasks, she found solace in internal solitude, where she felt in communion with God via her body, in the solitude of her heart. After years of seclusion, she transitioned to a more communal life. She attracted a following of devotees, drawn by her spiritual charisma and guidance. Among them were Hermits who abandoned solitary life, finding greater spiritual peace and advancement with her than in isolation.
8 It is worth pointing out that between her hagiography and her own writings, there is a marked difference: the former is overly spiritualised and fantastic, while her own writings are incredibly pragmatic.

References

Aino-Marjatta, M. (2023). "What Is Non-Negativisable Jouissance? From Negation to a Singular Norm." In D. Rousselle & M. G. Murphy (Eds.), *Negativity in Psychoanalysis: Theory and Clinic*. Routledge, Chapman & Hall, Incorporated.
Baldwin, A. B. (1987). *Catherine of Siena: A Biography*. Our Sunday Visitor Pub. Division.
Beattie, T. (2006). *New Catholic Feminism: Theology and Theory*. Psychology Press.
Beattie, T. (2013). *Theology After Postmodernity: Divining the Void – A Lacanian Reading of Thomas Aquinas*. OUP Oxford.
Curtayne, A. (1980). *Saint Catherine of Siena*. Tan Books.
Eagleton, T. (2018). *Radical Sacrifice*. Yale University Press.
Egan, J. (1999). *Power Suffering*. The New York Times Magazine. https://archive.nytimes.com/www.nytimes.com/library/magazine/millennium/m2/egan.html
Freud, S. (2003). *Beyond the Pleasure Principle*. Penguin UK.
Goetzmann, L., Eichenlaub, M., Siegel, A. M., Benden, C., Boehler, A., Jenewein, J., Seiler, A., Grytska, O., Hesse, K., Wutzler, U., & Ruettner, B. (2023). "Torus, Demand and Desire: Towards a Psychosomatic Structure of Lung Transplantation." *British Journal of Psychotherapy*, *39*(3), 466–485. https://doi.org/10.1111/bjp.12846
Gourgouris, S. (2010). *Freud and Fundamentalism: The Psychical Politics of Knowledge*. Fordham Univ. Press.
Grunbaum, A. (2010). "Psychoanalysis and Theism." In B. Beit-Hallahmi (Ed.), *Psychoanalysis and Theism: Critical Reflections on the Grünbaum Thesis* (pp. 3–44). Rowman & Littlefield.

Lacan, J. (1977). *Seminar XXIV Final-Sessions 1976–1977* (C. Gallagher, Trans.; 1st edn.). Lacan in Ireland. http://www.lacaninireland.com/web/translations/seminars/

Lacan, J. (1999). *The Seminars of Jacques Lacan Book XX: On Feminine Sexuality, the Limits of Love and Knowledge 1972–1973* (J.-A. Miller, Ed.; 2nd edn.). W. W. Norton & Company.

Lacan, J. (2001). *Autres écrits* (1st edn.). du Seuil.

Lacan, J. (2016). *The Sinthome: The Seminar of Jacques Lacan*. Wiley.

Mäki, A. M. (2023). "What Is Non-Negativisable Jouissance? From Negation to a Singular Norm." In D. Rousselle & M. G. Murphy (Eds.), *Negativity in Psychoanalysis: Theory and Clinic*. Routledge, Chapman & Hall, Incorporated.

Merton, T. (2013). *Thomas Merton—Spiritual Direction and Meditation*. Read Books Ltd.

Metzger, S. M. (2022). "Catherine of Siena's Medicinal Shaming of the Church." *Church Life Journal*. April 29. https://churchlifejournal.nd.edu/articles/catherine-of-sienas-medicinal-shaming-of-the-church/

Miller, J.-A. (2023). *Analysis Laid Bare*. Independently published.

Moncayo, R. (2019). *Lalangue, Sinthome, Jouissance, and Nomination: A Reading Companion and Commentary on Lacan's Seminar XXIII on the Sinthome*. Taylor & Francis Group.

Murphy, M. G., & Kim, W. (2023). "Anti-Antigone: From a Politics of Desire to a Politics of Love – Rethinking the Politics of the One-all-Alone." In N. A. Barria-Asenjo & S. Žižek (Eds.), *Psychoanalysis Between Philosophy and Politics* (1st edn., pp. 98–109). LOOK Publications of the Faculty of Humanities and Social Sciences Split and Multimedia Cultural Centre Split.

Pontalis, J. B. (1981). *Frontiers in Psychoanalysis: Between the Dream and Psychic Pain*. Hogarth Press.

Porcheret, B. (2007). "The Bodily Root of Symptoms." *Lacan Circle of Australia*. https://lacancircle.com.au/psychoanalysislacan-journal/psychoanalysislacan-volume-1/the-bodily-root-of-symptoms/

Regnault, F. (2010). "Saintliness and the Sainthood [excerpt]" (P. Bradley, Trans.). *Lacanian Ink*. https://www.lacan.com/lacinkXXXIII6.html

Reshe, J. (2020). "The Voice of Sadness Is Censored as Sick. What If It's Sane?" *Aeon*. https://aeon.co/essays/the-voice-of-sadness-is-censored-as-sick-what-if-its-sane

Siena, C. (2016). *The Dialogue of Saint Catherine of Siena*. CreateSpace Independent Publishing Platform.

Thurston, L. (2022). "Lacan's Analytic Goal Le Sinthome or the Feminine Way." In *Reinventing the Symptom* (pp. 59–82). Other Press, LLC.

Vauchez, A. (2018). *Catherine of Siena: A Life of Passion and Purpose*. Paulist Press.

Verhaeghe, P., & Declercq, F. (2016). "Lacan's Analytic Goal: Le sinthome or the Feminine Way." *Psychoanalytische Perspectieven*, *34*(4), pp. 234–300.

Wright, C. (2014). "Happiness Studies and Wellbeing: A Lacanian Critique of Contemporary Conceptualisations of the Cure." *Culture Unbound*, *6*(4), Article 4. https://doi.org/10.3384/cu.2000.1525.146791

Chapter 9

Death Driven by Love

Peter Prosen

Il y a des gens qui n'auraient jamais été amoureux, s'ils n'avaient jamais entendu paraler de l'amour [There are people who would never have been in love if they had never heard love mentioned] (La Rochefoucauld, 2007, pp. 38–39).

… Well? Is La Rochefoucauld in the right? I shall immediately raise an objection to his assertion but first, I would be remiss not to appreciate the insight of this lucid and trenchant aphorism; namely, that the experience of love, marred by the uncleanliness of language, suffers a profound disturbance to the point of utter misrecognition and that the *fantasies* of love are in no way truthful to the *experience* of love, quite on the contrary: *the experience of love is opposed and defended against by the fantasy of love*. One may fantasize only if one thinks and one may think only if one has had language encrusted upon one. Persons experience love more frequently than supposed but defend with all their might against it by erecting fantasies which they do not construct from themselves, as one would if one were a *causa sui*, but rather inherit them from without and then proceed with confidence to take them as the most intimate part of themselves.

Witness how popular thought describes love as the fortuitous meeting of two hearts and minds; an end of a protracted and painful search for the one who completes the other; or, worse still, the more rampant idea of love as a merely pragmatic arrangement between two bodies starved of enjoyment and substance – a heinous vision of love to be sure. The former is merely a cultural legacy bequeathed to us by Aristophanes in Plato's Symposium wherein he relates to us the fable of the pre-Christian fall of man, where the once perfect human being of circular shape, four pairs of limbs, two pairs of genitals, as well as two faces, is punished by Zeus for its hubris. The once perfect human has now been split in half in order to bring about a moderation in its ambition and mastery over its behavior; no longer shall it threaten the dominion of the Gods, and, thus weakened, the once mighty human being, no longer in possession of its former strength, preoccupies itself with seeking the lost half such that its ambition is no longer aimed at usurping the place of deity, but at seeking to refind the lost object. This myth has exerted an invincible influence upon the mind of man and continues to

DOI: 10.4324/9781032663487-11

supply it with pernicious material regarding love and the achievement of some sort of completeness though union with an external object. However lamentable this fantasy is, it pales into insignificance when stood against the latter: love as a pragmatic arrangement wherein the other occupies the position of a loved object solely on the grounds of its utility for the ego – once the well of utility runs dry, one simply turns to a novel object which promises to deliver the excess and narcissistic affirmation that the former had failed to. One would do well to heed the words of Schopenhauer when he states that "… love is an illusion like no other; it will induce a man to sacrifice everything he possesses in the world, in order to obtain this woman, who in reality will satisfy him no more than any other" (Schopenhauer, 1818, p. 165). Schopenhauer here quite unexpectedly and unseasonably prefigures the central tenets of psychoanalysis: the absolute impossibility of reaching complete sexual satisfaction and the tragic futility of seeking the perfect object.

I need not to belabour upon the reasons for the rising popularity of pragmatic love; it is sufficiently evident that a society suffering decays in social bonds and ethics produces subjects whose relating to other subjects takes the predominant form of relating – relation to commodities. We would be remiss to neglect the similarities between the two fantasies; both instances exhibit the logic of complementarity – the former through possession, the latter through consumption. The loved object is loved on the absolute condition that it not reveal the emptiness of identity, and furthermore, that it readily participates in the deception. Is it not popularly mandated that love ought not to cause distress? How dare one even begin to entertain thoughts that love is not a force of affirmation? How much bitterness and cynicism should rent a person's heart to deprive love of its sacred status as the benevolent force of unification amidst the icy indifference of the world? Our fatefully contemporary time makes the loudest (perhaps because they are the hollowest) claims regarding external obstacles of love; the logic runs thusly: love is natural, what is natural must perforce be positive and harmonious; should this harmonious nature be disturbed in some fashion, as for example when a love relationship fails to attain to the expectations of fantasy, then we are to conclude that some foreign element is disturbing the natural order of necessity and that it must be done away with, annihilated, extirpated. It does not occur to them that calamitous properties of love arise not from without but draw their strength from contradictions within. Consider the frequency with which persons in love report on losing their bearings, on having been disoriented by this malevolent force that turns quotidian actions into irrelevant dross and hinders one's ability to perform one's duties. The attendant disorientation brought about by the experience of love speaks more eloquently and with greater vivacity of the truth of love as it bypasses the lie of fantasy.

Plus on aime une maîtresse, et plus on est prés de la haïr
 [The more you love your beloved, the closer you are to hating her]. (La Rochefoucauld, 2007, pp. 32–33)

Freud long ago taught us of the principle of absolute interdependence thereby turning La Rochefoucauld's aphorism into a universal law. It states that any relationship which has attained to any depth will be replete with hostile and tender feeling alike; the object most loved is at once the object for whom greatest hatred is reserved. In love, one adopts the manifold mannerisms of the other; likewise, their inclinations and disinclinations, their enjoyments as well as their fears; one even assumes new enemies out of courtesy! Most importantly, one sacrifices a large portion of one's enjoyment, and grants partial ownership of it to the beloved. The beloved, therefore, grows immensely in strength for it now possesses the key to either gratification or frustration, neither of which readily lend themselves to moderation in a satisfactory manner; the moderation of enjoyment is perhaps the Sisyphean task *par excellence* for one, like a pendulum, tirelessly swings between absence and excess. For this reason, the other, whom one loves, is always at once the person whose warm touch turns most readily into a frozen blow.

Now, if we extend our inquiry to the point of harshness, we should ask ourselves in all earnestness: *how is love recognized? How does one know one is in love?* The banality of the question should not make us recoil for if the answer appears self-evident, we have already permitted ourselves to be swindled by the caprices of fantasy. We unwittingly misrecognize love when we begin to associate it with mere tender feelings and joyful sentiments for the real experience of love is *indistinguishable from anxiety*. One knows love only when one is overcome with dread and horror at the thought of losing the beloved; the eerie feeling of emptiness speaks the truth to us; the truth that the identity we inhabit and take as our own is not our sole possession; the image we take to be the proprietor of has different ownership. Whence anxiety? It is the experience of fading as a subject whose image had been corrupted from without. The envisaged disappearance of the other announces the hidden dependency of the self, a self that cannot stand on its own two feet without the other as a crutch. It is for this reason that persons whose romantic relationships have reached the ultimate end of their continuance take it upon themselves to substantially alter their physical appearance, for their present one has grown persecutory on account of its structural connection to the other whose traces continue to linger in their absence. Nothing causes us more bitterness and plants in us the most potent seeds of distrust than the experience of falling out of favour with our beloved for we have had to die countless deaths along the way. How frustrating it is, to have committed our identity to innumerable executions only to then be abandoned with a foreign image of ourselves, whose principal object of support had vanished. Alas, no amelioration of social conditions shall ever be able to undo the ravages of love – here, the subject stands alone with the echo of his ontological abyss.

Should one, therefore, conceive of love as a fortuitous blessing or as a categorical calamity? The conclusion one will draw will in large part depend on one's circumstance, temperament, and the unconscious architecture, but to say one is more valid than the other would be nonsense. The person of heightened sensibilities would find the truth of love rather appalling and disturbing; the person whose pride rests upon a sturdy intellectual conscience would instead find the truth of love of higher import.

Thus far, I have alluded to the truth of love a number of times, but it also goes by a different name: *self-alienation*. It is the privileged experience of the self, dying at the hands of the other. *Love is a form of death*, and its recognition is brought about through the effects of negating one's identity, the experience of which may only be transmitted by anxiety. This ought to ease the apprehensions of anyone who maintains the belief that the experience of love and fantasy of love are one and the same. The self-alienation in love presents itself to us with sufficient clarity when the object which previously held no import for us, and was on the whole regarded as either inconsequential or unknown, casts a long shadow over the self, granting the other an importance greater than the self. Therein arises yet another oddity, namely one cannot ever fully escape the tyranny of the ego for even when the ego suffers a diminution in worth by its being overshadowed by the other, it at once gains in value by virtue of it being the one doing the valuation. This self-alienating process is symbolic death, a slow death of a given identity, an act of Selbstüberwindung [*Self-overcoming*]. Formerly, I had thought of Nietzsche as the hereditary monarch of Schopenhauer's royal house of Hegelian hatred but this might have been a premature error in thought. In a peculiar and inconspicuous passage in the *Genealogy of Morals*, Book III, Nietzsche contradicts violently, in a strikingly Hegelian fashion, his later theory of Will to Power which lamentably confers upon him his infamous reputation.

> All great things perish by their own accord, by a deliberate act of self-destruction; this is the law of life, the law of necessary "self-overcoming" [*Selbstüberwindung*] in the essence of life. (Nietzsche, 2013, p. 65)

"The deliberate act of self-destruction" as *the law of life* would send most persons flying into a rage to voice objections against it, but to us, children of Freud, these words of Nietzsche's merely direct our attention to Freud's most salient and misunderstood concept of death drive. Love belongs to this dimension of self-destruction; it belongs to the realm of the death drive for one is pulled by what undoes one. In love, the loved object possesses a mysterious force (*objet a*) which pulls on our desire, but this force is vague, abstract, undefinable and unknowable. It is the function of desire and the function of fantasy to turn the destructiveness of drive in love into a sacrosanct image of the object which assumes the regal position in the psychical economy and has us imagine that this object is *it*, the final *Ersatz*. Love is a perilous force; it silently intimates insecurity upon the ego whose necessity is not to be underestimated even if ego is all falsity and pretense. Having said that, should it really come to us as a surprise that persons nowadays are deathly afraid of love? Is not the holy reverence through gentle coercion for (nearly) every form of identity the order of the day? So much for the secular age. The destructive tendencies and dispositions of love, once stripped bare of fantasy and desire, speak in favour of the necessity of the latter. But let us ask if love may produce enjoyment without the aid of fantasy. Perhaps it is an act of folly to even pose the question, but if we take the Freudian discovery of death drive seriously, i.e. the ontological inconsistency of the psychical apparatus, the answer stares us square in the eyes. The enjoyment of true love lies in the freedom of having the other become the executioner of one's identity. The melancholy beast, at last, ceases its fruitless search for the perfect object in exchange for having the other repeatedly destroy his identity; one becomes free to enjoy one's own destruction at the hands of the other. The enjoyment derived from fantasy is therefore replaced by the enjoyment of having the other become one's death drive.

Bibliography

La Rochefoucauld, F. (2007). *Collected Maxims and Other Reflections* (E. H. & A. M. Blackmore, Trans.; F. Giguere, Trans.). Oxford University Press.
Nietzsche, F. W. (1887, 2013). *On the Genealogy of Morals* (M. A. Scarpitti, Trans.). Penguin.
Schopenhauer, A. (1818). "Metaphysics of Love." In R. Dircks (Trans.), *Essays of Schopenhauer*. Penn State Electronic Classics Series Publication.

SECTION III

Beyond the Finite: Existentialism and Psychoanalysis in Interplay

Chapter 10

Existentialism After Finitude
The Transcendence of the Unconscious

Todd McGowan

The breach between existentialism and psychoanalysis appears irreconcilable. Existentialism takes finitude, the temporality of our being, as its point of departure, while psychoanalysis focuses on what is irreducible to time. From a psychoanalytic perspective, the unconscious is not the index of the subject's temporality but the point at which the subject reaches out beyond its finitude. Through the unconscious, the subject is infinite. Despite this chasm on the question of finitude, my claim is that psychoanalysis represents another – improved – version of existentialism. It confronts the problem of existence without remaining confined within finitude. Because it recognizes the infinitude of the subject, psychoanalytic thought offers a more compelling conception of freedom than the notable existentialist philosophers.[1]

Although Martin Heidegger and Jean-Paul Sartre have dramatically different conceptions of freedom, they both locate freedom in finitude. Freedom doesn't appear as central to Heidegger's thought as it does to Sartre's. Sartre makes freedom the basis of his philosophy, theorizing freedom as inhering in the basic structure of subjectivity. He is first and foremost a philosopher of freedom. The ability to freely break from one's surroundings and one's own past animates his thinking.

Sartre establishes freedom through the rejection of the standard notion of causality that would reduce any free act to the causes that led up to it. In his version of existentialism, our acts do not follow from an external causality but generate their own causes. We should think of causality operating in the opposite direction than we usually do. Or, as Sartre claims in *Being and Nothingness* (1956), "the cause, far from determining the action, appears only in and through the project of an action" (p. 578). Our existential project that we freely decide on validates causes and gives external causes whatever power they might have over us. A force has the ability to shape our actions only insofar as we grant it that power. This is where our freedom is located.[2]

This understanding of freedom depends on the subject's finitude. One is free in Sartre's eyes because one is always out ahead of oneself in time. Temporality generates a failure of self-identity that enables the subject to transform itself at any moment. Were the subject an infinite entity, it would also be a completely unfree one. Our limitations do not preclude our freedom in Sartre's view but generate it. The finite subject that confronts its finitude is necessarily the free subject.

For Heidegger, we discover freedom through our relationship to death. During the period when he wrote *Being and Time* (originally published 1927) and just afterward, Heidegger locates freedom in the anticipation of death. Most people spend most of their time submitting to the forces of social authority, what Heidegger calls the they (*das Man*). But by grasping one's impending death and orienting oneself around this inevitable future, he contends, one can escape the otherwise determinative constraints of the they.

The anticipation of death liberates us from our own tendency to conform to social pressure. This is because finitude, although it is universally shared, is not generalizable. Everyone must die alone, without anyone from the society accompanying them. The individuality of death renders it the site for freedom.

By anticipating my own death, I separate myself from everyone else. As Heidegger puts it in *Being and Time*, "*anticipation reveals to Dasein its lostness in the they-self, and brings it face to face with the possibility of being itself ... in an impassioned* **freedom towards death** *– a freedom which has been released from the illusions of the 'they'*" (1962, p. 311, emphasis in the original). Anticipating my death frees me from the social authority that depends on the denial of death. The they offers me constant reassurance about death, but anticipation dislodges the authority of this force by placing me in a realm where its authority cannot reach. Freedom emerges through my embrace of my own temporality that manifests itself in the approach of death. Rather than succumbing to the horror of it and seeking assuagement in the they, death provides an opportunity for me to assert my freedom.

Sartre prioritizes consciousness in a way that Heidegger does not. One doesn't arrive at Heidegger's anticipation of death through thinking but emotionally, through mood. It is not the product of consciousness. But neither is it unconscious. Like Sartre, Heidegger has no truck with Sigmund Freud's notion of the unconscious.[3] In his thought, we cannot reduce the unthought to the unconscious. To do so would be to fail to recognize our fundamental temporality. Insofar as Heidegger and Sartre want to keep their philosophy confined to temporality, they avoid the unconscious advisedly.[4]

Freud locates the unconscious outside of temporality. Although he acknowledges that subjectivity includes a sense of time passing, he theorizes temporality entirely in consciousness. In his essay "The Unconscious" (1957a), Freud notes, "The processes of the system *Ucs.* are *timeless*; i.e. they are not ordered temporally, are not altered by the passage of time; they have no reference to time at all" (p. 187). Temporal ordering of events results from the mechanism of perception and consciousness that defies the more fundamental logic that governs the unconscious. The timeless quality of events in the unconscious enables what occurred decades ago to retain the same power to traumatize as what happened yesterday.

In the psychoanalytic conception, we don't suffer from our finitude but from what time doesn't affect. We suffer from our infinitude – our ability to transcend the determinations that occur in time. As time passes, it doesn't grant us any unconscious distance from the traumas that we have experienced. They remain constantly alive for us. Their unconscious status augments rather than lessens how much we suffer from them. It is not that we seek out a social authority to assuage the horror of death, as Heidegger claims. We do so to find respite from our psychic traumas, not recognizing that this authority is itself a source of additional trauma.

Death is not a genuine problem for Freud. He spends little time on it because he views the fear of death as an epiphenomenon in the psyche. Freud argues that, since no one has ever had an experience of death, this rules it out as a source of fear. We fear only what we have already experienced in some form or another.

According to Freud, the fundamental affect that the subject experiences is the fear of castration. The fear of death is nothing but a translation of this more basic fear into a different form. As he states in *Inhibitions, Symptoms, and Anxiety* (1959), "the fear of death should be regarded as analogous to the fear of castration" (p. 130).[5] Unlike death, which no one has experienced and come back to recount, castration is universal. Every subject is a subject of symbolic castration. When we fear death, we unconsciously express a fear of the castration that we have already undergone as speaking beings.

Through the unconscious, the subject breaches its finitude. The timelessness of the unconscious distances the subject from the confines of its situation. This is why there is a link between the timelessness of the unconscious and freedom, a link that Freud himself doesn't recognize. According to Freud, a ruthless necessity governs the unconscious. To give in to unconscious desire is to accede to its mechanistic functioning. To the extent that he associates the unconscious with necessity, Freud doesn't grasp the radicality of his own discovery.

Because the unconscious interrupts the flow of time, it introduces a break between the subject and its external determinations. Without the unconscious, we have no possibility for gaining any purchase on the temporal determinations of our existence. Unconscious desire, not conscious choice, is the basis for the subject's freedom. The unconscious forms in response to what the social authority demands of us, but this response is always singular. The infinitude of the unconscious shatters the hold that social authority has over the subject.

Psychoanalytic theory, properly understood, is a form of existentialism. To see psychoanalysis as a form of existentialism is to grasp it as a project of freedom, a freedom rooted not in conscious decisions but in unconscious desire. In *Being and Nothingness*, Jean-Paul Sartre formulates an existential psychoanalysis, but in doing so, he strips the latter of the unconscious, which is the sine qua non of psychoanalysis. We should counter Sartre's existential psychoanalysis with a psychoanalytic existentialism, a way of thinking that emphasizes the freedom associated with an embrace of the unconscious.

The aim of psychoanalytic treatment is the elimination of the subject's reliance on a substantial figure of social authority. The subject comes to grasp that its symbolic identity, constituted through the social authority, has no foundation. The authority that would support the subject's identity itself has no support. When the subject reconciles itself with this truth, it frees itself from the social authority and takes responsibility for its own existence. The idea of the psychoanalytic cure – a point at which the subject takes responsibility for its unconscious – demonstrates its allegiance to the basic trajectory of existentialism. By including the unconscious within the ambit of the subject's responsibility, psychoanalytic thought takes a step further toward freedom beyond existentialism.

Achieving Isolation

The great discovery of existentialism is the subject's fundamental isolation and the freedom that redounds to the subject from this isolation. As a subject, I can know only my own existence, my own perspective, and never that of another subject, no matter how much I empathize with this other. Isolation condemns the subject to an intractable loneliness, but at the same time, it separates the subject from the collective that would simply imprint itself on the subject and deprive it of any singularity. Isolation is freedom because it is loneliness. To wish away the subject's fundamental loneliness would be implicitly to wish away its freedom.

The subject's inability to experience outside itself is an ontological fact for existentialism: the subject is condemned to solitude. One discovers the intractability of this solitude, for someone like Heidegger, in the unsurpassable encounter with one's own death. Finitude manifests itself as solitude. But the problem with this discovery of the subject's isolation is that the major existentialist thinkers assume that it is an immediate given of consciousness.

When we approach existence phenomenologically, the subject's isolation takes on the appearance of a fact of experience that layers of mediation serve to obscure. The wager of psychoanalysis moves in the opposite direction. As psychoanalytic thinking has it, the subject begins its existence already awash in the mediation of the symbolic structure. The social structure marks the subject's starting point. It is only through navigating this structure and discovering its point of failure that the subject can accede to its own isolation. Isolation is not an immediate given but the end point of subjectivity, emerging only through the collapse of the authority to which the subject initially submits.

Though the subject has no direct experience of other subjects, neither does it have a direct experience of its own identity or its own desire. For the subject, the social authority has a constitutive role in shaping its desire. This is what Jacques Lacan (1988) means when he claims that our "desire is the desire of the Other" (p. 146). The subject takes its cues for how to desire from the model that the authority provides, even though the subject must interpret this desire since it has no direct access to it. Even when a social authority tells us what to do, there is always an unconscious desire lurking within this command.

At the same time, the subject has no direct relation to itself. It approaches itself through the symbolic network laid down by the social authority and relates to its own experience through this network. In response to the mediation of the social order, the subject forms a fundamental fantasy that unconsciously determines its approach to its own experience. No subject has immediate access to its own experiences but relates to them through this unconscious fantasy structure.

The social authority is not an external force that the isolated subject encounters but the impetus that gives birth to subjectivity. This authority constitutes the subject through the demand that it imposes even prior to the individual's birth. But it is not a substantial entity. As a result, the subject cannot rely on it as a support for its identity. The subject supposes that the authority has a substantial identity and that it knows its own desire. This supposition always falls apart because the authority is just as much in the dark about its desire as the subject. The social authority that constitutes the subject dissolves when the subject grasps its insubstantiality. It is this dissolution that illuminates the subject's isolation. A subject is alone without any authority on which to rely. To discover this aloneness, psychoanalytic thinking suggests, one must go through the authority. Freedom becomes evident only after one's initial submission to a failed social authority.

The subject arrives at this point through the act of interpretation. The act of interpretation – or how theory understands it – marks a clear point of division between existentialism and psychoanalysis. For existentialism, interpretation obscures our immediate experience. As Heidegger puts it in *Being and Time*,

The achieving of phenomenological access to the entities which we encounter, consists rather in thrusting aside our interpretive tendencies, which keep thrusting themselves upon us and running along with us, and which conceal not only the phenomenon of such "concern," but even more those entities themselves as encountered of their own accord *in* our concern with them. (1962, p. 96)

Dasein has its own original involvement with things, but interpretation comes along to muck up the works. There is an original concern for the world that the subsequent act of interpretation obscures. The genesis for this interpretative act comes from the social authority. Dasein accepts the they's interpretation because it provides respite from the horror of its finitude.

The social authority functions as a lure for us to betray our isolation and its freedom. In Heidegger's terms, Dasein falls into the everyday interpretation of the they, whereas in Sartre's terms, the subject identifies itself with its social role through bad faith. The subject in bad faith accepts the authority's interpretation of its own identity as if that interpretation were definitive. The problem with both Heidegger and Sartre's denunciation of the act of interpretation that separates Dasein or the subject from its original relation to the world is that there is no original relation to the world outside of this detour through the social authority. The detour is constitutive, which is what psychoanalysis illuminates.

The error that the subject makes relative to the social authority when it assumes the substantiality of this authority is a necessary error. It serves to constitute the subject's own desire, its way of satisfying itself. In this sense, the social authority, though it is insubstantial, orients subjectivity. The social authority has primacy for the subject, and the index of this primacy is the unconscious. As the subject finds itself driven by an unconscious that it cannot master, interpretation provides the only avenue for finding a path out of the insubstantial authority's dominance.

Interpretation plays a radically different role in psychoanalysis than it does for Heidegger and Sartre. Rather than being the act whereby Dasein or the subject ensconces itself in the social order by betraying its original being in the world, interpretation is the path to the subject's freedom. The act of interpretation enables the subject to grasp its own investment in the social authority and the role that this investment plays in substantializing this authority. Through this act, the subject frees itself from its belief that the social authority can provide a ground for the subject's acts. Interpretation confronts the subject with its own isolation by dissolving the substantiality of the authority.

By transforming the position that the social authority occupies for the subject, psychoanalysis fundamentally alters the nature of existentialism. But this project remains within the existentialist orbit. The alteration is that we cannot assume isolation as a starting point but must arrive at it through psychoanalytic interpretation. In this vision, freedom becomes the product of interpretation rather than a given of existence. Sartre's insistence that we are condemned to freedom is nothing but a presupposition that he cannot prove. Psychoanalysis, in contrast, tries to account for the indications of the subject's lack of freedom – its obedience, its conformity, its capitulation – by showing how freedom must begin with the necessity of the social authority's imposition on the subject. It is only through this initial imposition that the subject can identify its own isolation, which serves as the basis for its freedom.

Existence Through Essence

The psychoanalytic conception of the unconscious is at once an affirmation of Sartre's well-known claim that existence precedes essence and a refinement of it. The subject makes itself in its act of speaking. It has no essential self prior to this act. By the same token, the act of speaking reveals the unconscious disruption that bespeaks the subject's essence. When the subject makes a verbal slip – saying the name of a former boyfriend instead of the current spouse, for instance – this slip reveals what the subject does not know about itself. The subject unconsciously desires the forsaken boyfriend while being consciously committed to the spouse. In this scenario, the subject's intended meaning is its commitment to the spouse, while it speaks its unconscious desire for the old boyfriend. This unconscious desire is the subject. It is a desire that becomes visible through one's acts, not prior to them.

The subject finds itself only after it has acted, but this act is already the subject's unconscious essence. This is how psychoanalysis reformulates the idea of existence preceding essence. The priority of existence emerges through the unconscious articulation of our essence. The act comes first, but our essence speaks in it.

What psychoanalysis adds to existentialism is an attention to the moments when the unconscious subverts our conscious mastery. This is where we can see our freedom. We are free not through our conscious successes but through our unconscious failures. When we escape our own conscious intentions, we act freely. We act according to our singular interpretation of what authority asks of us.

Unconscious desire never simply obeys. Even when it follows orders, it doesn't perfectly realize the command given to it. This is what Joan Copjec grasps in her theorization of the subject's relationship to authority. In *Read My Desire* (1994), she writes,

The subject emerges ... as a desiring being, that is to say, an effect of the law but certainly not a realization of it, since desire as such can never be conceived as realization. Desire fills no possibility but seeks after an impossibility; this makes desire always, constitutionally, contentless. (p. 36)

Although it undermines what the subject consciously wants, unconscious desire is not just the result of social authority's imprint. It distances the subject from this authority. This distance is the margin of freedom.

To create a psychoanalytic existentialism, we must perform a double maneuver. On the one hand, we must strip the emphasis on finitude from existentialism. Finitude is not the decisive problematic for the subject. Death is not itself the ultimate problem. On the other hand, we must introduce freedom into the deterministic schema of psychoanalysis. We can accomplish this by making the gap within social authority the pivot point. This gap reveals the incompletion of the authority and thus its inability to effectively determine the subject. The failure of every authority testifies to the infinitude of the subject. It always goes beyond what the authority would make of it. The subject's freedom lies in its infinitude that the subject itself cannot contain.

Notes

1. I will consider all the thinkers who accept Jean-Paul Sartre's mantra "existence precedes essence" as existentialists. This includes Martin Heidegger, though he explicitly rejected the label to dissociate himself from Sartre.
2. Although he has a much different understanding of the relationship between causality and freedom, Heidegger subsumes along with Sartre the problem of causality within the problem of freedom. In *The Essence of Human Freedom* (2002), he claims, "*Causality is grounded in freedom. The problem of causality is a problem of freedom and not vice versa*" (p. 205). This sounds quite a bit like something Sartre would say, but when Heidegger goes on to ground freedom in the question of being, he clearly parts company, before the fact, from Sartre.
3. While Sartre criticizes Freud, he nonetheless maintains a thoroughgoing respect for his insights as a thinker, so much so that Sartre writes the screenplay for a film on Freud's life that director John Huston will ultimately turn into *Freud: The Secret Passion* (1962). Although the film ended up well over two hours long, had Huston adapted Sartre's actual screenplay, it would have been more than twice that length.
4. Sartre contends that if we have an unconscious, we aren't free. Were the unconscious to play a determinative role relative to our conscious choices, all theorizations of freedom would run up against its necessity. The unconscious bespeaks the victory of necessity over freedom. This is a position that he shares with Simone de Beauvoir, who recounts precisely why she and Sartre rejected psychoanalysis when working out their philosophy of freedom. In *The Prime of Life* (1992), she writes, "Above all, the importance it attached to the unconscious and the rigidity of its mechanistic theories meant that Freudianism, as we conceived it, was bound to eradicate human free will" (p. 23). In Sartre and Beauvoir's understanding, accepting the unconscious meant acceding to

the past determining the present. As Beauvoir herself (to her credit) admits in a self-criticism, this is a tendentious interpretation of Freud. Although there are moments when Freud does locate the source for present symptoms in the traumas of the past, he also contends that current dynamics can activate past traumas that would otherwise lie dormant. This occurs through a process that he calls *Nachträglichkeit* or retroactivity.

5 Freud contends that we are unconsciously immortal. In "Thoughts on War and Death" (1957b), he states, "in the unconscious every one of us is convinced of his own immortality" (p. 289). The idea of death comes from consciousness, not from the unconscious. As Freud sees it, the fears that emerge out of the unconscious are always more horrifying. This marks a decisive break from Heidegger's thought.

References

Beauvoir, S. (1992). *The Prime of Life: 1929–1944* (P. Green, Trans.). Paragon House. Original work published in 1960.

Copjec, J. (1994). *Read My Desire: Lacan Against the Historicists*. MIT Press.

Freud, S. (1957a). "The Unconscious" (C. M. Baines, Trans.). In *The Standard Edition of the Complete Psychological Works of Sigmund Freud*, vol. 14 (J. Strachey, Ed.). Hogarth Press. Original work published in 1915.

Freud, S. (1957b). "Thoughts on War and Death" (E. C. Maine, Trans.). In *The Standard Edition of the Complete Psychological Works of Sigmund Freud*, vol. 14 (J. Strachey, Ed.). Hogarth Press. Original work published in 1915.

Freud, S. (1959). *Inhibitions, Symptoms and Anxiety* (A. Strachey, Trans.). In *The Standard Edition of the Complete Psychological Works of Sigmund Freud*, vol. 20. (J. Strachey, Ed.). Hogarth Press. Original work published in 1926.

Heidegger, M. (1962). *Being and Time* (J. Macquarrie and E. Robinson, Trans.) HarperCollins. Original work published in 1927.

Heidegger, M. (2002). *The Essence of Human Freedom: An Introduction to Philosophy* (T. Sadler, Trans.). Continuum. Original work published in 1982.

Lacan, J. (1988). *The Seminar, Book I: Freud's Papers on Technique* (Jacques-Alain Miller, Ed.; John Forrester, Trans.). Norton. Original work published in 1975.

Sartre, J.-P. (1956). *Being and Nothingness* (H. E. Barnes, Trans.). Washington Square Press. Original work published in 1943.

Chapter 11

Why Is the Death Drive Not Identical with Being-Toward-Death?

Simone A. Medina Polo

Undoing an Assumption

There is a commonplace assumption that the psychoanalytic notion of the death drive is identical with the existential phenomenological notion of being-toward-death. While there are affinities between both concepts, we will argue that the death drive and being-toward-death are not identical with each other. We argue that the death drive is rather a figure of infinity through its undead immortality, whereas being-towards-death is a figure of finitude contained to a determinate existential attunement towards mortality.

Through a reading of Hegel, Freud, and Lacan, we will demonstrate that the infinitude of the death drive is a self-limiting negativity; and through a reading of Kant and Heidegger, we will demonstrate that being-toward-death remains an articulation of the finite horizon of *Dasein*. Nonetheless, the affinities between the death drive and being-toward-death offers a speculative space for the transfinite link between these two concepts – love as an oscillating point between life and death as well as the infinite and the finite.

The Origin of an Assumption

The history between psychoanalysis and existential phenomenology depicts a tense relationship. Though Sigmund Freud and Martin Heidegger never met, there was a tension in their attitudes toward each other's discipline. Freud seldom concerned himself with philosophy and at most treated philosophy solely as a worldview (Freud, 1933/1989). Heidegger rejected Freudian psychoanalysis as a neo-Kantian scientistic substitution of philosophy and religion (Heidegger, 1987/2001).

Their dialogue was made explicitly by other thinkers and their contributions including Ludwig Binswanger's ontic anthropological psychiatric appropriation of Heidegger's ontological structures (Binswanger, 1958), Medard Boss' Daseinanalysis as a humanistic alternative to psychoanalysis (Boss, 1962/1982), and Jacques Lacan who disentangled Freud and psychoanalysis from its energetic scientisms and its resistance toward philosophy (Lacan, 1975/1991, 1966/2006a). There are two main trends in handling this tension: either philosophy was brought closer to psychoanalysis or psychoanalysis was brought closer to philosophy. In this chapter, we will focus on Lacan's intimations between the death drive and being-toward-death, since the death drive is untouched by Binswanger and Boss who emphasize being-with-others and care – in fact, Heidegger's remarks on the death drive were simply dismissive (Holzhey-Kunz, 1986).

Unlike Freud, Lacan met Heidegger when the latter visited him at Guitrancourt before delivering the "What is Philosophy?" lecture at Cerisy-la-Salle in 1955 (Janicaud, 2001).

And Lacan does offer some explicit commentary on Heidegger in general as well as on the death drive and being-toward-death. Lacan's interventions between philosophy and psychoanalysis can be understood on two ends. On one hand, Lacan remains committed to psychoanalysis and its fundamental concepts in asserting the "return to Freud" as a subversive style that nonetheless comprehends the meaning of Freud's interventions as genuine (Lacan, 1966/2006a, 1966/2006b, 1966/2006c, 1966/2006d, 1966/2006e). And on the other hand, Lacan engages with philosophy and regards himself as translating Heidegger (Lacan, 1966/2006e). Furthermore, Lacan is keen on concerning himself with philosophical truth and its revelation while acknowledging that science forecloses the grounding of truth as a cause in order to operate as science – this is a leftover concern for philosophers and theologians (Lacan, 1966/2006f, 1966/2006g, 1966/2006h). However, later Lacan contains his references to Heidegger (and any philosopher) into a didactic and propaedeutic prop for his psychoanalytic teaching – and the same cannot exactly be said the other way around (Lacan, 1973/1998). Nonetheless, these references towards the death drive and being-toward-death left an impression among some commonplace interpretations of Freud, Lacan, and Heidegger.

Figure 11.1 Left to right – Martin Heidegger, Kostas Axelos, Jacques Lacan, Jean Beaufret, Elfriede Heidegger, Sylvia Bataille-Lacan. *Roger Munier Archives.*

Being-Towards-Death and Existential Finitude

For the early Heidegger, being-towards-death can only be apprehended after the deconstruction of the history of metaphysics throughout part one of *Being and Time*. According to Heidegger, there are a number of prejudices and assumptions at work when we discuss the question of being such treating being as universal, indefinite, and self-evident. When we actually move on to ask any question with respect to being, this can only take place from an act of questioning which is itself implied in an understanding of being by the inquirer. For Heidegger, this is not circular reasoning but solely the act of laying the ground for metaphysics (Heidegger, 1929/1997, 1927/2010). Thus, the determinate being known as *Dasein* takes an ontological priority to any ontic focus insofar as *Dasein* is preoccupied with its own being. On this basis, Heidegger reinforces the difference between fundamental and regional ontology in order to clear the ground for fundamental ontology proper through the existential analysis of *Dasein*.

Heidegger distinguishes the existential analysis of *Dasein* from those focusing on anthropology, psychology, and biology and instead offers a phenomenological hermeneutic to interpret *Dasein* as it is being. *Dasein* is involved in the fundamental and constitutive orientations of its concerns such as being-in-the-world, being-with-others, and the ways in which *Dasein* gets caught up in the everydayness of being-with-others as the inauthentic anonymity of the "They." In any case, being-in as such shows the ways in which *Dasein* is attuned through existential moods into the equiprimordial structures around its way of being. Thus, Heidegger concludes the first part of *Being and Time* by disclosing the fundamental character of *Dasein* as care and letting truth be by making way for its revelations to be disclosed.

The second division of *Being and Time* addresses temporality as an existential horizon of *Dasein* that renders its care and existential projects intelligible. These concerns gain their authentic depth when *Dasein* confronts its being-towards-death as the fundamental existential interpretation of death and time that stands opposed to biologies, psychologies, theologies, and ontologies of life as well as the calculative temporalization of time (Heidegger, 1927/2010; Carel, 2006). For Heidegger, this existential sense of death matters because it constitutes *Dasein*'s ownmost possibility of being where only it can assume its own death. Thereby, *Dasein* is tempted to distract itself and cover-up its death-anxiety. Thus, Heidegger articulates the calls of conscience that confront *Dasein* with the indefiniteness of a future which only it can meet resolutely.

While *Being and Time* is notably an unfinished project, we can note that its concerns recur in Heidegger's later work. For example, in "What is Metaphysics?" Heidegger (1929/1993a) retains the attitude towards the question of being, regarding metaphysics as a basic happening of *Dasein* and *Dasein* itself as the truth of metaphysics hanging over "the groundless ground" of the nothing (p. 109). Similarly, existentially intelligible care remains in Heidegger's pastoralism of primordial truth and being, where they are poetically retrieved from their forgetting as in the instance of the scientific-technological appropriation of being (Heidegger,

1930/1993b, 1947/1993c, 1952/1993d, 1962/1993e, 1954/1993f). Lastly, we find this tendency insisting in the call of mortals towards dwelling as a primordial ontological imperative that we must take a hold of to build and to think (Heidegger, 1954/1993g).

Finitude remains one of the fundamental concepts of metaphysics for Heidegger, and this is informed by his readings of Kant's *Critique of Pure Reason* and the *Prolegomena to Any Future Metaphysics*. After finding itself in a world, there is a restlessness inspired in *Dasein*'s confrontation with the nothing insofar as this is our fundamental way of being and as this characterizes finitude in Heidegger's *The Fundamental Concepts of Metaphysics* (Heidegger, 1983/1995). Finitude is something to be cultivated and looked after since it properly constitutes individuation and the existential solitude of *Dasein*. Therefore, philosophy is an uncanny practice of being and time, a turbulence opposed to every comfort and assurance (Heidegger, 1983/1995, 1953/2000).

In these lectures, Heidegger sheds light on the significance of Kant in his philosophical project. On one end, it was Kant who fundamentally questioned the status of metaphysics due to the prevalence of dogmatism, thus metaphysics itself became a problem. However, on the other end, Kant withdrew from establishing the problem of human *Dasein* and finitude proper by opting for conceptions of the infinite and the absolute making the way for Hegel (Heidegger, 1983/1995). Heidegger's problem with Kant stems from Kant's attempt to systematize a science out of metaphysics for which the critique is only clearing the ground; and out of this groundwork, Kant is preparing the ends of reason through practical philosophy aiming towards the infinite and inconclusive project of cosmopolitanism and pure rational religion (Kant, 1783/1977, 1784/1983a, 1795/1983b, 1781/2003, 1793/2009). Thus, Heidegger claims that Kant's critical philosophy is not focused on the finitude of determinate existentiality and that Kant compromised his radical accomplishments for his more systematic ambitions. Being-towards-death can only be properly conceived of as an attitude of *Dasein* confronting its metaphysical horizon of being-in-the-world and confronting its solitude by virtue of finitude as a disclosure of the radical contingency of its given world and being.

Death Drive and the Absolute as Self-Limiting Infinity

While Heidegger regards Freud as a dogmatic psychologist and scientist, Freud's formulation of the death drive resists such a picture of Freud. In "Beyond the Pleasure Principle," Freud is critical about the dogmatic understandings of the economies between pleasure and pain as well as psychic life and the reality it tests. Freud's controversial arrival at the concept of the death drive is notably speculative, and it is often rejected as being unscientific and unverifiable. Alongside the expansion of the concept of sexuality, the death drive resulted in a crossroads between the early Freud's positive end of psychoanalysis and the later Freud's negative approach to psychoanalysis. This also marked a certain distancing from

Freud by the neo-Freudians, ego psychology, object-relation theorists, Adlerians, Reichians, and Jungians.

In many respects, Freud's formulation of the death drive is sketchy and fragmentary. In "Beyond the Pleasure Principle," Freud offers speculative descriptions of the death drive as something that is not merely involved in individual psychic lives, but rather it seems to be an elementary principle oscillating between organic life and the inorganic (Freud, 1920/1992). In *Civilization and Its Discontents*, the death drive now recurs in society, culture, and politics as an irreducible tension in their constitution for which we are finding ways to cope (Freud, 1930/1991). And while the death drive is often treated in opposition to the life drive, this figuration remains unclear since, in *New Introductory Lectures on Psycho-analysis*, Freud speculates that the life drive might also seek to return to an originary state like the death drive does – and this he leaves unanswered (Freud, 1933/1989).

This ambiguity in Freud's formulations of the death drive is certainly noted by Lacan (1986/1992) in *The Ethics of Psychoanalysis*: "I simply want to say that the articulation of the death drive in Freud is neither true not false. It is suspect; that's all I affirm." Furthermore, given the ambiguous similarity between the death drive and the life drive, Lacan points out that "Freud evokes there his sublimation concerning the death instinct insofar as that sublimation is fundamentally creationist" (p. 213). Therefore, the death drive creates as much as it destroys – an aspect that one can find in its earliest formulations by Sabina Spielrein (see Spielrein, 1912/1994).

This ambiguity of the death drive is articulated through Lacan's myth of the *lamella* which portrays the death drive as a dumb, undead impulse in spite all other aspects of life. The *lamella* is described as this undead persistence of the real and the drive without symbolic support for its articulation, as we are left with "immortal…irrepressible life" which makes itself apparent in the horizon of finitude as a radical constitutive failure (Lacan, 1973/1998, pp. 196–198). Therefore, we still need the symbolic to detect the drive, not as a primordial thing, but as something integrated in the kind of sexuated subjectivity that psychoanalysis articulates in the failures of speech in the clinic.

As Alenka Zupančič notes, the lamella is precisely the point in which the death drive and life drive are treated as one and the same by Lacan (Zupančič, 2023). After all, Lacan argues that every drive is virtually a death drive (Lacan, 1966/2006i). Not only is this destructive drive a challenge to everything that exists and the economy of life, but it will also create from nothing, as a will to begin again. This creative persistence of the death drive is precisely why it cannot be reduced to Heidegger's being-towards-death, as Žižek (2000) argues:

> In contrast to some attempts to identify them (found in Lacan's work of the early 1950s), one should insist on their radical incompatibility: "death drive" designates the "undead" *lamella*, the "immortal" insistence of drive that precedes the ontological disclosure of Being whose finitude confronts a human being in the experience of "being towards death." (p. 66)

Thus, the death drive is not so much being-toward-death, it is rather closer to the absolute idea and absolute spirit in Hegel's work. Why? Because each of them is a figure for expressing their infinities through their own respective self-limitation. In Hegel and Lacan, there is a transformation of our relation to the deadlocks that prevent the full embracement of our drive as well as the absolute. However, as Todd McGowan (2013) eloquently argues, it is that very impasse that it is the pass: "The infinitude of the concept is nothing but the concept's own self-limitation. The enjoyment that the death drive produces also achieves its infinitude through self-limitation" (p. 284). What is called "subjective destitution" in psychoanalysis is described by Hegel (1807/1977) as "letting go" or "knowing one's limit" when he writes in the *Phenomenology of Spirit*: "The self-knowing Spirit knows not only itself but also the negative of itself, or its limit: to know one's limit is to know how to sacrifice oneself" (p. 492). Therefore, the infinity of the death drive sets it diametrically opposed to the finitude of being-toward-death.

Although we introduced Freud's death drive by distancing it from Heidegger's critique of science, Lacan's approach revisits both the question of science and metaphysics positively. While for Heidegger, sciences are tied up to the metaphysical tradition that forgets the question of fundamental ontology; Lacan's psychoanalytic science breaks metaphysics with the metaphysical tradition of philosophy (Kurki, 2008). When Lacan thinks of the psychoanalytic science, the objectivity of psychoanalysis is understood within the analytic experience and the transference insofar as it is concerned with the metaphysical mirages and alienations that appear therein as forms of human madness (Lacan, 1966/2006b).

A fundamental decision happens there which short-circuits philosophy and psychoanalysis, as Zupančič notes in an interview with Frank Ruda and Agon Hamza (2019): "it is not these notions themselves that are problematic; what can be problematic in some ways of doing philosophy is the disavowal or effacement of the inherent contradiction, even antagonism, that these notions imply, and are part of" (p. 435). Where Heidegger sees the beginning of thinking at the end of the metaphysical tradition, Lacan intervenes through the metaphysical tradition by upholding this contradictory torsion that concerns the non-relationship of sex – a space that is prospective for the question of love.

Love as Transfinite

While Binswanger and Boss adopted Heidegger in their psychodynamic approaches by emphasizing being-with-others and care as a place for love, it is pertinent to note that a Heideggerian love would be one caught up in its finitude and solitude in the plenitude of being. And in order to love, it takes at least two – without which there is no love.

This is the crux of the difference between Heidegger's ontological difference and Lacan's sexual difference. What really makes a difference for Heidegger is the retrieval of fundamental ontology from the ontic preoccupations that obscure it for *Dasein* – *Dasein* turns away from the full extent of being-with-others in the form of the anonymity of *das Man* which makes it fall into inauthenticity. Thus, Heidegger's being-toward-death brings a difference in *Dasein* with respect to its self which is always in question. And what makes a difference for Lacan is the confrontation of the fundamental abyss of sexuality in the impasse of the non-relation. The analytic process requires the presence of the analyst, where the dynamics explored in the transference bring to light what are otherwise tensions that structure the everyday of the analysand.

The myth of the lamella as an articulation of the (death) drive depicts the irreducible real prior to attempts at symbolically appropriating it, what is otherwise the missing scene of sex. The drive articulates the locus of an ontological torsion where reality experiences itself as "missed encounters" at the threshold of what would be the horizon of finitude for Heidegger (Zupančič, 2008, 2017). While the nothing is owned up as the resolute solitude of *Dasein* unto death, the non-relation offers a possibility for love as a paradoxical sharing of a void among others with whom we negotiate the paradox of a truth that makes a difference in our lives (Badiou, 1996/2000; Lacan, 1975/1999). Therefore, love is transfinite, precisely because the death drive situates a happening where we expect nothing (Badiou, 2019/2012). As Žižek writes:

> It is in its capacity as the "drink of death" that it acts as the "drink of love" – the two lovers mistake it for the drink of death and, thinking that they are now on the brink of death, delivered from ordinary social obligations, feel free to acknowledge their passion. This immortal passion does not stand for biological life beyond the socio-symbolic universe: in it, carnal passion and pure spirituality paradoxically coincide, i.e. we are dealing with a kind of "denaturalization" of the natural instinct which inflates it into an immortal passion raised to the level of the Absolute, so that no actual, real object can ever fully satisfy it. (Žižek, n.d.)

References

Badiou, A. (2000). "What is Love?" (J. Clemens, Trans.). In R. Salecl (Ed.), *Sexuation* (pp. 263–281). Duke University Press. Original work published 1996.

Badiou, A., and Truong, T. (2012). *In Praise of Love*. (P. Bush, Trans.). The New Press. Original work published 2009.

Binswanger, L. (1958). "The Existential Analysis School of Thought." (E. Angel, Trans.). In R. May, E. Angel, and H. Ellenberger (Eds.), *Existence: A New Dimension in Psychiatry and Psychology* (pp. 191–213). Simon and Schuster.

Boss, M. (1982). *Psychoanalysis and Daseinsanalysis* (L. Lefebre, Trans.). Dacapo Press. Original work published 1962.

Carel, H. (2006). *Life and Death in Freud and Heidegger*. Rodopi.

Freud, S. (1992). "Beyond the Pleasure Principle" (J. Strachey, Trans.). In A. Richards (Ed.), *On Metapsychology, the Theory of Psychoanalysis* (pp. 275–338). Penguin Books. Original work published 1920.

Freud, S. (1991). *Civilizations and its Discontents* (J. Strachey, Trans.). In A. Dickson (Ed.), *Volume 12, Civilization, Society, and Religion: Group Psychology, Civilization and Its Discontents and Other Works* (pp. 251–340). Penguin Books. Original work published 1930.

Freud, S. (1989). *New Introductory Lectures on Psychoanalysis.* (J. Strachey, Trans.). W. W. Norton & Company. Original work published 1933.

Hegel, G. W. F. (1977). *Phenomenology of Spirit* (A. V. Miller, Trans.). Oxford University Press. Original work published 1807.

Heidegger, M. (1993a). "What is Metaphysics?" (F. Cohen, Trans.). In D. F. Krell (Ed.), *Basic Writings* (pp. 93–110). Harper Collins. Original work published 1929.

Heidegger, M. (1993b). "On the Essence of Truth" (J. Sallis, Trans.). In D. F. Krell (Ed.), *Basic Writings* (pp. 115–138). Harper Collins. Original work published 1930.

Heidegger, M. (1993c). "Letter on Humanism" (F. A. Capuzzi and J. G. Gray, Trans.). In D. F. Krell (Ed.), *Basic Writings* (pp. 217–265). Harper Collins. Original work published 1947.

Heidegger, M. (1993d). "What Calls for Thinking?" (F. D. Wieck and J. G. Gray, Trans.). In D. F. Krell (Ed.), *Basic Writings* (pp. 369–391). Harper Collins. Original work published 1952.

Heidegger, M. (1993e). "The Turning" (W. Lovitt, Trans.). In W. Lovitt (Ed.), *The Question Concerning Technology and Other Essays* (pp. 36–49). Harper Collins. Original work published 1962.

Heidegger, M. (1993f). "The Question Concerning Technology" (W. Lovitt, Trans.). In W. Lovitt (Ed.), *The Question Concerning Technology and Other Essays* (pp. 3–35). Harper Collins. Original work published 1954.

Heidegger, M. (1993g). Building Dwelling Thinking (A. Hofstadter, Trans.). In D. F. Krell (Ed.), *Basic Writings* (pp. 344–363). Harper Collins. Original work published 1954.

Heidegger, M. (1995). *The Fundamental Concepts of Metaphysics: World, Finitude, Solitude* (W. McNeill and N. Walker, Trans.). Indiana University Press. Original work published 1983.

Heidegger, M. (1997). *Kant and the Problem of Metaphysics.* (R. Taft, Trans.). Indiana University Press. Original work published 1929.

Heidegger, M. (2000). *Introduction to Metaphysics.* (G. Fried and R. Polt, Trans.). Yale University Press. Original work published 1953.

Heidegger, M. (2001). *Zollikon Seminars: Protocols – Conversations – Letters* (M. Boss, Ed.; F. Mayr and R. Askay, Trans.). Northwestern University Press. Original work published 1987.

Heidegger, M. (2010). *Being and Time* (J. Stambaugh, Trans.). State University of New York Press. Original work published 1927.

Holzhey-Kunz, A. (1986). "Todestrieb und Sein zum Tode." *Daseinsanalyse*, 3(2). https://doi.org/10.1159/000456136

Janicaud, D. (2001). *Heidegger en France II: entretiens.* Albin Michel.

Kant, I. (1977). *Prolegomena to Any Future Metaphysics* (P. Carus and J. W. Ellington, Trans.). Hackett Publishing Company. Original work published 1783.

Kant, I. (1983a). "Idea for a Universal History with a Cosmopolitan Intent" (T. Humphrey, Trans.). In *Perpetual Peace and Other Essays on Politics, History, and Morals* (pp. 29–40). Hackett Publishing Company. Original work published 1784.

Kant, I. (1983b). "To Perpetual Peace: A Philosophical Sketch" (T. Humphrey, Trans.). In *Perpetual Peace and Other Essays on Politics, History, and Morals* (pp. 107–143). Hackett Publishing Company. Original work published 1795.

Kant, I. (2003). *Critique of Pure Reason* (J. M. D. Meiklejohn, Trans.). Dover Publications. Original work published 1781.

Kant, I. (2003). *Religion within the Bounds of Bare Reason* (W.S. Pluhar, Trans.). Hackett Publishing Company. Original work published 1793.

Kurki, J. (2008). "Heidegger and Lacan: Their Most Important Difference." *The Symptom*, 9. https://www.lacan.com/symptom/heidegger-and.html#:~:text=For%20Heidegger%2C%20all%20sciences%20belong,the%20metaphysical%20tradition%20of%20philosophy

Lacan, J. (1991). *The Seminar of Jacques Lacan, Book I: Freud's Papers on Technique, 1953–1954* (J-A. Miller, Ed.; J. Forrester, Trans.). W. W. Norton & Company Inc. Original work published 1975.

Lacan, J. (1992). *The Seminar of Jacques Lacan, Book VII: The Ethics of Psychoanalysis, 1959–1960* (J-A. Miller, Ed.; D. Porter, Trans.). W. W. Norton & Company Inc. Original work published 1986.

Lacan, J. (1998). *The Seminar of Jacques Lacan, Book XI: The Four Fundamental Concepts of Psychoanalysis* (J-A. Miller, Ed.; A. Sheridan, Trans.). W. W. Norton & Company Inc. Original work published 1973.

Lacan, J. (1999). *Encore: The Seminar of Jacques Lacan Book XX: On Feminine Sexuality, the Limits of Love and Knowledge, 1972–1973* (J-A. Miller, Ed.; B. Fink, Trans.). W. W. Norton & Company. Original work published 1975.

Lacan, J. (2006a). "The Function and Field of Speech and Language in Psychoanalysis" (B. Fink, Trans.). In *Écrits* (pp. 197–268). W. W. Norton & Company. Original work published 1966.

Lacan, J. (2006b). "The Freudian Thing or the Meaning of the Return to Freud in Psychoanalysis" (B. Fink, Trans.). In *Écrits* (pp. 334–363). W. W. Norton & Company. Original work published 1966.

Lacan, J. (2006c). "On a Purpose" (B. Fink, Trans.). In *Écrits* (pp. 303–307). W. W. Norton & Company. Original work published 1966.

Lacan, J. (2006d). "Psychoanalysis and Its Teaching" (B. Fink, Trans.). In *Écrits* (pp. 364–383). W. W. Norton & Company. Original work published 1966.

Lacan, J. (2006e). "The Instance of the Letter in the Unconscious; or Reason since Freud" (B. Fink, Trans.). In *Écrits* (pp. 412–441). W.W. Norton & Company. Original work published 1966.

Lacan, J. (2006f). "Presentation on Psychical Causality" (B. Fink, Trans.). In *Écrits* (pp. 123–158). W. W. Norton & Company. Original work published 1966.

Lacan, J. (2006g). "On the Subject Who is Finally in Question" (B. Fink, Trans.). In *Écrits* (pp. 189–196). W. W. Norton & Company. Original work published 1966.

Lacan, J. (2006g). "Position of the Unconscious" (B. Fink, Trans.). In *Écrits* (pp. 703–721). W. W. Norton & Company. Original work published 1966.

Lacan, J. (2006h). "Science and Truth" (B. Fink, Trans.). In *Écrits* (pp. 726–745). W. W. Norton & Company. Original work published 1966.

Spielrein, S. (1994). "Destruction as the Cause of Coming into Being." *Journal of Analytical Psychology*, 39. https://doi.org/10.1111/j.1465-5922.1994.00155.x. Original work published 1912.

Žižek, S. (n.d.). "Why Lacan is Not a Heideggerian." *No Subject – Encyclopedia of Psychoanalysis*. Online. https://nosubject.com/Articles/Slavoj_Zizek/why-lacan-is-not-lacanian.html

Žižek, S. (2000). *The Ticklish Subject: The Absent Centre of Political Ontology*. Verso.

Zupančič, A. (2008). *Why Psychoanalysis? Three Interventions*. NSU Press.

Zupančič, A. (2017). *What Is Sex?* MIT Press.

Zupančič, A. (2023). *Let Them Rot: Antigone's Parallax*. Fordham University Press.

Zupančič, A., Hamza, A., and Ruda, F. (2019). "Interview with Alenka Zupančič: Philosophy or Psychoanalysis? Yes, Please!" *Crisis & Critique*, 6(1). https://crisiscritique.org/storage/app/media/2019-04-02/zupancic.pdf

SECTION IV

The Disintegrating Power of Love: Spielrein, Weil, and Kristeva

Chapter 12

Simone Weil on Death

Exploring Intersections with Freud and Spielrein's Death Drive

Wanyoung Kim-Murphy

Freud and Spielrein's Death Drive

While Simone Weil's philosophical framework may appear at odds with psychoanalytic theories, a deeper examination reveals nuanced connections, particularly in Weil's concept of self-denial. To comprehend the intersections between Simone Weil and the death drive, it is crucial to first explore the origins of this concept in psychoanalysis. Sigmund Freud introduced the death drive as an unconscious yearning for a return to a state of non-existence or the inorganic world. Freud initially introduced the concept of Thanatos, the death instinct, in his essay "Beyond the Pleasure Principle." His theory posited that humans possess an inherent inclination towards death and destruction, encapsulated in his famous statement that "the aim of all life is death" (1920). According to Freud, individuals typically externalize this death drive through aggression towards others. However, he also noted the potential for directing this instinct inward, leading to self-harm or suicidal tendencies. Freud derived this theory from clinical observations, highlighting that individuals who undergo traumatic experiences often reenact or relive those events. For instance, soldiers returning from World War I tended to revisit their traumatic encounters through recurring dreams of combat.

From these observations, Freud inferred that people harbor an unconscious desire for death, although life instincts generally moderate this inclination. He characterized the compulsion to repeat as something more primitive and instinctual than the pleasure principle it overrides, emphasizing the stark contrast between Thanatos and the drives for survival, procreation, and desire satisfaction. Sabina Spielrein, Freud's associate and the female pioneer of psychoanalysis, foreshadowed this concept by emphasizing the need to reconcile Eros with the death drive in the realms of love and creation (1912). This foundational understanding sets the stage for exploring how Simone Weil's ideas intersect with and contribute to this psychoanalytic discourse.

Simone Weil's Concept of Self-Denial

Simone Weil was a Jewish convert to the Catholic religion during World War II. She often protested on behalf of the poor and suffering. Weil proposes that self-denial serves as a strategy for channeling the dying instinct towards something noble. By consciously forgoing the self and embracing pain, individuals, according to Weil, can transcend their particular egos and connect with something larger. This philosophy of self-denial aligns with the unconscious yearning explored in the death drive. While Freud and Spielrein explore an involuntary pull towards non-existence, Weil suggests that consciously denying the self can lead to a higher purpose, mirroring the pursuit of meaning central to her broader philosophy. Simone Weil's examination of the modern world also provides another layer of connection with the death drive. She posits that the contemporary era has become so disconnected from the divine that it has lost its sense of meaning and purpose. This disconnect, according to Weil, represents a kind of collective death drive, where individuals seek to escape from a seemingly valueless world.

In "The Need for Roots," Weil articulates a profound exploration of the human condition, emphasizing the fundamental importance of rootedness and belonging. Weil asserts that a genuine connection to one's surroundings and a sense of belonging are essential for individuals to navigate the complexities of life with a deeper understanding and fulfillment. Rootedness, in Weil's perspective, serves as a stabilizing force, providing individuals with a firm foundation from which they can engage meaningfully with the world. Without this foundation, she argues, people are more prone to experiencing a pervasive sense of existential unease, potentially leading to a fear of death and a disconnection from their inherent humanity.

Weil's insights resonate with broader existential and psychological considerations, highlighting the profound impact of a lack of rootedness on the human psyche. The yearning for a sense of belonging is deeply embedded in the human experience, and Weil suggests that the absence of this connection can contribute to a sense of alienation and vulnerability. The fear of death, according to Weil, is intricately linked to this existential disquiet, as individuals without a solid sense of rootedness may grapple with a profound uncertainty about their place in the world, exacerbating anxiety and detachment.

Moreover, Weil's perspective on the need for roots extends beyond individual well-being to societal structures. She explores the idea that communities and societies also require a sense of shared values, traditions, and collective identity to thrive. In the absence of these roots, societies may face fragmentation and disintegration. Weil's call for rootedness, therefore, extends both to the personal and communal levels, advocating for a holistic understanding of human connection and the societal structures that contribute to a sense of belonging, resilience, and a more profound engagement with the mysteries of life, including the inevitability of death.

Weil's perspective on the modern world aligns with Freud and Spielrein's notions of the death drive, as the collective desire to escape reflects an unconscious yearning for non-existence. The modern world, in Weil's eyes, becomes a breeding ground for existential angst, mirroring the psychoanalytic concepts of Freud and Spielrein.

The Fear of Death in Simone Weil's Writings

Death, for Simone Weil, is both a necessary part of the human experience and a source of anxiety and despair for many. While not explicitly framed within the death drive, Weil's exploration of death aligns with Freud and Spielrein's concepts. The fear of death, according to Weil, can be seen as a manifestation of the death drive as individuals seek to escape the inevitability of their own mortality.

Within *Gravity and Grace*, Weil writes extensively about death and its relationship to the human condition. She argues that death is an essential part of life and that we must embrace it rather than fear it. Weil's exploration extends beyond the mere acknowledgment of mortality, as she advocates for a transformative perspective that encourages individuals to embrace death as an integral aspect of life. In her philosophical discourse, Weil contends that the acceptance of mortality is not an act of resignation but a profound act of grace and wisdom. By recognizing the impermanence of existence, individuals gain the opportunity to live authentically, appreciating the fleeting beauty of each moment. Weil challenges the prevalent cultural fear of death, inviting readers to confront the inevitability of their own mortality and find meaning in the transitory nature of human life.

Weil's insights go beyond conventional views on mortality, proposing that embracing death is a gateway to spiritual and existential growth. She suggests that our fear of death often hinders our ability to live fully and authentically. Instead of succumbing to existential anxiety, Weil encourages a profound engagement with the concept of mortality, urging individuals to confront the uncertainty of life with courage and humility. By integrating death into the fabric of our existence, Weil argues that we can discover a deeper connection to the human experience and a more profound sense of purpose.

Furthermore, Weil's perspective on death in her *Gravity and Grace* notebooks underscores the interconnectedness of life and death. She emphasizes that the awareness of our mortality should not lead to nihilism but rather to a heightened appreciation for the preciousness of existence. Weil's exploration of death transcends the boundaries of traditional philosophy, intertwining spiritual and existential dimensions to provide a holistic understanding of the human condition. In essence, "Gravity and Grace" serves as an invitation to reevaluate our relationship with death, fostering a perspective that transforms the inevitability of our mortality into a source of enlightenment and profound spiritual awakening.

"The Iliad, or the Poem of Force," an essay by Weil, serves as a thought-provoking commentary on Homer's epic poem, "The Iliad," exploring the profound theme of death and its intricate relationship with human conflict. Weil's analysis transcends the specific narrative of the Trojan War, offering a timeless exploration of the nature of violence and its roots in the human psyche. She contends that the fear of death is a primal force that propels individuals toward acts of brutality in times of conflict (2005). Weil's perspective invites readers to reflect on the universal nature of this human condition, as the fear of mortality becomes a driving force behind the tragic events depicted in the epic.

In the context of contemporary conflicts, such as those between Israel and Palestine or Ukraine and Russia, Weil's insights resonate with a haunting relevance. She suggests that the specter of death casts a long shadow over the battlefield, influencing the choices and actions of those engaged in conflict. Weil's argument extends beyond a mere analysis of historical events; it serves as a poignant lens through which to understand the motivations and consequences of contemporary wars. The ongoing struggles in these regions become poignant examples of Weil's thesis, where the fear of death plays a pivotal role in shaping the dynamics of violence and conflict.

Weil challenges the conventional notions of heroism and courage, proposing that true valor arises from an acceptance of the inevitability of death. In the face of mortality, individuals are called to confront their deepest fears and find a courage that transcends the mere physical act of combat. This philosophical exploration prompts readers to critically examine the motivations behind human conflicts and to seek a deeper understanding of the profound interplay between mortality, violence, and the human spirit. Weil's insights, rooted in the ancient narrative of "The Iliad," reverberate across time and space, inviting contemplation on the enduring complexities of war and the quest for genuine courage in the face of mortality.

Waiting for God, a compilation of essays and letters by Weil, presents a profound exploration of spirituality and the human experience, with death emerging as a recurring theme throughout the collection (1970). In the essay titled "Reflections on the Right Use of School Studies with a View to the Love of God," Weil introduces the transformative idea that death can serve as a teacher in our journey towards a deeper understanding of life and its ultimate meaning. Her perspective challenges conventional views of death as a mere endpoint, positioning it as a profound source of wisdom if approached with the right mindset.

Weil's assertion that death can be a teacher aligns with her broader philosophical outlook, emphasizing the spiritual dimension of human existence. In seeking to learn from death, she encourages a contemplative engagement with the transitory nature of life, prompting individuals to reflect on the significance of their actions and pursuits. By acknowledging death as an inevitable part of the human condition, Weil suggests that it can become a guiding force, inspiring individuals to live with greater purpose and authenticity.

The notion that death can be a teacher finds resonance in various cultural and religious traditions, but Weil's approach is deeply personal and introspective. Her writings invite readers to embrace mortality not as a source of fear but as a catalyst for personal and spiritual growth. In the context of *Waiting for God*, Weil's exploration of death transcends the conventional boundaries of philosophical discourse, weaving together insights from her own experiences and reflections on the broader human condition (1970).

Ultimately, *Waiting for God* serves as a poignant invitation to reconsider our relationship with mortality and to view death not as an endpoint but as a transformative force that can guide us towards a more profound understanding of ourselves and the divine. Weil's essays and letters within the collection offer a rich tapestry of thought, encouraging readers to embark on a contemplative journey that extends beyond the fear of death to a more enlightened perspective on the meaning of life.

Overall, death is a recurring theme in Weil's writings, and she approaches the subject with a deep sense of thoughtfulness and compassion. Weil's nuanced understanding of death delves into its multifaceted nature, encompassing both acceptance and fear. Her exploration resonates with Freud and Spielrein's emphasis on the unconscious forces that drive human behavior, revealing shared themes in their disparate perspectives.

Conclusion: Intersections and Connections

Comparing key themes in Weil's writings with Freud and Spielrein's concepts reveals rich intersections and connections. Weil's philosophy of self-denial aligns with the unconscious yearning explored in the death drive, while her critique of the modern world as a source of collective death drive adds another layer to the discourse. The fear of death as both a necessary human experience and a manifestation of the death drive bridges Weil's ideas with the psychoanalytic concepts of Freud and Spielrein. Simone Weil's emphasis on the human experience of suffering and the search for meaning in a seemingly bleak world resonates with Freud and Spielrein's psychoanalytic exploration of the death drive. Weil thus contributes a unique perspective, enriching the discourse on the human condition and the pursuit of meaning.

In conclusion, Weil's work, while not explicitly focused on the death drive, intertwines with Freud and Spielrein's psychoanalytic theories in profound ways. The intersections between Weil's ideas and the death drive shed light on the complexity of human experience, suffering, and the search for meaning in a world that can sometimes seem bleak and meaningless. Exploring these connections deepens our understanding of the intricate interplay between philosophy and psychoanalysis, highlighting the enduring relevance of these ideas in our quest for meaning and purpose.

References

Freud, S. (1920). "Beyond the Pleasure Principle." Internationaler Psychoanalytischer Verlag.
Spielrein, S. (1912). Destruction as the Cause of Coming Into Being. *Jahrbuch für psychoanalytische und psychopathologische Forschungen.*
Weil, S. (1952). *Gravity and Grace*. Routledge & Kegan Paul.

Weil, S. (1947). *The Need for Roots*. Routledge & Kegan Paul.
Weil, S. (1970). *Waiting for God*. Harper One.
Weil, S. (2005). "The Iliad, or the Poem of Force." In R. C. Kuhn (Ed. & Trans.), *Simone Weil:*
Writings on War (pp. 1–33). Wesleyan University Press.

Chapter 13

In Search for Adult Sexual Tenderness in Freud, Kristeva, and Bersani

Stephanie Koziej

As various texts within this book suggest, Freud's concept of the death drive places self-destruction at the core of human existence, presenting death as a fundamental force operating within life. In this chapter, I aim to explore how a much earlier Freudian concept, predating the death drive, may offer insights into placing self-destruction at the center of life. I am referring to Freud's underexplored notion of tenderness or *Zärtlichkeit*, a word he borrows from his earliest patients, the so-called hysterics. While Freud himself does not explicitly articulate this idea, I will argue how an idiosyncratic interpretation of Kristeva's work on "reliance" and Bersani's exploration of the "shattering of the self" during sexual experiences, can support this assertion. However, before delving into this theoretical discourse, it is essential to set the stage by sharing a personal anecdote – a scene that sparked my interest in tenderness in the first place.[1]

The Primary Scene

He was one of my first lovers, but I had a hard time connecting with him. Until one evening. With our clothes off, we aimlessly caressed and kissed each other. My fingertips softly stroking his skin, our bodies co-creating a rhythm we both submitted to. Each movement of his responded with one of mine, and vice versa. Until, whether it was his hand or mine, conducting the rhythm, no longer mattered. Skins and eyes talking a wordless dialogue, to the point of unison and bliss. Then his hands started to make their way to my genitals. Without words, I tried to convey to him how I did not want that. I knew it would lead to the "conventional sex" we had had before. This sex was nice, but I had never felt as connected as now. Here, while lingering in mutual caresses, I felt a closeness of a higher intensity. So I tell him: "Can we keep doing this instead? I feel so connected to you." But he isn't having it. "You give me nothing!" he busted out in anger, while adding "you're hysteric" and "frigid" to the insults. He put on his clothes and left, loudly slamming the door.

Since that encounter, I've been captivated by the paradox it presented: how could something dismissed as "nothing" by him hold such profound meaning for me? And how could the rhythmic caresses and kisses, which brought me sexual pleasure, be labelled as "frigid" by him? The very term "hysteric," intended as an insult to my desire, paradoxically became the starting point for unravelling the complexities from this pivotal moment.

Freud and the Pathologizing of the Hysteric's Tender Desire

Tenderness – or preferably *Zärtlichkeit* – is the name the so-called hysterics in Freud's early writings use to refer to their peculiar desire. Unfortunately, Strachey's translation of *Zärtlichkeit* as "affection" (and occasionally as "love," with rare instances of "tenderness") has led to a lack of exploration regarding its importance.[2] However, a thorough examination of Freud's early works reveals that figures such as Miss Lucy R and Elizabeth von R in *Studies on Hysteria* (Breuer and Freud, 1895), as well as Dora in *An Analysis of a Case of Hysteria* (Freud, 1905a), employ the term *Zärtlichkeit* or tenderness to articulate their (often unreciprocated) desires.[3] Freud himself subsequently incorporates this term into his *Three Essays on the Theory of Sexuality* (1905b) and the lesser-known essay *On the Universal Debasement in the Sphere of Love* (1912), granting it a pivotal role in his theory of sexuality.

It is in the early bond between mother and infant. Freud writes in his *Three Essays*, specifically in acts like caressing, kissing, rocking, and cleaning that the infants' sexuality first blossoms and his or her erogenous zones bud.[4] Characteristic for this infantile sexuality, Freud emphasizes, is its non-teleologic and non-goal-oriented nature. The infant is polymorphous perverse, and its' partial drives and erogenous zones exist without hierarchies, seeking pleasure independent of each other. However, Freud famously contends that this dynamic undergoes significant transformation during puberty.

> With the arrival of puberty, changes set in which are destined to give infantile sexual life its final, normal shape. […] Its activity has hitherto been derived from a number of separate instincts and erotogenic zones, which, independently of one another, have pursued a certain sort of pleasure as their sole sexual aim. Now, however, a new sexual aim appears, and all the component instincts combine to attain it, while the erotogenic zones become subordinated to the primacy of the genital zone. (1905b, p. 207)

What this primacy of the genital zones entails, Freud clarifies, is that all partial drives and erogenous zones will have to seek their pleasures in function of the *ultimate* pleasure, genital pleasure, and this through coitus. All non-genital pleasure he coins "fore-pleasure," which he assigns a preparatory role in function of the ultimate orgasmic "end pleasure" (1905b, p. 210). Freud warns us about the "dangers of fore-pleasure," which he claims arises

> if at any point in the preparatory sexual processes the fore-pleasure turns out to be too great and the element of tension too small. The motive for proceeding further with the sexual process then disappears, the whole path is cut short, and

the preparatory act in question takes the place of the normal sexual aim. (1905b, p. 211)

With the publication of his *On the Universal Debasement in Love* (1912) essay, Freud will speak of a split in the libido. The libido consists of two streams or currents – the early "tender stream" of infantile sexuality, in which erogenous zones and partial drives independently seek pleasure for the sake of pleasure, and the later "sensual stream" of puberty and adulthood, with its teleologic fore-pleasure and end-pleasure. In his 1915 edition of the *Three Essays*, Freud will introduce this language of the "tender current"[5] and "sensual current" into his *Three Essays* (1905b, p. 207). He will additionally urge how the repression of this tender current is a precondition for "healthy" "normal" adult sexuality.

With this new jargon, the "dangers of fore-pleasure" could equally be described as "the dangers of tenderness," since this is exactly at stake when Freud describes the mechanisms of hysteria:

> At every stage in the course of development through which all human beings ought by rights to pass, a certain number are held back. [...] They are mostly girls, who, to the delight of their parents, have persisted in all their childish love far beyond puberty. It is most instructive to find that it is precisely these girls who in their later marriage lack the capacity to give their husbands what is due to them; they make cold wives and remain sexually anaesthetic. [...] Girls with an exaggerated need for affection [*Zärtlichkeit*/tenderness] and an equally exaggerated horror of the real demands made by sexual life have an irresistible temptation on the one hand to realize the ideal of asexual love in their lives and on the other hand to conceal their libido behind an affection [*Zärtlichkeit*/tenderness] which they can express without self-reproaches by holding fast throughout their lives to their infantile fondness, revived at puberty, for their parents or brothers and sisters. (1905b, p. 227)

What this passage reveals, is how for Freud tender sexual acts – like caressing for the sake of caressing, or kissing for the sake of kissing – do not belong to the realm of adult sexuality. For Freud, these non-genital-oriented actions are always already "infantile," belonging to "childish love." And although Freud had previously referred to tenderness as sexual – when it occurred in the caregiving bond between mother and child – now that he is describing tenderness between two adults, he can only refer to it as "asexual love" and "sexually anaesthetic" (1905b, p. 227).

In other words, at the centre of this blatant misogynistic passage we find the anaesthetization and repression of adult sexual tenderness as a cornerstone of Freud's understanding of adult sexuality. Any desire for (sexual) tenderness becomes always already infantilized and pathologized as a symptom of hysteria. For Freud, tenderness in adulthood can only be a fixation of a kind of sexual desire that belongs to infancy.

Hence tenderness, Freud suggests implicitly, does *not* belong to the sexual life between two adults; it belongs merely to the infantile and maternal sexuality between mother and child. The "barrier against incest" – as Freud still refers to it in 1905 – thus entails not merely a letting go of the incestuous sexual objects, but equally a letting go of the non-genital-oriented desire of tender sexuality (p. 225). In adulthood, according to Freud, tenderness should become repressed and any adult desire for tenderness from an adult sexual partner becomes understood as a "regressive" and infantile symptom of hysteria.

What this critical reading of Freud's *Three Essays*, attentive to the notion of *Zärtlichkeit* or tenderness as sexual, shows us, is double. Firstly, *that Freud's theory of adult sexuality is built upon the radical split between tender and sensual sexuality*. Anticipating the discussion of Kristeva, we could refer to this tenderness and sensuality as two different economies of desire.[6] Tenderness as a non-goal-oriented economy, in which care-like acts such as caressing, kissing, rocking, and cleaning are valued as legitimately sexual and pleasurable in their own right, and a teleologic and goal-oriented economy in which all these acts become considered as fore-pleasure in function of genital end-pleasure.

Secondly, a focus on tenderness shows us how *Freud's notion of adult sexuality implies the repression of adult sexual tenderness*. I have previously referred to this as Freud's "*taboo of adult erotic tenderness*" (Koziej 2019, 2020, 2023b). This taboo entails that according to Freud, when it comes to the sexuality between adult lovers, acts according to the tender economy of desire are always already pathologic, incestuous, frigid, and hysteric.

When we return to my primary scene, we notice that my partner was not alone in his disdain of my desire for kissing for the sake of kissing and caressing for the sake of caressing, nor in his pathologizing of this desire as asexual and frigid. He had the authority of the father of psychoanalysis behind him. Next, I will turn to Kristeva, in order to take a closer look at what might be at stake in these moments of adult erotic tenderness. However, Kristeva's relationship with tenderness is not without its own problems.[7]

Kristeva on Reliance

In her 2014 article "Reliance or the Maternal Erotic," Kristeva scolds contemporary psychoanalysis (and especially attachment theorists and infant-caretaker researchers) for their avoidance of defining the infant-caretaker relationship as sexual. She urges psychoanalysis to focus on maternal eroticism and recognize it as a "different economy of the drives" (p. 82).

Kristeva's insights on reliance will turn out crucial towards a better understanding of tenderness. Before proceeding, it is important to point out that Kristeva's paper has its own problems. Firstly, she completely omits reference to the passage on infantile and maternal tenderness in Freud's *Three Essays*. Secondly – and probably related to the first point – she echoes Freud's silencing of adult erotic tenderness, by choosing to oppose reliance to the libido of sexually active adult lovers.[8] In doing so, she claims that this specific economy of the libido merely belongs to the sexuality of the infantile and the maternal – an argument she will echo in a later paper *Prelude to an Ethics of the Feminine* (2019).[9] This is a lost opportunity that widens the split between tenderness and sexuality even more and feeds into the taboo on adult erotic tenderness.

What we take from Kristeva, however, is a clue as to what might be at stake in adult sexual tenderness. Her analysis portrays reliance as a specific economy of the libido, with a libidinal logic of its own (p. 71). She describes reliance as a multiplicity, a vacillation between two states: (a) First "a state of emergency," or "abject state."[10] In such an abject state, there is "not yet either a subject or an object […] but only abjects" (p. 76). This first stage which defies rationality, she explains as some kind of "falling apart of the Self" (p. 73), and a "returning to a pre-Self before the mirror stage" (p. 80). For Kristeva this entails a return to a pre-discursive, pre-signifying state of the *Khora* or the semiotic.[11] This state would be unbearable and leading to insanity, was it not followed up by a *second state*. (b) This second state consists in a re-linking, a re-attaching and re-connecting of this fallen-apart-Self, through careful actions of caretaking:

> The maternal transforms the abjects (which the death drive has re-jected into the not-yet space of mother-child) into objects of care, into survival, and into life. Always inside and outside, self and other, neither self nor other, an intervening space, maternal eroticism separates and rejoins [*relie*]: hiatus and junction. (p. 76)

From this account, we gather that reliance/tenderness happens in the *movement between* these two states, a falling apart of a coherent self, followed by a mending of the self. And it is through this oscillation that the self enters into a significantly close bond or relation with another.

What we gather from Kristeva is the insight that the *abject* is the vehicle through which tenderness moves. Tenderness moves through that which *defies* the integrity and stability of a perfectly rational, integrated, independent and bounded self. In other words, *what's at stake in adult sexual tenderness, is nothing less than the cornerstone of modern subjectivity: the integrity and stability of rational, integrated, independent, and bounded selfhood – the sovereign subject.* This might explain why both Freud and Kristeva limit and *other* tender sexuality to the mother and the child, and why Freud "had" to pathologize an adult desire for tender sexuality as asexual, frigid, and hysteric.

However, an idiosyncratic reading of Kristeva's appreciation of tender erotics offers us the insight that what characterizes the "hysteric's" tender desire, is specifically this significantly close bond, which moves through abjection. In other words, what might be "dangerous" about the so called "hysterics" is that they are not faced by this abjection – outside of the confines of motherhood and infancy. On the contrary, they find pleasure in this vacillation between self-disintegration and re-linking, with and through an (adult) other.

Queer theorist Leo Bersani has also focused on the disintegrating dimension of sexuality. However, much like Kristeva, his relationship to tenderness is not without its own problems. And yet, his appreciation of what he refers to as the "self-shattering potential of sexuality" offers a pathway towards deeper comprehension of the implications inherent in instances of adult erotic tenderness.

Bersani on the Shattering of Proud Subjectivity

Emancipating non-normative sexuality has been the main goal of queer theory. And yet, despite their so-called "aberrant," "abnormal" and "pathological" sexuality, the hysteric has remained a blind spot in queer theory. This is surprising, given queer studies' investment in "exploring the ways in which non-normative sexualities and desires have been marginalized and pathologized within culture" and their attempts "to disrupt these oppressive structures through critical inquiry critiquing normative sexuality and emancipating abnormal sexuality" (de Lauretis, 1987).

The binary split between tender and sensual sexuality upon which Freud's normative theory of sexuality is built, forms another blind spot for queer theory – both blind spots are probably directly related. This is equally surprising, given queer studies' investment in "challenging and deconstructing normative understandings of sexuality […], and examining the ways in which these categories are constructed, regulated, and policed within society, [in order] to disrupt the binary thinking that underpins conventional understandings of sexuality and desire." (Sedgwick, 1990). However, an idiosyncratic reading of Freud's *Three Essays* unearths how the split between tenderness and sensuality is one of the foundations of (Freud's) hegemonic heteronormative and phallic sexuality.

In a similar vein, tender sexuality remains a blind spot for queer theory. Tenderness' radical potential to re-think normative (read sensual) sexuality, remains unexplored. On the contrary, when it comes to queer theory, tenderness has quite a bad reputation.[12]

Queer theorist Leo Bersani's body of work introduces a re-reading of Freud's *Three Essays* as a generative tool for queer theory. In his article "Is the Rectum a Grave?" (1987), he answers the eponymous question affirmatively. The rectum but also the mouth and the vagina, all penetrable orifices, have the potential to be graves in which "proud subjectivity is buried" (p. 222). In "strong physical orgasms," we experience a "powerlessness" and "loss of control" that should be valued as a "radical disintegration" of the self, Bersani explains (p. 217). He refers to this as the "self-shattering" capacity of sexuality, and for him this experience is sexuality's queer potential to rethink dominant phallocentric and heteronormative notions of both subjectivity and sexuality.

Instead of embracing, celebrating, and valuing the self-shattering nature of sexuality, Bersani argues, hegemonic heteronormative culture introduces all kinds of mechanisms to save the sacrosanct self from falling apart (p. 222). According to him, the "pastoral impulse" – an (implicit or explicit) agreement of "what sex should be: a wholesome sexuality, a natural and healthy conjunction between sex, tenderness and love" – is one of these mechanisms (pp. 215, 221). This idealization,

Bersani claims, is built on "chimerically nonviolent ideals of tenderness and nurturing," and denies sexualities' self-erasing side.

Hence, when it comes to tender sexuality, Bersani is ruthless. He can only identify this "chimera" as perpetuating self-hyperbolic and idealized notions of both sexuality and tenderness, which deny the queer self-erasing or self-shattering side of sexuality. Put differently, according to Bersani, tender sexuality perpetuates wholesome sex and wholesome subjects.

But when we bring our earlier findings on tenderness to bare on Bersani's claims, two problematic assumptions come to light in Bersani's argumentation. Firstly, Bersani presumes that only penetrative and orgasmic sex can result into a shattering of proud self-hyperbolic subjectivity. Secondly, he can only understand this radical disintegration or self-shattering as anti-loving and anti-tender. These presumptions result in two blindspots, which Kristeva's work on reliance helps us indicate: self-shattering tender sexuality, as well as the tender dimensions of self-disintegration.

Bersani's analysis fails to see that his own concept of the pastoral impulse – which critiques the wish to unite the seemingly distinct phenomena of sex and tenderness – is already at the "other side" of the split between tenderness and sex. Bersani misses curiosity regarding the genesis of this split between tenderness and sexuality. This is particularly noteworthy since Freud's *Three Essays* play a major role in Bersani's argumentation.

Bersani's sexual framework conforms to the radical split between tenderness and sensuality. He conforms to Freud's monopoly of goal-oriented sexual pleasure, in which the tender stream is already repressed and sexuality becomes equated with sensuality. Put differently, instead of problematizing the dichotomous split between tenderness and sensuality, at the heart of Freud's theory of adult sexuality, Bersani *perpetuates* this dichotomy. Like Freud, Bersani would only be able to understand the search for adult erotic tenderness as something negative. For Freud it was hysteric or frigid, where for Bersani it is always already parochial and always in function of a self-hyperbolic subject, because based on the allegedly nonviolent ideals of nurture, love, and tenderness. In doing so, Bersani perpetuates the taboo against adult sexual tenderness.

However, when we follow the hysteric's insistence that tenderness *is* sexual, and when we follow Kristeva's insight that tenderness results in a kind of self-disintegration which is not necessarily anti-loving, anti-nurturing, nor anti-tender, we could conclude that tender sexuality too, harbours a radically queer potential.

The Self-Shattering of Adult Erotic Tenderness

In his book *Intimacies* (2008) co-written with Adam Philips, Bersani seems to move towards such a redeemed notion of adult sexual tenderness as self-shattering (Berlant, 2009).[13] However, it should be pointed out that the word "tenderness" is nowhere to be seen. Despite this fact, Bersani and Philips suggest how we need a new vocabulary and new story about intimacy, a "radical redescription of love" (p.

92). Their answer to this call is "impersonal narcissism," which entails a radical "undoing of the opposition between the active lover and the passive loved one, by instituting a kind of reciprocal self-recognition in which the very opposition between sameness and difference becomes irrelevant as a structuring category of being" (pp. 85–86).

What characterizes this impersonal narcissism is simultaneously its radical potential: a self-shattering of the ego, the shattering of the modern "sacrosanct value of selfhood" (p. 96). The desire which characterizes this impersonal narcissism is the desire of the ego for such a self-shattering (p. 92). In this account, masochism – "the capacity to bear, the capacity to desire the ultimately over-whelming intensities of feeling that we are subject to" – is no longer seen as a pathology, but instead "a developmental achievement" (p. 94).

After our de-tour through Kristeva, we can now add the hysteric to this list of figures whose desire is characterized by a shattering of the ego and subversively claim hysteria as a "developmental achievement."

"Now more than ever [...] psychoanalysis has become something [...] to be going on from. It has become the discipline of useful errors, of instructive (and destructive) mistakes, of radical roads not taken" (p. vii): with these words Bersani opens *Intimacies*. In a similar vein, I have tried to argue for tenderness or *Zärtlichkeit* as such a "radical road not taken." Simultaneously, I aim to point at the hysteric, as an under-explored (queer) figure (*avant la letter*), who might still have much to teach us about the underlying modern ideologies behind hegemonic notions of both sexuality and subjectivity.

Or how an insult during a not-so-tender night, paved the way towards a deep-dive into the queer potential of tender sexuality and a potential answer to the questions at the heart of this primary scene. What was at stake in my desire for caressing for the sake of caressing or kissing for the sake of kissing, was my lovers' proud subjectivity, his modern notion of individualism. Much like Freud – as Whitebook argues in *Freud, An Intellectual Biography* (2017) – this analysis suggests that both men feared the disintegration of their sacrosanct selfhood.

What both men had a hard time valuing – unlike the so-called "hysterics" – was the peculiar intersubjectivity that could have been gained from such a disintegration. In line with a "hysterical" reinterpretation of Kristeva's notion of reliance, the tender encounter does not culminate in self-annihilation but rather oscillates towards a re-establishment of the self. However, this is not the self of modern and proud subjectivity. This is a significantly altered self, altered through abjection as well as through the deep bond and connection it is able to foster.

Notes

1 In her book *Sexuality, Disability and Aging* (2019) Gallop uses personal and sexual anecdotes of the struggles in her sex life as a "catalyst and focus for an extended critical and theoretical inquiry" (p. 26). Like Gallop, I frame my text as an attempt to "read" this personal anecdote for the theoretical insights it affords. Similar to Gallop, my text will combine psychoanalytic, feminist, and queer theory.

2 For more on the inconsistent translation of *Zärtlichkeit* by Strachey in the *Standard Edition*, see Koziej (2019) and Koziej (2020).
3 For a close-reading and tracing of *Zärtlichkeit* throughout *Studies on Hysteria, An Analysis of a Case of Hysteria*, and *Three Essays* see Koziej (2020). For a more in-depth analysis of tenderness in *Dora*, see also Koziej (2023a).
4 For a more in depth analysis of tenderness in Freud's *Three Essays* see Koziej (2019) and Koziej (2020).
5 Again, Strachey translates *Zärtlichkeit* here into "affection," referring to this first and earliest current as the "affectionate current" (1905b, p. 207).
6 More on this in the next section.
7 This is a summary of an argument I previously developed in my 2019 paper (Koziej, 2019).
8 "Psychoanalysis assigns sexuality exclusively to the lover and the unbearable destiny of object relations to the maternal" (p. 62). And more obviously: "But while the lover's libido is dominated by the satisfaction of drives, maternal eroticism deploys (or "sprouts" [*fait tendre*]) its libidinal force as tender-ness. Beyond abjection and separation, tenderness is the basic affect of reliance" (p. 75).
9 Here Kristeva repeats: "But while the *female lover's libido* is dominated by the satisfaction of drives, *maternal eroticism* deploys its libidinal thrust as tenderness; beyond *expulsion, abjection*, and *separation*, tenderness is the basic affect of *reliance*" (Kristeva, 2019).
10 I call *ab-jection*: the inevitable process of fascination-repulsion, where there is not yet either a subject or an object, or even *objeux* (Francis Ponge here anticipates Winnicott), but only "abjects" (Kristeva 1980). The child "loses" me ("kills" me) in order to leave me: Orestes before Oedipus. From my perspective, in order to separate from the child and re-become an "I," I leave him by "abjecting" him. Simultaneously, I abject the Thing into which we were fused, the biopsychical continuum I had become (2014, p. 76).
11 "This biopsychical zone that surrounds maternal reliance defies rationality. It haunts philosophy and literature. Plato alludes to it in the *Timaeus* when he apologizes for using "a kind of bastard reasoning" (p. 52). *Khora*, as he calls it, is a space before space, a nurturer-and-devourer at once, prior to the One, the Father, the word, and even the syllable. It is a modality of *sense* prior to *signification*, what I call 'the semiotic'" (pp. 72–73).
12 For a preliminary list of queer theorists engaging with tenderness, see Koziej (2023b). In that paper, I share some of my thoughts on Bersani's problematic relationship towards tenderness.
13 In *Neither Monstrous nor Pastoral, but Scary and Sweet* (2009), queer and affect scholar Lauren Berlant describes *Intimacies* as a "reparative book," in the sense that after so many years of equating sex and sexuality with loss, from shattering to shame and melancholia, Bersani and Phillips try to imagine *something* in sex (p. 264). Sexuality undoes the subject, but this is not all that negative as it opens the subject up to a radically new relationality and attachment, a "potential extension of the ego into the other not as an annihilative threat to sovereignty but as the ego's dissemination" (p. 268). This sexuality, she stresses, occurs through a kind of love, which they refer to as "impersonal narcissism" because the self the subject sees reflected in the other is not the unique personality vital to modern notions of individualism" (p. 268).

Bibliography

Berlant, L. (2009), Neither Monstrous nor Pastoral, but Scary and Sweet. *Women & Performance: a journal of feminist theory* 19(2): 261–273.

Bersani, L. (1987), Is the Rectum a Grave? *October*, 43: 197–222.
Bersani, L. & Philips, A. (2008), *Intimacies*. Chicago, IL: The University of Chicago Press.
de Lauretis, T. (1987), *Technologies of Gender: Essays on Theory, Film, and Fiction*. Bloomington, IN: Indiana University Press.
Freud, S. & Breuer, J. (1895), Studies on Hysteria. *Standard Edition*, 2: 3–124. London: Hogarth Press, 1955.
Freud, S. (1905a), Fragment of an Analysis of a Case of Hysteria. *Standard Edition*, 7: 125–248. London: Hogarth Press, 1953.
Freud, S. (1905b), Three Essays on the Theory of Sexuality. *Standard Edition*, 7: 125–248. London: Hogarth Press, 1953.
Freud, S. (1912), On the Universal Tendency to Debasement in the Sphere of Love. *Standard Edition*, 11: 177–190. London: Hogarth Press, 1957.
Gallop, J. (2019), *Sexuality, Disability, and Aging: Queer Temporalities of the Phallus*. Durham, NC: Duke University Press.
Koziej, S. (2019), Towards a Tender Sexuality. From Freud's implicit Taboo on Adult Erotic Tenderness, to the Unexplored Tender Critical Potential of Mitchell and Perel's Clinical Practice. *Psychoanalytic Psychology*, 36(4): 342–450.
Koziej, S. (2020), *Tender Rhythms: Re-thinking Sexuality, Selfhood and Sociality through the Hysteric's Desire for Tenderness*. [unpublished doctoral dissertation]. Emory University.
Koziej, S. (2023a), "De (on)mogelijkheid van volwassen tederheid. #MeToo en een hedendaags geval van volwassen Confusion of Tongues". In: *Het Kinderlijk Trauma*. Franckx C. & Hebbrecht M. (eds.). Antwerp: Gompes & Svacina.
Koziej, S. (2023b), Carving out a Sonorous Space for Erotic Tenderness: A Deleuzo-Guattarian Reading of Björk's Becoming-Tender as Queer. *Deleuze and Guattari Studies* 17(3): 424–448.
Kristeva, J. (2014), Reliance, or Maternal Eroticism. *Journal of the American Psychoanalytic Association*, 62(1): 69–85.
Kristeva, J. (2019, July), *Prelude to an Ethics of the Feminine*. [Key-note address]. International Psychoanalytic Association, The Feminine. London, UK. http://www.kristeva.fr/prelude-to-an-ethics-of-the-feminine.html.
Sedgwick, E. (1990), *Epistemology of the Closet*. Berkeley, CA: University of California Press.
Whitebook, J. (2017), *Freud. An Intellectual Biography*. Cambridge: Cambridge University Press.

Chapter 14

The Spielreinian Death Drive and Negative Affect Regulation Processes

Arvin Bains

In the not-so-distant past, psychoanalysis has moved away from placing exclusive importance on sexuality in the service of individual pleasure to understanding the psyche through subject-subject interactions. Affective regulatory processes offer central links to these subject-subject relationships. Affect comprises the somatic, representational, perceptual, and feeling states of the psyche. Contemporary scholarship has defined affect regulation as the process of identifying and monitoring the experience and expression of affect, much of which occurs in the implicit, unconscious mind. This process is inherently relational; for example, a subject affectively thinks about others, manifesting empathy. The word "empathy" is "derived from the German *Einfühlung,* the term 'empathy' refers to the ego's capacity to transiently identify with someone else in order to grasp his or her subjective experience" (Akhtar, 2009). During the early phase of his theory's development, Freud suggested that the qualities of empathy were instrumental in psychoanalysts' work with patients (Freud, 1912).

More than a hundred years ago when Freud was simultaneously developing his theory, Sabina Spielrein explored the weakness in Freud's work, convincingly arguing for the death drive as the central mechanism of the mind. In doing so, she pushed the envelope of Freudian theorizing at the time and laid the groundwork for modern affect regulation theory. As Freud developed his theory, Spielrein, also working within the classical psychoanalytic framework, extended the meaning of empathy through the lens of the death drive to include affect, which meant "mentalizing" to feel another's emotions and affective states. Through the clinical case synopses of patients suffering from dementia praecox, hysteria, discussions of dreams, and exploration of dynamic unconscious experiences of artists and neurotics, Spielrein presents a remarkable anticipation of contemporary psychoanalysis. Her work comprehensively explores the patients' conditions and examines various thoughts on mythology. Accordingly, one can engage with Spielrein's complex paper in multiple ways, including understanding the patients' conditions and exploring thoughts on mythology. My concentration is restricted with this chapter being devoted to the processes of the Spielreinian death drive as illuminated in her paper, "Destruction as the Cause of Coming into Being" (Spielrein, 1994). I draw from Spielrein's clinical documentation, particularly an exemplary vignette from her analysis of a young patient, to support my conceptual understanding of the Spielreinian death drive processes within current research on affect regulation processes.

Spielrein's Theory: A Forerunner to Contemporary Affective Regulatory Processes

Critiquing Freud's teleological approach to pleasure and repression of the sexual instinct, Spielrein argues that Freud's conceptualization lacks an investigation into the motivations behind pleasure. According to Freud, pleasure is an innate force of the human psyche necessitating a constant energy release in affective forms. In Freud's early stage of his theory, pleasure is the primary element that governs our psychological functioning with external factors potentially disrupting the inner psyche, leading to intense feelings that the individual must discharge. Severe negative affect experiences are repressed (Laplanche and Pontalis, 1973). Freud believed that drives and affects interfere with our perception of reality, arguing that the sensory perception of the external world is considered objective. Freudian psychoanalysis aims to remove these distortions that drives cause and preserve mental representation. However, Freud's tension reduction model of the mind (Laplanche and Pontalis, 1973) overlooks the importance of interpersonal relationships in shaping our psychological development.

Spielrein challenges the Freudian instinct impulse (affect derivative) model centered on extraction, discharge, and the recovery of the pristine core. In examining the origins of subjective experiences with negative affect as central to them, she begins to view affect in qualitative rather than quantitative ways. Spielrein underscores the significance of intersubjectivity or the "We-psyche" concept which is fundamental and relates to the other in having the mind-to-mind linkage and sexuality as a manifestation of the species dimension. However, in Freud's libido conceptualization, it is the following:

> The theory that sexual urges provide a motivation for psychic functioning from earliest infancy, and that the focus of sexual attention shifts from one erogenous zone to another during the course of development – from the oral to the anal and to the genital. The theory assumes that the sources of the sexual instincts are derived from somatic processes, and these are connected with certain aims or wishes that arouse sensual pleasure associated with fantasies about an object.
> (Tyson and Tyson, 1990)

Conversely Spielrein positions sexuality (pleasure) as a motivating instinct that does not have a superior position. Spielrein begins her paper with a synopsis of a child patient, highlighting the function of "toned-feeling" as a form of affect. She posits that "everything that moves us aims to be felt as important and understood," with past experience embedded in the present. Developmental history is implicit as the patient can invoke memories of her relationship with her mother; therefore, this patient's experience takes a developmental trajectory.

While Spielrein supports Freud's idea of past experiences in present psychological states, she compellingly introduces the concept of subject-subject interactive processes in psychoanalysis.

> A young girl read stories of witches with great joy; as a child, she often played at being a witch; analysis shows that the witch in the girl's fantasies represents the mother with whom the girl identifies. For the girl, the stories are pleasurably tinged only in so far as the mother's life is pleasurable for her. The girl may even choose to emulate her mother's life. The stories are mere allegories on which the feeling-tone is displaced; they are a substitute for the "desired," the life story lived by the mother. The witch stories would not be pleasurable for the girl without the experience of the mother. In this sense, "all passing things" are only allegories, perhaps of the unknown primal experiences, that seek analogues in the present. Thus, we experience nothing in the present since we project a feeling-tone onto a current Image. (Spielrein, 1994, p. 157)

Spielrein introduces the idea of internal working models, exemplified in the above-mentioned account, revealing striking correlations between the internal working models and her concept of the death drive, marking a significant milestone in psychoanalytic theory. Fonagy and his colleagues (2002, p. 416) note the following:

> Thus a key developmental attainment of the internal working model is the creation of a processing system for the self (and significant others) in terms of a set of stable and generalized intentional attributes, such as desires, emotions, intentions, and beliefs inferred from recurring invariant patterns in the history of previous interactions.

Notably, the Spielreinian unconscious constitutes the home for self-sacrifice where the maternal figure teaches the developing child how to think and feel what others are thinking and feeling. This impartation to the developing subject is precisely because mother herself learned through experience what caring implies.

The Dutch phrase for caring is "*zorgen*," which appears to convey an increased magnitude of the more severe and concerning aspects of caring. The expression "*kinderzorg*" refers to childcare, and a "*zorgenkind*" denotes a child who requires special care and causes significant perturbation (van Manen, p. 58, 1990). While *zorgenkind* does not necessarily contain a negative affect, the term may signify anxiety as a central negative affective experience. For example, a mother participating in the infant-mother dyad offers her participation in ways that can lead to trepidations, disruptions, and strains. Motherhood extends beyond being a mere responsibility embodying a journey of self-sacrifice that demands a mother's active participation in her infant's survival. It is a beautiful yet dynamic "dying" process that requires immense dedication and commitment in the form of love. This appears to be a natural, biological result of mothering. Moreover, one may contend within modern psychoanalysis, as Spielrein's significant work corpus demonstrates, that motherhood involves an inherent act of self-sacrifice as it necessitates active engagement within love to ensure the infant's survival. In Spielrein's perspective, altruism, or the selfless act of helping others, is believed to be influenced by the collective unconscious mind, a shared pool of memories, beliefs, and experiences beyond conscious awareness. Notably, crucial situations can activate the death drive and affect regulation processes, highlighting their interconnectedness.

The mother-child relationship represents a unique and special bond that requires a particular type of engagement, often referred to as mirroring (Fonagy et al., 2002). A child actively seeks out their mother's attention and interacts with her, demonstrating a natural propensity towards engagement. According to mirroring theory, the process is instinctive and does not require formal training for the mother to become a mirror for her child. Through largely unconscious processes, a mother can understand and relate to her child's emotional states, attuning herself to their inner needs and helping the child to identify, label, and regulate their feelings, thereby aiding in regulating their affect. By communicating to her child that she is receptive and empathetic to her child's mental state, a mother fosters an environment in which the child can perceive their own mind reflected in hers through facial expressions, how she holds them, and how she cradles them.

A maternal figure repeatedly provides her child with affect regulation through a process of monotonous engagement that happens daily. Repeated interactions are essential to help the child learn how to regulate their feelings and become more adaptive to their social environment. One of the main processes of mirroring is providing room for negative emotions; it focuses on regulating negative affect rather than eliminating negative affective experiences. This, I think, suggests that love is a substrate within affect regulation processes. The implicit affect exchanges are completely present at birth, and the memory patterns are formed through repetition (Fonagy et al., 2002).

Emphasizing how past experiences guide a patient's current response to a situation, Spielrein notes that one must understand any meaning assigned to the present from "previously feeling toned" material. This perspective is illustrated by a young patient who engaged in stories (in the example) for her mother. As mentioned earlier, Spielrein notes: "For the girl, the stories are pleasurably tinged only in so far as the mother's life is pleasurable for her" (Spielrein, 1994, p. 157). The narrative captures the idea of self-sacrifice and the experience of "pain in joy." Spielrein ponders, "Do the basic drives of preservation (self and species) possesses a similar value for the whole of psychic life and the ego viz., pleasure and displeasure?" (Spielrein, 1994, pp. 159–160). She explores the interplay between the primary (id) and the secondary (ego) processes suggesting that the patient's interaction with the stories is not about her. Notably, the Freudian sense of pleasure (Freud, 1911) does not have a superordinate status in Spielrein's understanding of this patient. Spielrein later reflects in the paper: "The purely personal can never be understood by others" (Spielrein, 1994, p. 164). To be "understood" transcends the function of the rational, logical mind; the subject's deep consciousness is the key.

Within the Spielreinian framework, the idea of feeling understood overlaps with the current concept of mentalization which acknowledges that it is not reasonably possible to know exactly what others think and feel. However, one can seek clarification on what others have in their minds. This is mentalization. Individuals engage in "emotional dwelling," and are attuned to how others think and feel and reflect on their own feelings (Atwood and Stolorow, 2019). For example, forgiveness can be a complex process that involves perspective taking and appreciating others' affective experiences. It is considered as one of the significant themes of "good mentalization" (Bateman and Fonagy, 2006). Forgiveness requires one to accept and move past the wrongdoings of others while still acknowledging the emotional and mental state of the person who caused the pain. This mentalization process is crucial to achieving forgiveness because it guides in tolerating affect, particularly enduring negative affect. Mentalization also entails the increasing ability to appreciate the differences in how human minds function, such as the distinction between 2-year-olds and 5-year-olds. The mentalizing process is core to identifying, labeling, and monitoring the experience and expression of feelings. The concept of mentalization closely aligns with Spielrein's theory of the stages of the death drive.

Spielreinian "Dying" and Implications for Negative Affect Regulation Processes

Two distinct stages within Spielreinian theory illustrate the Spielreinian death drive processes. Initially, the activation of ego particles in the first stage is due to emotional information through the senses drawing dynamic information from the depth of the psyche, the We. The We-psyche is an unconscious, non-verbal, symbolic procedure. In this phase, the ego participates in individual comprehension of others, limited to the reactions of pleasure and displeasure. Subsequently, in the second stage, the now "feeling-tones" ego particle is assimilated and dissolved in the We-psyche seeking an analog to the person or situation that initially activated the ego particle. This blending results in de-differentiation which occurs when the ego particle combines with similar (not identical) aspects of the species' psyche. This novel mental state, the ego particle, now enriched with the relevant characteristics of the collective psyche (ancestral and parental), "re-emerges." This new particle seeks the other through love, art, or empathy by being a responsive listener to the other. The destruction of the ego particle is a must because: "Where love reigns, the ego, the ominous despot, dies" (Spielrein, 1994, p. 174).

The transformed ego particle, now bearing more negative feelings, avails itself to the other for "When one is in love, the blending of the ego in the beloved is the strongest affirmation of self, a new ego existence in the person of the beloved" (Spielrein, 1994, p. 174). This completes the death drive process. This process is more than empathic, representing a universal comprehension of the other. It seeks a "relational home," and Spielrein notes the following:

> Each image searches for equivalent, non-identical yet similar, material with which it can be blended and transformed. This similar material produces an understanding based on analogous image contents through which the other person makes sense of our image. Comprehension evokes a sympathetic feeling that means nothing to others. When understood, no further words need to be uttered. (Spielrein, 1994, p. 164)

In this context, comprehension is the sensory registration of perception of the objective external world. For Spielrein comprehension appears to be representational and therefore devoid of affect with the deep unconscious, the dynamic We-psyche, governing the conscious mind. Thus, understanding is experienced when the unconscious interacts with the conscious, comprising a complex, reflective process in which affect is fundamental.

Contemporary studies in affect regulation within neurobiology also follow the interaction between the unconscious and the conscious (Hill, 2015; Wallin, 2007). In the realm of emotional regulation analysis, it is discernible that an individual's first response to a situation can trigger a hyper or hypo-aroused state in the body. The limbic system, which is responsible for governing emotions, automatically analyzes the body's condition and initially interprets it at a subcortical level (Wallin, 2007), similar to the Spielreinian We-psyche. Subsequently, the left brain, which is responsible for our ego self, consciously processes the interpretation for intentional secondary processing at the cortical level. This interpretation is subsequently consolidated again by the right brain (Hill, 2015), which can be seen as a We-psyche process. Thus, a simultaneous process occurs in which the ego is formed through a complex interplay with the We.

Furthermore, drawing from Spielrein's hypothesis, it is conceivable to assert that the destruction of ego particles and the creation of new ones occur concurrently. At any moment, the ego self reflects exactly the dynamic mental states of the We-psyche in play at the time:

> Close to our desire to maintain our personal condition, there lies a desire for transformation. A personal image-content, derived from material from times past, blends with similar content and comes into being as a typically collective wish at the expense of the individual. One seeks likeness (parents or ancestors) with which an ego particle can blend because merging in similars is not rapidly destructive but proceeds unnoticed. And what does this merger signify for the ego-particle? Is it not death? (Spielrein, 1994, p. 163)

From early development, individuals engage in a process of self-reproduction by projecting their mental states onto others, such as their mothers. Implicit processes encoded through repetition from birth onward have a significant impact on these projections.

The relationship between the We-psyche and the ego psyche is central to the death drive, contributing significantly to the "understanding" of affect regulation and the process of mentalizing. In Spielreinian theory, patients lack proper awareness due to isolated experiences within the We-psyche rather than distorted perceptions due to bodily instincts. The Spielreinian death drive is not accomplished by releasing accurate, sense-based representation (within ego) from distorting dynamic forces but rather by placing "I-summation" in the increasingly essential Spielreinian We. For Freud, Spielrein notes: "the unconscious is timeless since it consists only of wishes that it exhibits for fulfillment in the present" (Spielrein, 1994, pp. 184–185). Conversely, from Spielrein's view, experience is timeless because, in their psyche, patients have not been able to integrate their disparate experiences. In terms of attachment, they live in a sequence of secluded presents in which one experience replaces another rather than being combined with it (Hill, 2015). According to Freud, within the realm of sexual instinct, the expression of impulses substitutes the act of remembering (Laplanche and Pontalis, 1973).

From Spielrein's viewpoint and based on current research, acting out and remembering can both be considered forms of memory. In acting out, mental and physical aspects are indistinct within the collective We. Conversely, remembering allows for a distinction between mental and physical realms permitting a patient to act mentally with or without concurrent physical action (e.g., the young patient reading stories and not physically playing a witch). In Spielrein's theory, patients may perceive their thoughts as reality and disregard external reality because they conflate their internal thoughts and feelings with outer reality, a phenomenon that occurs in the collective We-psyche. For the patient, the evidence is self-explanatory and requires no further explanation as they are unaware of their interpretive role. Thus, a thought or perception carries instant and absolute belief. In Freud's terms, experience is the criterion for reality, and the patient is oblivious to their environment (Freud, 1911). However, from Spielrein's perspective, the subject knows they are interacting with the other. The external object is not experienced as separate or independent from the patient. This dynamic refers to psychic equivalence, which is central to current mentalization and dissociation studies (Fonagy et al., 2002; Hill, 2015).

Dissociation can be understood through the example of an anesthetized patient who does not feel pain due to the lack of connection between their primary and secondary processes, as described in Spielrein's framework. However, patients at the We-psyche level are aware of what is happening to them. Similarly, another patient does not feel pain while anesthetized but can perceive their body from the outside. Adopting a Spielreinian perspective, within affect regulation theory, dissociation occurs as a hyper or hypo state when the ego psyche struggles to link with the Spielreinian We. Hyper-aroused states, such as flashbacks, lead to terror and panic and are often experienced by patients with hysteria. Derealization and other hypo states cause a reduction in the level of consciousness, leading to a state of lowered awareness and detachment from one's surroundings. During dissociation, a patient may experience a sudden blankness, causing their thinking to slow down significantly. Their thought processes become disrupted, impairing clarity and memory recall. This mental fog can be disorienting and frustrating, often leading to feelings of confusion and disconnection from one's surroundings. When various self-states or ego particles struggle to connect within the We-psyche, it can lead to dissociation as seen from the Spielreinian theoretical perspective manifesting as hyper or hypo states. Nevertheless, in these negative states, a patient relates with others, even though they are consciously unaware of their relatedness (Wallin, 2007).

Concluding Remarks

Freud's commitment to the theory of infantile narcissism limited his ability to acknowledge Spielrein's theory. Freud did not assign primacy to nurturance, which is a two-person psychology. Freud viewed sexuality as the mind's central psychic force, with seeking pleasure and wish fulfillment as critical aspects of human functioning (Laplanche and Pontalis, 1973). Within this framework, instinct drives are considered motivational energy that must be discharged for pleasurable feelings. However, this model of energy cannot explain how affects such as anxiety can be defined in terms of the quantity discharged, portraying the Freudian self as a psychic energy reservoir.

In contrast, it is not what the death drive does (as a source) but what it is that warrants attention (Reshe, 2023). The term "dying" more appropriately seems to highlight the intricate process that is the death drive. Spielrein's patient discussed at the beginning of this paper appears to be experiencing a successful "dying" via psychological transformation, facilitating mentalizing and negative affect regulation. Here the patient experiences deep empathy and the other feels "understood." Because of dissociation, other patients continue to make an effort to survive; they relate and are not narcissistically bodily-focused. In essence, patients do not lose their relational nature toward the external environment during dysregulation. It is implicit in Spielrein's work that regulated and dysregulated patients do not seek the discharge of affect as their primary motive. Thus, the Spielreinian death drive creates a central space for subject-subject interaction rather than focusing on achieving libidinal satisfaction. This perspective, alongside contemporary research on negative affect regulation, can offer profound insights into human attachment and love by examining Spielrein's death drive theory.

Focusing on the subjective and relational nature of the human mind reveals the implicit cognitive aspect of affect, as observed in Spielrein's patients. Spielrein performed intensive research at the intersection of psychoanalysis, psychology, and biology postulating the following:

> I have come to the conclusion that the chief characteristic of an individual is that he is "dividual." The closer we approach our conscious thoughts, the more differentiated our images; the deeper we penetrate the unconscious, the more universal and typical the images. The depth of our psyche knows no "I," but only its summation, the "We." (Spielrein, 1994, p. 160)

In the evolving landscape of psychoanalytic theory, the leap from Freud's focus on sexuality to Spielrein's conceptualization of the death drive and affect regulation marks a pivotal shift. While Spielrein's work has garnered growing attention over the past few years, the omission of her work in affect regulation theory remains perplexing. Future research could consider the interdisciplinary understanding of Spielrein's theory, particularly at the intersection of philosophy, neurobiology, and psychoanalysis.

References

Akhtar, S. (2009). *Comprehensive dictionary of psychoanalysis*. London: Karnak.

Atwood, G., and Stolorow, A. (2019). *The power of phenomenology: Psychoanalytic and philosophical perspectives*. New York: Routledge.

Bateman, A., and Fonagy, P. (2006). *Mentalization-based treatment of borderline personality disorder*. Oxford University Press.

Fonagy, P., Gergely, G., Jurist, E. J., and Target, M.I. (2002). *Affect regulation, mentalization, and the development of the self.* New York: Other Press.

Freud, S. (1911). *Formulations on the two principles of mental functioning*. Standard Edition, 12. The Hogarth Press.

Freud, S. (1912). *Recommendations to physicians practicing psycho-analysis*. Standard Edition, 12. The Hogarth Press.

Hill, D. (2015). *Affect regulation theory: a clinical model*. New York: W. W. Norton and Company.

Laplanche, J., and Pontalis, J. B. (1973). *The language of psycho-analysis* (Trans. Donald Nicholson-Smith). New York: W. W. Norton and Company.

Reshe, J. (2023). Personal communication with the author, March 19.

Spielrein, S. (1994). Destruction as the cause of coming into being. *Journal of analytic psychology* 39, pp. 155–186.

Tyson, P., and Tyson, R. (1990). *Psychoanalytic developmental theory.* New Haven: Yale University Press.

van Manen, M. (1990). *Researching lived experience: Human science for an action sensitive pedagogy*. Ontario. State University of New York Press.

Wallin, D. (2007). *Attachment in psychotherapy.* New York: The Guilford Press.

Chapter 15

Spielrein's Negative Psychoanalysis
Mother Death Calling

Julie Reshe

Getting to Know Sabina Spielrein

The name of Sabina Spielrein has been forgotten, and erased from memory. She suffered brutal, repeated murders. Alongside her two daughters, Spielrein fell victim to Nazi gunfire in 'Snake Ravine' near Rostov-on-Don. Even before her tragic end, her name had begun to fade. Those who once hailed her as their teacher started to forget her.

Sabina Spielrein was of Jewish origin, born in 1885 in Rostov-on-Don. She is referred to as a Russian-Jewish-Soviet psychoanalyst. Although, taking into account that, until 1887, Rostov-on-Don was part of the Ekaterinoslav Governorate, historically linked with Ukraine, she could be regarded as a Ukrainian-Jewish-Soviet psychoanalyst.

Spielrein's ideas transcend the boundaries of psychoanalysis, weaving through the crossroads of psychiatry, philosophy, biology, and mythology. Her intellectual legacy encompasses some of the most fundamental concepts in psychoanalysis. Yet, as time went on, many of her ideas became exclusively associated with the names of Freud and Jung. She introduced the idea of collective unconscious structures within the psyche, which Jung later incorporated into his concept of the collective unconscious. Most notably, Spielrein formulated the hypothesis of the death instinct, an idea subsequently adopted by Freud. Despite Freud and Jung's admiration for her ideas, they allocated scant credit to her. Their primary focus lay in assimilating her concepts into their own theories while safeguarding their theoretical legacies.

In the early days of psychoanalysis, Spielrein gained significant recognition. It could be that Freud and Jung refrained from emphasizing her contributions to the ideas they adopted, deeming it superfluous, given that it was already quite apparent during that time (Sells, 2017). Regrettably, what was once self-evident gradually faded into obscurity, leading to Spielrein's authorship being nearly erased from memory.

The Curse on Psychoanalysis

Spielrein developed the concept of the death instinct nearly a decade before Freud accepted it and incorporated it into his theory of the death drive. In November 1911, Spielrein presented it in her report "Destruction as the Cause of Becoming" (working title "On the Death Instinct") at a meeting of the Vienna Psychoanalytic Society, where Freud was among the attendees. Spielrein's concept faced initial resistance, later acknowledged by Freud: "I remember my own defensive attitude when the idea of destruction first emerged in psychoanalytic literature, and how long it took before I became receptive to it" (1961, p. 79).

Freud developed his concept of the death drive in one of his key later works, "Beyond the Pleasure Principle" (1920). He mentions Spielrein in a footnote, stating, "A considerable part of this speculation has been anticipated in a work which is full of valuable matter and ideas but is unfortunately not entirely clear to me" (p. 328). Although the late Freud, like Spielrein, began to lean toward the idea that the death drive is crucial to understanding the human psyche, one might speculate that her work remained not fully comprehensible to him.

One could suggest that his failure to fully grasp Spielrein's work reflects a defence mechanism that aided Freud in safeguarding his psychoanalytic theory and practice. As Freud explores the notion of the death drive in Beyond the Pleasure Principle, one can discern his resistance and its inherent incongruity with his already-established perspective. The concept of the death drive fundamentally clashes with Freud's original psychoanalytic framework. In relation to his earlier psychoanalytic paradigm, the concept of the death drive not only appears foreign but also destructive.

In "Beyond the Pleasure Principle," Freud attempts to integrate Spielrein's theory of the death instinct into his general framework while also adapting his own theory to incorporate Spielrein's concept. However, despite his efforts, the death drive remains an outsider within his theory. When sincerely acknowledged and authentically integrated into the Freudian framework, the concept of the death drive disrupts the very foundation of Freud's theory, challenging its core principles and the purpose of psychoanalysis itself.

In essence, this is partially the trajectory that unfolded. Freud found himself profoundly disenchanted with psychoanalysis in later life. In Todd McGowan's exploration of the death drive, he notes the "seemingly absolute pessimism of the later Freud, Freud after 1920, who appears to have abandoned his belief in the efficaciousness of the psychoanalytic cure" (2013, p. 19). This shift is evident in a particular regressive style that is inherent to "Beyond the Pleasure Principle." Freud makes several attempts to reconceptualize the death drive and attribute to it a central significance. Yet, each time he reverts to his previous way of thinking, resulting in the failure of each attempt. McGowan further observes,

> When Freud discovered the death drive in 1920, this optimism became theoretically untenable and disappeared from Freud's writings. While Freud's discovery

of the unconscious disrupted the thought of others, the discovery of the death drive disrupted his own and that of his followers – and this disruption makes itself felt in the halting and backtracking style of Beyond the Pleasure Principle. (2013, p. 10)

Alexander Etkind also acknowledges this shift in his analysis of Spielrein's influence on Freud's "Beyond the Pleasure Principle." He states: "One sees the striking image of a normally bold and self-assured thinker coming up against an alien tradition" (2019, p. 153). According to Etkind, in this context, Freud finds himself deeply immersed in an unfamiliar tradition, subjecting himself to an entirely new logic. Etkind elaborates,

The idea of attraction to death switches psychoanalytic discourse [...] to a completely different way of thinking [...] Freud's clear, rational, and heterosexual thoughts were unfolding before the reader's eyes with the help of discordant ideas [...] a contradiction that might have necessitated a fundamental reevaluation of the basic values of psychoanalysis, had Freud not stopped just in time. (2019, p. 154)

I would argue that the concept of the death drive is the point at which Freud's psychoanalysis, both in theory and practice, loses its foundation and collapses. What exactly lies at the core of the profound incompatibility between Freud and the death drive? The fundamental way of understanding a subject in Freudian psychoanalysis, as well as in the broader realm of conventional scientific and quasi-scientific knowledge, revolves around the idea of a subject enclosed within the boundaries of their individual psyche, driven by self-interest. In Freud's lexicon, this embodies a subject guided by the pleasure principle, driven to seek pleasure while avoiding displeasure. This foundational logic shapes the trajectory of Freudian psychoanalytic practice, which aims to facilitate the fulfilment of the pleasure principle and alleviate the suffering of the analysand.

Freud's subject is a living being driven by the desire to live and experience pleasure. Incorporating the death drive into his theory would necessitate Freud's abandonment of this foundational theory – a theory that underscores psychoanalysis' fundamental understanding of what defines a subject.

Spielrein's concept of the subject significantly diverges from that found in Freudian psychoanalysis, as her subject is inherently oriented towards death. It not only lacks self-centeredness and selfishness but also existence itself. While Spielrein occasionally touches upon the pursuit of pleasure, it holds minor significance compared to the overarching theme of the death instinct. In Spielrein's view, the subject is not isolated but profoundly interconnected with others. Individuality and self take on secondary roles in relation to this deep interconnectedness. Perhaps this is because, unlike Freud's human, Spielrein's human is a woman, not a man. She primarily loves rather than seeks pleasure. She gives and wastes herself rather than appropriates. She dies rather than lives.

Love is Pain

Since Freud's primary focus is centred on the individual, his integration of the concept of the death drive involves defining it as a property of the individual psyche. In contrast, Spielrein's concept of the death instinct operates within a pre-individual and inter-subjective dimension. To put it more plainly, the death instinct does not reside within the individual but exists between individuals as an intersubjective principle, blurring the boundaries of individuality.

Spielrein's concept of the death instinct carries an inherent quality of intersubjectivity, encompassing forms such as love and sexuality. As early as 1909, Spielrein articulated the fundamental aspects of her concept of the death instinct in her diary:

> This demonic force, whose very essence is destruction (evil), at the same time is the creative force, since out of the destruction (of two individuals) a new one arises. That is in fact the sexual drive, which is by nature a destructive drive, an exterminating drive for the individual, and for that reason, in my opinion, must overcome such great resistance in everyone. (as cited in Carotenuto, 1982, p. 108)

This demonic force bears responsibility for both destruction and creation, rendering love and death inseparable.

At the beginning of her work "Destruction as the Cause of Becoming," Spielrein emphasizes her observation that apparently positive phenomena associated with unity and reproduction, such as love and sexual attraction, are not only accompanied by positive emotions but also by negative ones, including anxiety (Angst) and disgust (Ekel). In the young women undergoing psychoanalysis with Spielrein, self-destructive impulses take centre stage. Her analysands feel their own love passion as an inner adversary that "compels her with an iron necessity to do what she does not want; she feels the end, the passing away [das Vergängliche], from which she might try in vain to escape into unknown distant lands" (1995, p. 466). For Spielrein, the negative emotions that colour sexuality are not merely elements of the human psyche. The prominence of destructive emotions at the subjective level mirrors the significance of the destructive process at the existential intersubjective level.

The emphasis on the centrality of negative emotions distinguishes Spielrein's stance from that of Freud. It challenges early Freudian doctrine, which posits that a subject's fundamental drive is the pursuit of pleasure. According to this perspective, positive emotions naturally align with Eros, while negative emotions are considered secondary and contingent. Spielrein criticizes Freud for commencing with the concept of infantile pleasure as his foundational premise. She doubts that negative emotions intertwined with sexuality stem solely from societal constraints. In her view, they epitomize the most fundamental essence of love, rather than being mere byproducts of cultural pressures. While Freud begins with the concept of a self-centered pursuit of pleasure, Spielrein uncovers something even more primal underneath it, maintaining that love's core essence is deeply intertwined with these negative emotions.

In Spielrein's interpretation, sexuality and love, among other phenomena, are "only different forms and degrees of self-destruction" (1995, p. 484). Love passion is, in essence, a manifestation of the self-destructive impulse, which is at the heart of the death instinct, or, to use a more Freudian term, the death drive. I would suggest that, despite Spielrein's use of terminology, it is more fitting to describe what Spielrein discusses without employing the terms "instinct" and "drive," as these terms imply a desire inherent to the subject. Instead, it seems more fitting to describe it as a "call" or "enchantment." The call of death summons a subject from an external realm, echoing within as something intrinsically foreign to them.

Spielrein's analysis combines a biological perspective with the use of mythopoetic imagery. From a biological standpoint, Spielrein emphasizes destructiveness by referencing elementary aspects of reproduction. For instance, fertilization involves the fusion of female and male germ cells, ultimately leading to the emergence of a new living entity. This process may seem to adhere to the straightforward logic of addition, as in "1 + 1 = 2," where the combination of two entities results in a new entity. However, this positive logic overlooks the inherent element of destructiveness. Even in this elementary and seemingly entirely positive process, destruction is at play. In fact, it can be regarded as the driving force. From this perspective, all positive entities can be seen as the outcome or consequence of destruction. When cells merge, they undergo dissolution as individual entities. A new life emerges as the remnants of this dissolution, and this new life, in turn, seeks its own annihilation. To illustrate this logic, we can use a formula that employs multiplication by zero as a symbol of destruction. Let's consider, for instance, "$(1 \cdot 0) + (1 \cdot 0) = (1 \cdot 0)$." In this equation, the entities exist only fleetingly, driven by their inherent longing for self-annihilation. It is through a combination of self-negations that a new (self-negating) entity arises.

The inherent connection between destruction and reproduction is even more evident in some animals. Within various species, individuals perish at different stages of their reproductive cycle – some during the act of mating, others after providing essential care to their offspring. Spielrein's perspective paints their demise as a sacrifice for the emergence of a new life. According to Spielrein, a similar process unfolds within the human species. While it may seem that humans are fortunate, experiencing only a partial demise during reproduction, as only germ cells are sacrificed during fertilization rather than the entire organism, Spielrein asserts that, nonetheless, "The transformation affects the entire organism" (1995, p. 467).

According to her perspective, all facets of human love and sexuality can be understood as expressions of the underlying principle of destruction. In line with this reasoning, during intercourse, bodies undergo a process of merging and intertwining, with their boundaries fading away, representing a form of destruction. The core of passionate love, too, is an expression of self-destruction. The feeling of love strips the individual of their own identity, leading to the dissolution of one's self into another. The example of motherhood, from both a biological and mythopoetic viewpoint, stands out as the most obvious form of self-elimination. Spielrein emphasizes the physical harm of pregnancy on a woman's body, stating, "one is destroyed in pregnancy by the child, which develops at the expense of the mother, like a malignant tumor" (1995, p. 481).

It is important to note that while both Spielrein and Freud engage in extensive discussions about sexuality, it plays significantly different roles in their views. For Freud, it is obvious that the sexual instinct serves as the primary driving force behind the human psyche. He sees sexual desire as inherently self-centred, revolving around the pursuit of personal pleasure. Love, in Freud's framework, emerges as a sublimated expression of the sexual instinct. In contrast, Spielrein's central point of consideration shifts away from sexuality to destruction.

Sexual desire represents just one of the myriad ways in which destruction finds its embodiment, alongside love, motherhood, and art. While Freud views love as a sublimation of sexual desire, Spielrein considers love and sexuality as various embodiments of destruction. In Freud's theory, which gravitates around the male perspective, sexual desire is entwined with the notion of dominance. In this framework, positive logic takes centre stage, revolving around the desires of the individual. On the other hand, Spielrein's viewpoint introduces a contrasting narrative where sexual desire embodies dissolution and self-sacrifice. As a result, this perspective is rooted in negative logic, placing emphasis on the collective "We" rather than the individual "I."

We-psyche

Spielrein challenges the notion that our psychic existence is confined to the realm of the self. According to her, our individual psyche, including the unconscious, represents a secondary and acquired formation. There exists a deeper dimension that precedes and encompasses the self, which she refers to as the "We-psyche" or the collective psyche. Spielrein articulates this concept by saying, "The depth of our psyche knows no 'I,' but only its summation, the 'We' [das 'Wir']" (1995, p. 472). The "I" is but an ephemeral and ever-changing aspect within the "We"-dimension. To a greater extent, we embody this space itself rather than our individual selves. The "We"-dimension precedes and encompasses the "I"-dimension, serving as the foundation of our individual selves. Consequently, at its core, the "I" yearns for self-negation. When we descend into the depths of our being, we discover the 'We.' In other words, at the heart of oneself, there exists no self.

In relation to this deeper dimension, the individual is rendered insignificant. What lies beneath the individual psyche is indifferent to personal pleasure, individual interests, and the preservation of one's own life. According to Spielrein, this collective dimension resonates within us as a call to self-destruction. She writes, "there is something in our depth which, as paradoxical as it may sound, wants this self-damaging" (1995, p. 471). The call of the We-psyche does not align with the personal desires of the I; it remains indifferent and negates the "I" entirely. This call emerges from the depths of the soul, beyond the realm of the I, where the

"I" ceases to exist. The dissolution of the "I" is experienced as self-loss, a process of depersonalization. The I-psyche is in opposition to the We-psyche. While the I-psyche strives for self-preservation, the We-psyche seeks to assimilate the I-psyche into itself. Our yearning for death represents the impulse to return to the We, signifying the rejection of oneself as a distinct, separate entity.

Moreover, Spielrein suggests that the self is not a constant, indivisible entity; instead, it is mutable and fluid. Beneath the illusion of the self's integrity lie fragmentation, impermanence, and inner conflicts. The self is merely a transient amalgamation of various complexes. An individual is not a singular self; they are a Dividuum, characterized not by indivisibility but by divisibility and fragmentation.

It is crucial not to perceive the We-psyche as a confined formation. It is neither the collective psyche of a specific social group nor the entirety of humanity. It is not something beyond the individual that belongs to a larger collective individuality. "We" does not refer to a particular, differentiated collective "We" confined by a specific culture but rather to the realm of negation beyond the bounds of individuality at any scale.

Spielrein portrays the realm of the We-psyche using mythopoetic imagery of the primordial sea and nurturing maternal waters. This mother-being [*Muttersein*] is a dark, undifferentiated dimension where linear time and boundaries fade away. Within the realm of *Muttersein*, all differentiation dissolves. Concerning all forms of differentiation, this dimension fulfils the role of erasure and dissolution. We all inevitably partake in this collective undifferentiated realm. We discover it in the depths of ourselves, where our self dissolves and negates itself.

Spielrein points out the alignment of the mythological image of the grave with that of the mother's womb. While motherhood is commonly regarded as a symbol of the creation of life, it is equally intertwined with death. It carries a negative aspect – sacrifice, dying, lack of differentiation, and the blurring of boundaries. It encompasses both the act of offering life as a sacrifice and the emergence of new life.

Spielrein often turns to Nietzsche's image of Zarathustra, which, for her, symbolizes motherhood and self-annihilation, a merging of death and love. To illustrate Zarathustra's longing to dissolve into his children, Spielrein quotes his words, "I lay enchained to the love of my children: Desire set this snare for me, the desire, that I would become my children's prey and lose myself to them" (1995, p. 485).

According to Zarathustra's teachings, a human is something that must be overcome. Zarathustra sacrifices himself for what comes after the demise of humanity. He is the one who simultaneously carries death and bears life into existence. For Spielrein, he embodies the image of a mother who self-destructs, dissolving into her children, essentially sacrificing herself for a new creation. Zarathustra surpasses himself, thus participating in the creation of something different from himself. The merging with one's depths, where the self is dissolved, signifies becoming a mother. Spielrein writes, "Through uniting in love with the mother, Nietzsche himself becomes the generating, creating, becoming mother" (1995, p. 482). In the depths of ourselves, we discover our mother – her womb and our grave, and in doing so, we ourselves become mothers.

In Freud's psychoanalytic framework, the father figure holds a prominent position, while in Spielrein's reflective realm, the mother takes the spotlight. Traditional psychoanalytic thought upholds the symbolic authority of the father, establishing a hierarchical relationship between father and mother. Here, the process of individualization and the transition into the symbolic sphere revolves around the dominant figure of the father. Conversely, the mother is associated with the primitive, the pre-symbolic, and the pre-individual.

While Freud and Lacan contemplate the idea of transcending the mother's domain, Spielrein's reflections express a different perspective. In her theory, the mother's domain extends as an all-encompassing space, embracing every aspect of existence. It's within this expansive dimension that individualization unfolds, always cradled within its nurturing embrace. Here, the prevailing principle is not hierarchical authority, but rather a dynamic of care and mutual sacrifice.

For Spielrein, the symbolic is not linked to individualization but conversely, to entering the realm of the collective, a maternal realm. In this view, individualization stands as a relative concept, perpetually enfolded within the collective as a fleeting, temporal phenomenon.

A Matter of Taste

While in Freud's interpretation, the longing for death is seen as a repetition of the same and a yearning for a return to an inorganic existence, for Spielrein, the call of death is intimately tied to transformation. In her perspective, the impulse for self-preservation is indeed static and positive, aimed at maintaining the current state of the self. In contrast, the longing of the We-psyche is dynamic and marked by ambivalence, where its positive facet carries a simultaneous negative charge. In this realm, transformation unfolds by engendering a new state that negates the previous one, thus bringing about a convergence of death and resurrection.

Spielrein posits that through immersion in the undifferentiated realm of the "We" and undergoing its demise, the "I"-particle can reemerge "in a new, perhaps more beautiful form" (1995, p. 476). Apart from love, this dissolution and reemergence can take on various other forms. Spielrein illustrates this with the example of depressive depersonalization observed in schizophrenia. This process unfolds as a profound estrangement from both self and the world, wherein the self and the world become uncanny ("'I am a complete stranger to myself,' 'The world is changed, eerily strange; it is like a theater play'" [1995, p. 474]), and a pervasive indifference takes hold ("The patients no longer take anything personally" [1995, p. 474]). Thus, the self undergoes a form of inner death, fades away, and submerges into the depths of undifferentiation. The demise of the self can assume both beautiful and unsettling forms, sometimes even simultaneously. The key idea is that any transformation implies the death of the old state, as Spielrein states, "No transformation can proceed without the destruction of the old state" (1995, p. 491).

Contemplating transformation in alignment with death, Spielrein suggests that the resurrected self is "not the same particle of self, but another, born at the cost of the death of the former, like a tree sprouted from a seed, though it belongs to the same species, it is not the same tree" (1995, p. 476). She then makes an important remark: "it is actually more a matter of taste whether we prefer to emphasize the existence in the new product developed at the expense of the old, or the deliberate fading of the old life" (1995, p. 476). Prevailing tastes tend to perceive this process of transformation as positive in the end, akin to the idea of renewal or rebirth. Destruction and death are comprehended in this perspective as negative stages within a broader positive context of becoming. In this interpretation, death assumes a secondary role, serving the renewal of life. Ultimately, life negates death and triumphs over it. This embodies a positive logic that places the negative element under the dominion of the positive process, making destruction secondary to becoming. This does not allow destruction to assume a central place. One can identify this logic even in Spielrein's own work; for instance, when she asserts that "destruction leads to becoming" (1995, p. 487). However, such an interpretation of Spielrein is only possible if one disregards her important remark about taste.

When one equates birth and death, as Spielrein does, the inclination is to accentuate birth as the pivotal element. Conventional tastes tend to place death in subservience to birth, perceiving it as a mere step towards rebirth. Spielrein, however, proposes a shift in focus towards the destructive element of death. Because there's an equal sign between death and birth, it implies that the reverse position with an emphasis on the centrality of death is also valid. Spielrein's conceptual taste leans towards seeing death as a defining phenomenon.

The negative taste would rather perceive the rebirth of the self as a triumph of death. The renewed self is one with death within it, never reverting to its former state, as the experience of inner death leaves an indelible scar. Rather than becoming more alive, it surrendered to deeper nonexistence. "I" merged with the collective "We."

One can assess their taste by contemplating the mythical figure of the Phoenix – a bird capable of burning itself and being reborn from the ashes. Conventional taste emphasizes the rebirth following its demise, often overlooking death as if its resurrection nullifies or redeems it. However, death is no less significant; it's the very transformation into ashes that can be seen as the defining process. From this perspective, the Phoenix's image symbolizes not so much eternal return and triumph over death, but rather perpetual dying – an unending process prolonged by resurrection, preventing it from reaching its completion.

Becoming a mother provides yet another illustration of how destruction plays a central role in the cycle of dying and rebirth. Undergoing a transformative dissolution, the maternal self emerges as a distinct entity diverging from its former pre-maternal state. Motherhood, at its core, demands the self-sacrifice of one's existence for the sake of nurturing another. A mother weaves her child's life from the threads of her own. Maternal sacrifice may be seen as the triumph of life over death, as the outcome of the mother's sacrificing herself is the life of her child. However, this perspective, rooted in positive logic, offers just one possible interpretation of motherhood. The child's life does not compensate for the mother's demise. The new life emerges as an immediate effect of her self-sacrifice, inseparable from it. The maternal self is the self offered as a sacrifice – a new, half-existing subject who has surrendered her "self." At the heart of maternal existence, it is no longer her self but her deceased former self and the self of her child. This newfound self can be viewed as a rebirth into a new and more beautiful form. However, using negative logic, this new self can also be seen as uncanny, ephemeral, treading the delicate line between life and death.

The Practice of Loving and Dying

It's worth contemplating what form psychoanalytic practice might take if we were to sincerely embrace the Spielreinian concept of the call of death, recognizing it as the most profound aspect of being human. Psychoanalytic practice came into being alongside the early theoretical framework of Freudian psychoanalysis and was never reconciled with the later, Spielrein-influenced, revelation of Freud. This means that psychoanalytic practice, which left Freud disillusioned in his later years, originated from his early bias towards the primacy of the pleasure principle. It is fundamentally incompatible with Spielrein's assertion regarding the centrality of the call of death. Psychoanalytic practice, even today, clings to the intention of overcoming destruction and healing from the death drive, as if it were not only non-central but also avoidable. Clearly, a psychoanalytic approach that places the role of destruction in the forefront suggests an entirely different trajectory. While Spielrein doesn't explicitly discuss this alternative path, one can speculate that such a practice would diverge significantly from the classical Freudian struggle against repression in the name of pleasure. If human beings fundamentally seek their own demise rather than pleasure, how can and should one assist them?

What emerges from Spielrein's insights is that in the human experience, the choice between life and death remains elusive; we are destined for death while being alive. What, to some extent, lingers within our control is the manner in which we undergo our demise. Possibly, a revised negative practice would not concern itself with individuality, personal well-being, or the pursuit of pleasure, but would instead engage with destructiveness and interconnectedness. The involvement of the psychoanalyst and the analysand would not happen with the intention of escaping the call of death but within it. Such a practice could work with the form of its embodiment, at the intersection between destruction and creation. In Spielreinian psychoanalytic practice, the emphasis wouldn't lie on aiding survival but on involvement in the process of self-dissolution through practising the art of loving and dying. In such a practice, the individual self would not be seen as something to be exalted, but rather as destined for loss. Perhaps it would be offered as a sacrificial gift to others, to the world, or to nothingness. This wouldn't be a practice of indifference but a practice of care. It would no longer entail alienation under the guidance of the symbolic father but rather loving and dying in the embrace of the mythical primordial mother.

References

Carotenuto, A. (1982). *A Secret Symmetry: Sabina Spielrein Between Jung and Freud.* Pantheon.

Etkind, A. (2019). *Eros of the Impossible: The History of Psychoanalysis in Russia.* Routledge.

Freud, S. (1920/1961). *Beyond the Pleasure Principle* (The Standard Edition). (J. Strachey, Trans.). Liveright Publishing Corporation.

Freud, S. (1930/1961). *Civilization and Its Discontents* (J. Strachey, Trans. & Ed.). W. W. Norton.

McGowan, T. (2013). *Enjoying What We Don't Have: The Political Project of Psychoanalysis.* University of Nebraska Press.

Sells, A. (2017). *Sabina Spielrein: The Woman and the Myth.* SUNY Press.

Spielrein, S. (1912/1995). "Destruction as Cause of Becoming." *Psychoanalysis and Contemporary Thought*, 18, 85–118.

Index

A
affect regulation 137–138, 140–145
alienation 6, 30, 44, 46, 114, 122, 155
ambivalence 153
anxiety 6, 34, 95–96, 111, 122–123, 139, 144, 149
authenticity 124
attachment 46, 51, 130, 135, 143–144
autonomy 30, 34

B
Badiou, Alain 14, 55–57, 69–78, 115
Beauvoir, Simone de 107–108
Bersani, Leo 127, 131–134
being-toward-death (Heidegger) 109–110, 114–115
being-with-others 110
Binswanger, Ludwig 109–110, 114
Boss, Medard 109–110, 114

C
care
  Heidegger 110–111, 114
  Spielrein 150, 153, 155
  caretaking 131
categorical imperative (Kant) 31
Chaucer, Geoffrey 32–33, 35–36
collective unconscious 140, 146
collective death drive 122, 125

D
Dasein (Heidegger) 102, 105–106, 109, 111–112, 114–115
Daseinanalysis 109
Dederer, Claire 38, 40–41, 44–46
death drive (Spielrein, Freud, Lacan) 16–19, 22, 25–27, 29–30, 32–36, 44, 47, 52–53, 74, 80–83, 89, 96–97, 109–110, 112–115, 121–123, 125, 127, 131, 137–144, 147–150, 155;
  repetition compulsion 18, 23, 24, 26
  death instinct 113, 121, 146–150
  Thanatos 29, 52, 63, 80, 82–83, 121
depersonalization 53, 152–153
depression 22, 24–26
desire 5–8, 10–11, 13–14, 18, 20–27, 29, 32, 34, 36, 39–40, 42–43, 45, 54–55, 57–58, 60, 70, 72–76, 84, 86–88, 96, 103–107, 128–132, 134, 148, 151
Diotima 55, 61–67
duty 30–31
Dolar, Mladen 30–32, 34, 35

E
Eros and Thanatos 29, 34, 52–53, 55, 61, 65, 80, 82, 121, 149
erotic 51, 57, 130–135
ethical subject 29–30, 34, 36
event (Badiou) 69, 71, 75–78
enjoyment 12–14, 27, 29, 34, 41–44, 46–47, 78, 81, 84, 89, 95–97, 114
existential phenomenology 109
existential psychoanalysis 103
extimacy 18, 20, 29–30, 34

F
fate 30–31, 34
fear of death 32, 60, 82, 103, 122–125
finitude (see mortality) 29, 61, 75, 101–107, 109, 111–115
freedom 16–17, 19–20, 22, 26–27, 29–31, 34, 101–107
Freud, Sigmund 21, 31, 45, 51–54, 57, 72, 80–83, 90, 95–97, 102–103, 107–108,

109–110, 112–114, 121–123, 125, 127–135, 137–140, 143–144, 146–151, 153, 155

G
gaze (Lacan) 22, 35, 42–43
guilt 40–43, 46

H
Hegel, Georg Wilhelm Friedrich 96, 109, 112, 114
Hegelian dialectics 71
Heidegger, Martin 101–108, 109–115
human condition 29, 122–125
human subject 29, 84–85
hysterical subject 19, 21, 34, 70, 127–135, 137, 143

I
intersubjectivity 134, 138, 149
intimacy 56, 57, 71, 133

J
jouissance (Lacan) 11, 17–19, 22, 24–27, 29, 32–34, 36, 39–46, 53–54, 80, 84–89
Jung, Carl 88, 113, 146

K
Kant, Immanuel 30, 31, 33–34, 109, 112
Kristeva, Julia 130–131, 133–135

L
lamella (Lacan) 113, 115
lack 3–14, 16–27, 38–40, 42, 44, 54–55, 72, 84, 87
libido 82, 129–131, 135, 138
life drive 29, 82, 113
loss 12–14, 29, 43–44, 55

M
masochism 22, 27, 134
mother, maternal 128–131, 135, 139–140, 142, 150, 152–155
melancholia 52, 135
mentalization 141, 143
mirror stage (Lacan) 80, 131
mortality (*see finitude*) 29, 62–63, 65, 67, 82, 85, 109, 123–125
mourning 51
mystical theology 80, 88

N
narcissism 6, 10, 51–52, 57, 59, 61, 134–135, 144
negation 63, 78, 80–81, 86, 88, 150–152
Nietzsche, Friedrich 96, 152
non-relation 55, 85, 114–115
Normal People, Sally Rooney 16–28

O
objet petit a 29, 35
ontology 35, 56, 109, 111–112, 113, 114–115

P
pain 13–14, 17, 32, 34, 42, 86, 112, 122, 140, 143, 149
passion 33, 55–57, 83, 86, 115, 149–150
Neruda, Pablo 12–14
Phoenix 59–67, 154
pleasure principle 17–19, 29, 34, 44–47, 112, 121, 148, 155
pregnancy 65–67, 151
psychoanalytic existentialism 103, 107

R
the Real (Lacan) 4, 5, 8, 11, 26–27, 30–31, 35, 44–45, 52, 55, 57, 77, 85, 87, 89–90, 113, 129
reliance 127, 130–135
Ruti, Mari 11, 51, 54–55

S
sacrifice 7–8, 38–42, 46, 56, 64–66, 89, 94, 114, 139, 150–155
Sartre, Jean-Paul 101–103, 105–107
Schopenhauer, Arthur 94, 96
self-destruction 96, 127, 150–151
self-negation 83, 150–151
sublimation 35, 53, 65, 113, 151
suffering 26, 80–86, 89–91, 122, 125
suicide 11, 14, 25
sinthome (Lacan) 27, 84–86, 88, 89, 91

T
tenderness 127–135
Thanatos 29, 52, 63, 80, 82–83, 121
the Thing (Lacan) 31, 35, 54–55, 57–58, 135
transference 3–4, 16, 53, 114–115
trauma 5, 29, 82, 102–103, 108, 121
truth 66, 71, 76, 78, 95–96, 110–111, 115

U

unconscious 95, 101–108, 121–122, 125, 137, 139–144, 146, 148, 151

V

violence 25, 123–124

W

well-being 122, 155

Z

Zupančič, Alenka 30, 35, 43, 45, 73
Žižek, Slavoj 29–31, 34, 35–36, 38–39, 44, 46, 113, 115

For Product Safety Concerns and Information please contact our EU representative GPSR@taylorandfrancis.com
Taylor & Francis Verlag GmbH, Kaufingerstraße 24, 80331 München, Germany

www.ingramcontent.com/pod-product-compliance
Lightning Source LLC
Chambersburg PA
CBHW051401290426
44108CB00015B/2105